Praise for *Three Year*

"*Three Years on the Great Mountain* is not only a compelling recount of Cristina Moon's own personal journey to Zen but a universal exploration of belonging and the profound liberation available to all of us through dedication and training. From the front lines of Burma's resistance movement to the meditation mats of Chozen-ji, Moon's call for all of us to take seriously each moment is an important one for this time."

—Prentis Hemphill, author of
What It Takes to Heal

"*Three Years on the Great Mountain* is a powerful expression of awakening through the Zen path. This story is a teaching of going beyond our small self as training in freedom. The grounding wisdom of this path of practice emerges whether one skillfully wields a cup of tea, a sword, a broom, or the breath. The path is not about Cristina, you, or I; it is about how wholehearted commitment transforms our fear into fearlessness. This book is about how to live the Buddhadharma fully."

—Koshin Paley Ellison, Zen teacher and author of
*Untangled: Walking the Eightfold Path to Clarity,
Courage, and Compassion*

"Cristina Moon's engaging memoir reveals the spirit of Zen and local Hawaii culture at her training temple Chozen-ji and in so doing, steps into a lineage of no fear, of moving seamlessly in the world. The book makes the case for an embodied Buddhist training, the type of Zen where skin, flesh, bones, and marrow are offered fully to the life of attention and awakening. An invitation to discover one's true self and home."

—Duncan Ryūken Williams, author of *American Sutra*

"Rev. Cristina Moon spells out in profound detail the rigor and resonance of Zen training at Chozen-ji. For those of us who may be intrigued—but also intimidated—she guides us through her own inner narrative as she introduces us to her teacher and community, masters unfamiliar forms, and cuts through self-imposed limitations. This is a memoir that inspires us to train, to embody an attentive way of being, and to cultivate spiritual strength."

—Rima Vesely-Flad, author of
Black Buddhists and the Black Radical Tradition

"In this striking portrait of a Zen priest in training, Rev. Cristina Moon shares her singular journey from the streets of Rangoon to a dojo on Oahu: from activism to Buddhism, kotonk to senpai, doubt to conviction. Told with honesty, humor, and crackling detail, the stories in this memoir offer the gift of spiritual vigor for all seekers. Ferocity and grace, striving and sincerity—this book, like its author, contains multitudes."

—Chenxing Han, author of
Be the Refuge and *one long listening*

THREE YEARS ON THE GREAT MOUNTAIN

A Memoir of Zen and Fearlessness

CRISTINA MOON

SHAMBHALA

Shambhala Publications, Inc.
2129 13th Street
Boulder, Colorado 80302
www.shambhala.com

Cover design: Amanda Weiss
Interior design: Claudine Mansour Design

9 8 7 6 5 4 3 2 1

First Edition
Printed in the United States of America

Shambhala Publications makes every effort to print on acid-free, recycled paper.
Shambhala Publications is distributed worldwide by Penguin Random House, Inc., and its subsidiaries.

Library of Congress Cataloging-in-Publication Data
Names: Moon, Cristina, author.
Title: Three years on the great mountain: a memoir of Zen and fearlessness / Cristina Moon.
Description: Boulder: Shambhala Publications, 2024.
Identifiers: LCCN 2023033025 | ISBN 9781645472827 (trade paperback)
Subjects: LCSH: Moon, Cristina. | Zen priests—Biography. | Martial arts—Religious aspects—Buddhism. | Zen Buddhism—Essence, genius, nature.
Classification: LCC BQ972.M66 A3 2024 | DDC 294.3/927092 [B]—dc23/eng/20231023
LC record available at https://lccn.loc.gov/2023033025

For Michael,
who brought me home

CONTENTS

PROLOGUE

As soon as the last tea was served and the last bow performed, I was out the door of the *Budo Dojo.** I walked briskly; there was no time. This feeling had become so familiar over the past two years—the constant motion and a crackling awareness of how fleeting each moment could be.

The rice cracker in its plastic wrapper crinkled against my skin where I had tucked it away inside my thick, indigo *gi*. Behind me, beyond the crunch of gravel under my feet and the thick, cottony swoosh of my *hakama*, I could hear people putting away meditation cushions and running to fetch folding chairs. The large, square cushions made booming sounds as they were thrown one on top of the other.

I ducked into the tea house, removing my slippers and making my way to the bathroom. There hung my kimono: simple, cotton, white.

After a week of intensive Zen training marked often by frantic unease and doubt—*What's coming next? Where am I supposed to be?*—putting on the kimono was a sweet respite. This, I knew how to do. As my hands pulled the front of the kimono across my

---

* Throughout the book, I italicize the first instance of Japanese, ʻŌlelo Hawaiʻi (Native Hawaiian), Hawaiian Pidgin, and other non-English words and phrases. Translations and guidance on pronunciation for these italicized terms can be found in the glossary. I also use diacritical marks for words in ʻŌlelo Hawaiʻi. A macron, called *kahakō*, is signified by a straight bar ˉ over a vowel and indicates that it's a long vowel. A left single quotation mark signifies an *ʻokina*, which sounds like a glottal stop, similar to the sound between the syllables of "oh-oh."

body—first the right side, then the left—I sighed into this rare moment of creature comfort. The familiar drape and hug of the fabric pulled together all of the events of the past week and, even beyond that, my years of wandering and searching. For on this morning, December 8, 2019, I was doing something that I had never anticipated. In fact, I had never even given thought to it before. But when it presented itself, it felt so obvious that it could easily have been predetermined. Today, I was getting ordained as a Zen priest.

I pulled the kimono tight in the middle with a thin strap to account for the curve of my hips and the narrowing of my waist. I pulled until it was cinched and shapely and tight enough in the middle that it was just a little hard to breathe. In my right hand, I held one end of my white *obi*, the cloth belt that would wrap around my body and then around itself in the front, folding just right so that the cloth belt secured itself in a perfect square resembling a giant buckle. Holding the obi up to my waist, I spun slowly in a circle several times as I had learned to do over a year of dressing in kimono for weekly classes in *Chado* (the Way of Tea, or Japanese tea ceremony).

My priest robes were voluminous and cumbersome, with long, wide sleeves and a *kesa* worn formally on top, while a *rakusu* was worn for informal occasions. Practicing putting it all on the day before, I had looked in the mirror and admired how the robes changed my presence and shape. They made me bigger and more substantial—an appearance, I thought, befitting a Zen priest whose highest directive was to give courage and take away fear. I had had many occasions to contemplate what taking away fear meant, especially when passing the calligraphies around our temple bearing this invocation: 無畏—*Mu I* (fearless; lit., "Void Fear").

After slipping on two *tabi*, white split-toed socks that fastened high up around the ankles with dime-sized metal tabs, I gathered up the other items that had been given to me for this day: a black rope belt, my rakusu, *juzu*, and a paper fan. Finally, I grabbed the hanger from which my new robes hung and made for the door.

In many ways, a Zen priest ordination resembles a funeral. In a Japanese context, the simple white kimono lends a clean feeling and an unquestionably funereal air; it is the same garment that Japanese corpses wear on their last journeys into the ground or to the cremation chamber. At ordination, one is also given a new, Buddhist name, which would otherwise be reserved in Japan for after someone has died. Today, however, I would receive my full Buddhist name on a certificate of ordination as a new Zen priest. The renaming was a nod to how, as a priest, I would straddle this world of the living and whatever else there is that this world is not.

I hung my robes and placed my other accoutrement on a bench on the side of the Budo Dojo, where they would remain for the beginning of my ordination ceremony. Then, I walked slowly toward the entrance. Through the windows, I saw the small audience that had come for the ceremony, sitting in silence and waiting. Seated on the tatami floor were the other students with whom I'd been training all week in an intensive period called *sesshin*, all in matching navy-blue gi and hakama. The few Dojo members—close mentors and friends—whom I had invited sat behind them in chairs, dressed in pressed slacks and aloha shirts.

Approaching the threshold, I exchanged looks with an older priest standing next to the Peace Bell on the hill just opposite the Budo Dojo. He nodded solemnly and, turning away from me, stepped toward the bell. He grabbed hold of the thick rope that dangled from the striker and pulled it all the way forward toward the bell until it was almost touching. Then, releasing it, he let it swing backward and then forward again. At the very end of its arc, he coaxed it further, just enough to strike. A tremendous sound emerged. He rang the bell five times in all, each low reverberation filling the hollow in the Koʻolau Mountain Range that was home to Chozen-ji, the Zen temple and martial arts dojo where I had been living and training as a monk for the past two years.

As the bell rang, I tried to gather my thoughts and remember the sequence of the ceremony, but it was fruitless; I could not. Everything was just . . . blank. Although an outsider might mistake the clean expression on my face as tranquility, I was actually just exhausted. Over the past six days, I had generally gotten only a few hours of sleep a night. But the night before, I had not slept at all. As is usually the case on the last night of sesshin, the hours from ten at night until three thirty in the morning had been filled with alternating periods of seated meditation, some chores, and martial arts. After cleaning the kitchen, I had meditated again with the others and run through our now familiar morning schedule of chanting and calligraphy. Then, a short tea ceremony ended the intensive training period.

Now, I was here, trying—and failing—to remember the previous night's rehearsal and what I was supposed to do next.

On the fourth ring of the Peace Bell, I made a guess and stepped forward, my palms held together in *gassho*. On the fifth, I stepped over the threshold with my left foot, then my right, bowed, and proceeded into the dojo. After a few steps forward, I hesitantly passed a small, high table set in the center of the room. A rectangular, red lacquer box sat on top. Behind the table stood my teacher, Sayama Daian *Roshi*, in a white kimono that mirrored my own but which, unlike mine, was topped with robes that were brilliant purple and gold. He did nothing to stop me, so I cautiously continued on until I was just a few steps away from the *butsudan*, the altar on the far side of the room. On the butsudan's back wall hung a huge calligraphy of a circle, called an *enso* in Japanese, painted onto a panel of wood. The grain of the wood glistened under the bright spotlight in the butsudan. The whole butsudan glowed, in fact, with the warmth of the wood and with the light bouncing off the bright red felt draping the table within.

On top of that table were a half dozen religious objects, including two black *ihai*, or memorial tablets, for our temple's founders. I felt a sudden surge of gratitude as, upon seeing them, they sparked my memory of what came next. I bowed to the ihai and retrieved a small pinch of flaked incense from another red lacquer box identical to the one in front of Sayama Roshi. After bringing the incense briefly up to the height of my forehead, I released the flakes just above the box so that they fell onto the small, rectangular coal burning inside the box. The incense immediately smoldered, releasing a plume of smoke upward into the heart of the enso. Then, I stepped back and, circling both arms up overhead, began *sampai*, a set of three full-body prostrations, in front of the butsudan. Afterward, I turned and walked back to where Sayama Roshi stood. Positioning myself between him and the door, I completed another sampai.

Sayama Roshi offered his own pinch of incense. Then, everyone in the room—Sayama Roshi, myself, a handful of priests, and the assembled crowd—all recited a short chant, calling out the names of the various buddhas. This was followed by more chanting, many voices making the air thick with sound and expectation.

My past two years in the temple had been filled with hard work, mostly chores and physical Zen training. Throughout the days, I had tried to remain disciplined and focused on the goal that brought me to Chozen-ji: to realize my True Self. Despite whatever assumptions I had had about what life at a Zen temple would be like, the reality here was always, "Go, go, go." I was up before the sun and in bed long past dark and, through such training, had cultivated the ability to endure tiredness, pain, and all manner of discomfort to a degree that I had previously thought impossible. Yet I lived most days back on my heels, never quite able to anticipate the demands of the Dojo and never feeling like I was close enough to my goal. I always carried with me the vague but persistent feeling that, despite my efforts and the generosity of my teachers, I had not learned nearly enough.

Now, standing in front of Sayama Roshi, my mind, though still far from clear, was at least not racing with thoughts.

What now? I wondered. This was, in fact, an appropriate question for the whole of my situation. I knew little about what to expect of being a Zen priest aside from the fact that it meant, in many ways, a new beginning and not the end of my training. One thing

I knew for sure was that my ordination came with the responsibility to take away fear. And while the training had taught me how to conquer many of my own anxieties and habits, I couldn't yet comprehend the mechanics of this greater No Fear. Could I embody it myself? What would it mean to achieve a state of fearlessness and complete, total courage?

I stood, looking dumbly at Sayama Roshi, whose face showed that he was just as exhausted as I was. Although he was already in his late sixties, he had sat almost every period of meditation over the past week, training alongside those of us more than twenty and thirty years his junior. He was so tired, I could tell, that he didn't even have the energy to be annoyed by my forgetfulness. About that, I was relieved. But still, I stood and waited for my next cue for what felt like an eternity, our small audience looking on in silence. It was only after several more such moments that he finally bade me outside with a wave of his hand.

Putting my palms back together in gassho, I bowed and retreated toward the door. At the threshold, I bowed again and stepped outside. Too caught up, perhaps, in the formalities of the moment, trying to adhere to the sequence of the ceremony and remember what came next, the fact that this was the last time I would step out of the Budo Dojo as just me, just Cristina Moon, slipped by me unnoticed. Once I put on my robes and began walking back to the Budo Dojo, I would be on my way to being someone else: 緑水妙安—*Ryoku Sui Myo An*.

Back outside the Budo Dojo, I took the robes off their hanger and put them on. I wrapped the black corded belt around myself, tying it in a knot in the front and tucking the ends neatly. I picked up my fan and beads. The new robes did not add much certainty in terms of what came next. But I did feel an undoubtable momentum forward, a smooth and silent tide pulling me swiftly from the shore of the known. I had only one thing to do: keep putting one foot in front of the other. I did not know what exactly lay on the other side of all of this, even after two years of training, day in and day out, but I knew enough to still go forward.

Hands together, I stepped in, bowed, and approached my teacher again. The strength and stoicism on his face broke into kindness, warmth, and pride. Handing me my rakusu with two hands, he began to speak to the assembled crowd about my new name. I listened and waited for its meaning, "Mysterious Peace Arising from the Green Water," to sink in, as if, through this ceremony, it would permeate my body and I would understand it, or perhaps become it by osmosis.

Eventually, it came time for me to join the other priests, dressed in their flowing black robes and sitting on low, brocade chairs. There, they chanted in unison. I turned around and walked over to join them, my new brothers in arms. To me, a Chozen-ji priest was the picture of poise and courage. Fashioned through great effort and determination, they were capable of transcending the depths of human suffering through spiritual strength. They could face down any threat, utterly ferocious, while also able to comfort those who needed it with care. They were big and they were bright, the kinds of people you would want by your side in battle and at both the hardest and the most joyful moments of your life.

Standing beside them, I matched outwardly, dressed as I was in my new robes. But, on the inside, I felt still so very green. I added my voice to their chanting as best I could. I had been welcomed into their ranks. Now I was one of them, and I should sound the part. I looked straight ahead, trying my best to inspire courage in myself and everyone around me, but I could barely get out a sound. Tears streamed down my cheeks, so hard and so fast that I could barely see.

INTRODUCTION

My only true regret in life is that I did not start training in Zen sooner and, specifically, that I didn't start training much earlier in Chozen-ji Zen, the line of Zen Buddhism headquartered at Daihonzan Chozen-ji, a Rinzai Zen temple and dojo on the Hawaiian island of Oʻahu.

Though my very first taste of Buddhism came early on, the particular kind I encountered first was just not for me. This isn't a slight to other schools of Buddhism. There are a tremendous number of different Buddhist sects and even multiple lines within said sects. These schools and the personalities they attract are as varied as the geographies in which they've taken root over the millennia, spanning thousands of miles and many cultures. With many flavors and adaptations to its far-flung homelands, Buddhism around the world often beautifully reveals the mixtures of people and the trading of goods and ideas at some of the greater historical crossroads of humankind. Amid this diversity are also some schools that evolved in such isolation, on cloistered mountaintops and among remote island chains, that they became totally distinct. It would have been impossible for them to come into existence anywhere else—and this, I believe, is the case with Chozen-ji Zen.

I had to explore several kinds of Buddhism before finding this one—the one that is, without doubt or hesitation, my spiritual home. Sometimes I reflect on all of that searching and wandering, and I do ask myself with impatience why I couldn't have made this homecoming sooner. In those moments, I try to remind myself that things had to happen as they did, if only because that's how they did happen.

Like the young oxherd depicted in the famous Zen paintings, *The Ten Ox-Herding Pictures*, I spent a long time adrift, not just in search of home but also in search of some understanding of myself, why the world was the way it was, and what I was supposed to do with it all. This was often illuminating, and I don't doubt that I grew along the way. Once my spiritual searching had been definitively set in motion, I also never faltered in keeping at least one foot on the Path. But throughout, I often felt lost, at least a little unsure of where to turn while at the same time quite confident that I had not yet found "it": the Truth, a teacher, or a method through which to make progress toward enlightenment or at least less suffering.

"In the pasture of the world," reads a twelfth-century poem accompanying one version of *The Ten Ox-Herding Pictures*, "I endlessly push aside the tall / grasses in search of the Ox." Here, the ox is a metaphor for the mind and an understanding of the nature of reality.

> Following unnamed rivers,
> lost upon the interpenetrating
> paths of distant mountains,
> My strength failing and my vitality exhausted,
> I cannot find the Ox.[1]

That about sums it up! If I am being honest, it would have been wonderful to have avoided feeling lost and on my own for quite so long. I spent many years losing the strength and vitality the poem speaks of, working too much and supported only by a bricolage spiritual practice that I now regard, in retrospect, as grasping at straws. When I finally did arrive at Zen, I was already too old to engage in the kind of all-out, intense training I craved and that I might have been able to do when I was in my twenties, which I remember as a time of endless energy and physical resilience. But again, I know that I cannot turn back time and change how my path unfolded.

I have Mr. Mike Brown to thank for my very first exposure to the *buddhadharma*, or the collected teachings of Buddhism. Mr. Brown was my middle school biology teacher, and one day, he chanced upon me browsing the Buddha figurines in a hippie and occult store—the kind selling glow-in-the-dark Grateful Dead posters, marijuana paraphernalia, and sarongs. Whether it was profound intuition or just a whim that moved Mr. Brown to give me a small cast metal figurine like the ones I'd been admiring in the store that day, he sensed correctly that I had a karmic affinity for Buddhism and that it would one day end up being my path.

I still have the statue he gave me. The Buddha depicted is young— thin and muscular, with one hand extended to the earth, representing the moment that the historical Buddha, Siddhartha Gautama, asked the earth to witness his final and complete enlightenment, perhaps around 500 B.C.E. Along with the figurine, Mr. Brown gave me a copy of a book by the renowned Soto Zen teacher Shunryu Suzuki called *Zen Mind, Beginner's Mind*.

Zen Mind, Beginner's Mind is a treasured text in the Buddhist world. But even my precocious, thirteen-year-old mind could not comprehend it. The extent of what I remember is picking up on a few spare instructions for meditation. I recall trying it out on a hill near Mr. Brown's fluorescent-lit classroom, where I helped feed rats to the class boa constrictor and where he taught us about species, genus, and the inner workings of cells.

"What are you doing?" I remember a classmate of mine asking, sticking her head out of a window as I sat on the grassy knoll during free period.

"I'm meditating," I said. Her only reply was to quietly pull her head back inside and slide the window shut.

I only attempted to meditate with Suzuki's instructions once more, after convincing another classmate to try it with me. But she did not share my curiosity or interest and had no similar karmic affinity, no inexplicable pull to just sit and count her breaths. She eventually became bored and then just got up and walked away. I returned *Zen Mind, Beginner's Mind* to Mr. Brown and stopped trying to meditate after that.

I finally returned to Buddhism at the age of twenty-six. At that time, I dove in with the kind of full-throated zeal I would've liked to have had as a teenager, with little regard for what my peers, parents, or schoolteachers thought. But it would have been very unlikely for me to find that kind of determination at such a young age. That is the rarest of the rare, either inexplicable and to be understood only as karma or the result of an unreasonably hard childhood. Those who have experienced the latter can possess a deep understanding of the difficult truths of Buddhism—suffering, sickness, old age, and death—and may find that they are more willing to do the hard work of Zen training.

At twenty-six, I was, myself, a little worn for my years because of my work advocating for human rights and democracy in the Southeast Asian country of Burma, also known as Myanmar, a calling in my teenaged years. I suffered from vicarious trauma and PTSD from living with the stories of horrific abuse and violence perpetrated by Burma's military regime, and from losing friends and acquaintances to the dictators' ethnic cleansing and political persecution. If not for a sobering need to do something radical in the face of the life-and-death circumstances I confronted in that work, I would never have started meditating seriously. It was the difficulties I encountered as an activist that brought me face to face with the purpose of meditation, the teachings of Buddhism, and, eventually, to the end of my work for a free Burma. Yet still, it would require pushes from beyond the world of rational explanation for me to take the leap so that I would finally, fully, and irreversibly jump in with both feet.

This book is the story of many such reaches, jumps, and leaps of faith, small and large, but primarily those I took once I arrived at Chozen-ji, the temple and dojo established by Tanouye Tenshin Rotaishi and Omori Sogen Rotaishi to bring *shugyo*, or the deepest possible spiritual training, to the West. My hope is that, in sharing my experience of monastic rigor that is at once traditional and modern, Old World and New, a new generation may gain a broader understanding of what it can mean to live fully and less governed by fear. Society's consensus today as to the best use of our incredible human bodies and precious human lives is, frankly, insufficient and shortsighted. It is possible to transcend such self- and societally imposed limitations. The key is in cultivating the body, the mind, and the spirit to be far more sensitive and far stronger than we normally think is possible. This book is a testament to the fact that there are time-tested ways to do so.

For my first thirty-five years, I had only an inexplicable yearning and the nagging suspicion that such a way of living existed. I knew of the Shaolin Temple, and I had even considered the more familiar monastic path of renunciation in places like Burma or Thailand. But, as an incorrigible political activist, I also felt a strong calling to remain of and in the world in a way I knew I would not be able to as a Buddhist nun. Resigned to a more mundane and mainstream life, I tried to fit myself into the boxes I more readily found in society. But I only ever met with dissatisfaction in the form of the nagging and persistent question: "Is this all there is?"

I eventually found my answer in the back of a valley all the way out in the middle of the Pacific Ocean. Here, a training method of surprising rigor and liveliness thrives at the crossroads of East and West, equidistant between America and Japan. At the same time, Chozen-ji has been geographically and culturally isolated, at least partially protected from the forces that have exploited and dulled so much of the world and so many of our spirits.

Here, I also experienced a different kind of homecoming, not just a spiritual arrival but also the chance to feel truly comfortable in my own skin as a woman of Asian ancestry. After I had begun to meditate seriously in my mid-twenties, I always sought out Buddhist communities to sit and meditate with wherever I went. It surprised me how much these various schools and sects differed— and also that they held certain things in common. The Tibetan and Zen Buddhist schools I encountered had strong lineages with clear cultural roots. There was usually a Tibetan monk or maybe second-generation Tibetan American, or a Japanese priest or Japanese American community member around, making me not the only Asian there. But sometimes, other members, who were almost uniformly white, would assume my Asian face meant that that this one other Asian person and I were related. Or they would assume I was Tibetan or Japanese or a recent arrival from Asia for whom English was a second language.

As insight meditation and secular mindfulness grew in popularity, I found myself sitting more and more with these groups, especially in the larger cities I lived in like Washington, New York, and San Francisco. I appreciated their commitment to simple, seated meditation. But I also struggled in these groups with the assumptions that the mostly older, white members projected onto me. I was confused and then later chafed when people asked about my Buddhist upbringing, assuming I had been raised Buddhist because I was Asian. But actually, my paternal grandmother and great-grandmother had converted to Christianity after the Korean War, and I grew up going, on and off, to an Episcopalian church. The disappointment I saw on their faces when I wasn't familiar with certain Buddhist sutras or philosophy made me feel as if I had failed an exam and as if they were casting judgment on my upbringing. It was also in these spaces that I heard the racist reasoning that Asian Buddhists weren't good Buddhists like us Americans because they didn't sit and meditate. Instead, theirs was a folk religion, obsessed with superstition and gaining merit through making offerings at temple. Not knowing any better at the time and full of zeal for meditation, I regrettably repeated this racist and imperialist trope.

As times changed and more meditation centers held sits aimed at people of color (POC), I gravitated toward these. These groups applied a racial justice lens to the teachings of Buddhism, or the dharma, and provided a space to meditate and listen to talks, all with other nonwhite people. But here, also, I could feel unwelcome or out of place. At that time, I wasn't yet able to see the root of my discomfort in the systemic erasure of Asian people and culture in predominantly white Buddhist spaces. I couldn't figure out why I felt uncomfortable; I only knew that I did. But at least in the POC groups, I didn't have to steel myself against the inevitable question about where I was "really from," and I was not addressed by non-Japanese people as Cristina-*san*.

Upon learning about Chozen-ji and then later arriving on the temple grounds, there wasn't just one thing that made me feel that I had come home. It was an accumulation of different things, beginning with how the use of the martial arts and physical labor as Zen training made my body feel strong and alive. I was not asked to believe in anything, except in the best intentions of the teachers and in whatever value I derived from my own training, and I wasn't asked to subscribe to any doctrine. Nor was I asked for money.

There was also an audacity in the ethos and spirit of the place that resonated with my own worldviews and personality. One thing that exemplified this was the fact that Chozen-ji has always been a place for people from all walks of life to find a home and a method to develop themselves, including seekers, businessmen, artists, laborers, and even Catholic nuns and priests. Here, I have found myself challenged to grow every way that I turn. As one of the Catholic sisters who long trained at Chozen-ji is said to have commented, the training made her a better Christian—and I feel that it's through my training that I've become simply a better human.

My experience at Chozen-ji has been one of becoming more and more comfortable in my own skin, and this was aided in no small part by the physical and cultural environment of Chozen-ji and Hawaiʻi. In fact, I cannot understate how important a role local Hawaiʻi culture has played in the development of Chozen-ji Zen and in my own training.

To share a sense of this, I've written this book to reflect, as much as I can, what it is like to live here. Throughout my time at Chozen-ji, this has meant that words can go untranslated for a while and that people expect me to behave in ways that may feel unfamiliar to me, as obvious as they may seem to someone who's, as they say in Hawaiʻi, "local." Sometimes, I can feel like a foreigner or a time traveler, challenged to take in the whole rich tapestry in front of me while also grasping at its threads as I try to comprehend certain cultural subtleties and nuances before they slip away. So sometimes, in this book, I leave Japanese, ʻŌlelo Hawaiʻi (Native Hawaiian), and Hawaiian Pidgin words without immediate translation, which is how they're often experienced in conversation at Chozen-ji. Keep reading, and I will translate them eventually! But if you feel the need to know what they mean right away, I have also included a glossary in the back of the book.

My greatest wish for you is that you may find your True Self—a version of you that is still you but just happy and free, beyond fear and any self-imposed limitation. To aid you in getting there, I also wish that you may find your own Chozen-ji, whether it's in the city or the country, in the middle of the ocean or on a high mountain plain. When you read this book, please find encouragement in its pages—encouragement that it is really possible to make progress toward your True Self in our modern, fast-paced world and that there are means to help you do so that have been tested and refined by millions of people over thousands of years, standing the tests of time. May you find in these pages the confirmation that yes, there can be more to being human and that there are ways to train so as to perfect human being. And that, in training hard, it is possible to find your way home.

1

IN THE PASTURE
OF THE WORLD

Aung Din was used to how cavalier—how American—I could be. That was why, on my last day in our cramped advocacy office in Washington, DC, he was giving me the sternest dressing down I'd ever received. The tension was as thick as the scent of garlic and spices that regularly filled the room, rising from containers of noodles and curries that Aung Din brought from home and then kept under his desk throughout the morning. Only inches apart, we sat at his one desk. The door was closed.

"You're not a blonde, blue-eyed American," Aung Din said to me sternly. "The secret police might think you are Burmese. You could be arrested. Did you think about that?"

Aung Din sat looking off into space for several moments, silent. It was a while before he spoke again.

"You could be tortured," he finally said.

He looked at me and then quickly waved his hand to dismiss any response. He knew me so well. With equal parts frustration and concern, he was trying to make me take my upcoming trip to Rangoon, Burma's capital, more seriously. No matter what altruistic goals I might have and how important we both felt our work for human rights and democracy in that country was, Aung Din felt that I needed to accept the reality of what I could face "inside."

I trusted Aung Din—he spoke from experience. Curt and soft-spoken, he had spent four years as a political prisoner for his part in organizing pro-democracy protests in Burma in the late 1980s, when he was just a university student. I had only heard him describe in broad strokes what his time in prison was like; he did not share specifics. But after working in the Free Burma Movement with refugees, dissidents, former political prisoners, and exiles for seven years, I knew well enough what he might have gone through.

For the entirety of my college career and a few years after that, I had spent most of my waking hours thinking, reading, and talking about Burma. My dedication—my infatuation—confused my friends, who asked if I ever took a day off. I didn't even know how to respond to that except to laugh. Of course I didn't. How could I? People were dying at the hands of a brutal military regime that belonged in the farthest reaches of fiction. Even if we lived on the other side of the planet, otherwise untouched by what was happening inside Burma, I held the immovable conviction that it was an affront to all of us that such horrors occurred unchecked in our world.

Aung Din and I continued talking for almost an hour, and over that time, his frustration with me only grew. I tried to reason with him that I had been working out the plans of my trip for a long time. I had done my homework, crossed my t's and dotted my i's. I reminded him that I was well versed in the international statutes and human rights conventions routinely flouted in Burma vis-à-vis forced labor, arbitrary detention, extrajudicial killings, military rape, and ethnic cleansing. I was familiar with the methods of torture and interrogation the Burmese military regime used against their detractors. After all, I had been sending briefings with such details to congressional staff and the State Department for the past seven years. Every time our organization and the Free Burma Movement pushed for a new round of sanctions on the Burmese regime or for more humanitarian aid, there was always the same old litany of political abuses to enumerate, as well as new evidence of ethnic cleansing to share.

Although I was only twenty-six years old, I had already regularly crossed the border into eastern Burma with armed rebels, visiting camps for internally displaced peoples, transporting aid, and outfitting jungle clinics. My senior year in college, I had founded a school for displaced children from the persecuted Karen ethnic minority. I had spent summers while in college living on the Thai-Burma border, working alongside refugees and exiled activists to build international legal cases against the Burmese regime, interviewing rebel generals and defected Burmese soldiers, and teaching the next generation of movement leaders the same basics of international human rights law I learned myself in college. But every time I mobilized such a defense to Aung Din, he only waved at me dismissively, the snap of his wrist getting sharper and sharper each time.

I did eventually concede to him. I spoke my thoughts aloud as the pieces came together, explaining that, up until this conversation, I had indeed only thought things through to the point of possible arrest and detention. All my energy had gone into avoiding that outcome, learning how to encrypt meeting notes and dispose of incriminating evidence. I had not thought about what would happen if I were actually picked up.

Finally, Aung Din asked me what seemed like a peculiar question, referring to the democracy activists that I was set to meet and interview while inside Burma.

"Why didn't you tell them that you're Korean?"

The question confused me.

"They thought you were American," he continued. "Now they're worried about you. They think it might be too dangerous."

It took a moment for what Aung Din was saying to add up in my head.

"Oh," I finally responded, "you mean they didn't know I'm *Korean American*."

"Yes."

"So they think the secret police would mistake me for Burmese," I said, continuing to think out loud.

"Yes. Probably," Aung Din said and then, after he had thought it over for a second, "as long as you don't talk."

In the long, quiet gap in conversation that followed, my thoughts went to a group of international college students who had been arrested in Rangoon in 1998, known as the Rangoon 18. The Rangoon 18 had staged small solidarity protests around the capital, wearing T-shirts printed with activist slogans, and they had leafletted temples and markets with messages of solidarity and freedom. The Americans, which included some Asian Americans, were given the most dangerous areas to hand out literature under the assumption that the US consulate would come to their aid if they were arrested, which they ultimately were. All the students—who hailed from the United States, Australia, Thailand, Malaysia, Indonesia, and the Philippines—ended up being detained for a week by the Burmese regime and were then sentenced, after a sham trial, to five years' hard labor and summarily deported. Back home, they were regarded among Burmese exiles as both heroic and naive. Two of the American students in the group were quoted in the newspaper comparing their experience in detention to summer camp. They had been allowed to remain together as a group and sang songs. They had had clean water, food, and were allowed to bathe, which was more than real political prisoners were granted. But I also remembered how a colleague whispered to me once that he thought one or two of the Asian and Asian American students might have gotten "slapped around a little."

"I'm so sorry, Aung Din," I finally stammered. "It didn't occur to me to tell them I'm Asian. But please tell them I still want to come. I'll be very careful."

"Have you even thought about how you could be putting them in danger?"

"Yes, of course," I said.

My carefully constructed demeanor faltered now, threatening to erase all the progress we'd made. I could not quell my pride, even despite all the obvious reasons that I should've been, at this point, fully humbled into contrition.

"But that's their decision to make," I said. My defiance, my arrogance, and my naivete ballooned to fill the tiny room.

Aung Din paused, looking at me with hard eyes. He took several breaths. By the time he spoke again, he had softened.

"You have done a lot for Burma and a lot for them," he said, referring to my years of advocacy, including times when I had helped rally international pressure to get some of the very dissidents I was going to meet out of prison. "We're not going to say no. But if something happens to you, we will be responsible."

There wasn't much left to say. I was out of defenses, and Aung Din knew there was no point in trying to convince me to cancel my trip. I made a few empty assurances that I would be careful, for myself and for anyone I would meet. I at least knew that he was acting out of care for me, not just trying to control me. And I knew that he worried for the activists inside who also happened to be some of his oldest friends. If something were to happen to them, he and I would both hold ourselves responsible for the rest of our lives. Only, Aung Din had a clearer sense of what that meant.

I said goodbye to Aung Din. Stepping out of the elevator, I rolled my bicycle into the bustle of lobbyists and otherwise nondescript office workers making their ways to the DC Metro. Like every other day when I left work, everyone else was in a black or navy suit. I zipped up my leather jacket, rolled up the right leg of my jeans, and then hopped onto my slender steel road bike, a vintage Schwinn I rode around Washington, DC, like a trusty steed, weaving in and out of traffic and racing past the besuited masses. Entering the portage road and then climbing northeast along the avenues, I headed home. Along the way, I tried to keep my mind on avoiding potholes and traffic rather than on the distant and more troubling dangers ahead.

2

"FOCUS HERE."

Miles and miles of empty fields, blanketed in snow, lined my approach to a vipassana meditation retreat center in rural Illinois. I arrived beyond relieved that I had completed the scary and snow-bound journey from Washington, DC. Over the long trip—driving alone and carrying in my station wagon everything I owned—the snow had gotten thicker and thicker until I almost couldn't see the road in front of me. I passed tractor-trailers jackknifed along the side of the interstate, recently crashed so that the deep snowdrifts had only just started to work their ways up the sides of the cabs. Some of the containers had even been torn open by the force of their careening on the ice, ripped into sharp points and with the trucks' contents strewn about the highway's snowy shoulders.

Now, upon my arrival, all I could see was silent, white winter farmland in every direction. The already short winter day had disappeared over many hours of driving. By the time I arrived, I could see the nearest city's faint orange glow on the horizon.

A few weeks earlier, I had decided that a ten-day silent meditation retreat was the best way to prepare for my upcoming trip to Burma. The idea had come from two friends, two of the toughest people I'd ever met. One was a wilderness rescue and first-aid trainer in Maine; in her twenties, she had solo hiked part or the entirety of all three trails of the rare and esteemed triple crown of American hiking: the Appalachian Trail, the Pacific Crest Trail, and the Continental Divide Trail. The other was a soccer player and a cyclist who had biked across Southeast Asia alone and done a stint in the Naval Reserve Officer Training Corps of the US Marines. Both had also completed ten-day meditation retreats in the S. N. Goenka school of vipassana, a style of Buddhist meditation. Despite having biked and hiked to the point of bleeding sores, dehydration, hypoxia, hunger, and exhaustion, the most extreme exercises in discipline and fortitude I could imagine, they still described these meditation retreats as the hardest things they had ever done.

The way my friends described their retreat experiences made it sound like torture. They spoke of excruciating pain in their legs from eight hours of sitting on the floor each day; back pain that made them spasm and shake; sleeplessness; a strict code of conduct in which they were prohibited from any kind of communication or even eye contact with others; and mental and emotional duress, subjected to an unending soundtrack of their harshest inner critics and minds that tried to trick them into giving up. But most importantly, both of my friends also said their meditation retreats were punctuated by moments of serene transcendence. These were times when they were so completely absorbed in meditation that their pain disappeared, at first momentarily and then later for extended periods. Whatever discomfort they experienced was eventually acceptable, if not actually perceived as a gift—a chance to investigate deeply the Buddhist truths of nonself and impermanence. I had never heard anything like it, and, facing the possibility of arrest and torture, it sounded like exactly what I was looking for.

My Burmese exile friends agreed. All of them had grown up with Buddhism and meditation indelibly woven into their lives. Some had been on retreats, as well, either in the Goenka school or in Buddhist monasteries. They described these retreats as hardcore—I would be meditating for eight to ten hours a day, often sitting through excruciating pain. And they agreed with me that, in that way, it could be a good way to prepare for the possibility of torture. They also encouraged me out of generous concern for my karmic merit, a common aspect of Buddhist belief in Asia that incentivizes good behavior with promises of a better life and rebirth. On those grounds alone, they would have encouraged me to sit a retreat. But it also couldn't hurt, they figured, if I did run into trouble.

So I registered for a standard ten-day silent vipassana meditation retreat. It began early in the morning, the day after my arrival. All of us "retreatants," which is what the staff called us, shuffled in two lines through the newly fallen snow, making what would soon become a daily trek from our dorms to the meditation hall. The women used a small bridge to cross over the pond in front of our separate, women's-only entrance. In its repurposing as a retreat center, much of the homeyness and character of what used to be a farmhouse had been scrubbed away and painted over in favor of an institutional aesthetic. It had been a long time since the fireplace was used, so long that I doubted it still worked. Above it, two boxy televisions were mounted on metal arms anchored to the wall. We sat on metal folding chairs in the dining hall, where we ate practical, bland vegetarian food. We slept on thin, twin-sized mattresses encased in vinyl, which squeaked whenever I moved and woke me repeatedly through my first night.

Entering the meditation hall for the first time, I could tell that a few of the retreatants had been here before, so I followed their leads as they made stations for themselves around the room. A utility closet off the hall held high metal shelves stocked with a rainbow of meditation cushions and benches, blankets, shawls, and throw pillows. I followed the more experienced retreatants as they fetched cushions and blankets and set them up in rows facing the fireplace. When it came time for the retreat to officially begin, nobody spoke, dutifully adhering to the vow of "noble silence" we'd taken the night before. To support the quieting of our minds, we committed to not speaking, pantomiming, or writing except if absolutely necessary. Finally, the televisions flickered on, and S. N. Goenka, the Indian Burmese teacher who had developed this style of retreat, appeared on-screen to welcome us.

Back in the 1960s, Goenka built on the work of his teacher U Ba Khin and other modern Burmese meditation masters, transposing the daily schedules of Burmese Buddhist monks so that serious meditative practice could be made more widely available for non-monks and regular people. Now there were hundreds of retreat centers like this one around the world practicing his method. Almost all the instructions and lectures, or dharma talks, we received over the following ten days came from Goenka-*ji*'s round, brown face on the TV, speaking to us, I guessed, from his home in India and filmed sometime in the distant past, judging by the quality of the video.

We listened to Goenka-ji, meditated, walked in the snow, and ate in silence. At first, we were instructed to sit, eyes closed, and to "focus here" on the areas of our upper lips, where, if we paid enough attention, we would soon perceive the soft inflow and outflow of our breaths entering and exiting our nostrils. For two days, that was almost all the instruction we received. Just "focus here" and to count our breaths. I quickly realized that to just sit in silence, eyes closed and "focusing here," was quite difficult. It was hard to sustain my attention for so long without succumbing to some sort of distraction. It took me those two whole days before I could even consistently count ten breaths without losing track. The rest of the time, my mind wandered, and I wove myself a web of daydreams, rumination, and planning.

Just like my friends had described, my body soon began to ache. My hips, knees, and ankles hurt, the pain increasing in intensity and frequency each day. I could only assume the other retreatants were feeling the same because they slowly accumulated more and more cushions—cushions propped under knees, second and third cushions under their rears, and cushions wrapped in blankets until some of them had built themselves whole recliners made of cushions. I was young, strong, and limber—and unable to empathize with the physical limitations of the other older retreatants. Rather than finding compassion in the pain that we shared, I instead reproached them in my mind. The silent spaces within each day were taken up by self-comparison and judgment. If this retreat had been a competition in suffering, I would have been determined to win it. After all, I was here to learn to withstand torture!

I looked down my nose at all the cushion thrones around me, even as I, too, broke. I concocted a bevy of excuses that finally justified my walking to the cushion closet to fetch a second meditation cushion and a small pillow to fold under my knee. Cushion accumulation proved to be a slippery slope. It wasn't long before I fetched another pillow for the other knee and then started playing Goldilocks with my main meditation cushion, thinking that if I tried enough different ones, I'd finally find one that relieved the pain in my buttocks. My behavior began to feel desperate, like an addict's. I was becoming a fiend for comfort. I became a more frequent visitor to the cushion closet. But finally, I arrived only to find that every single spare cushion had already been taken. I stood in the closet for what felt like a long time staring at the empty shelves. Only a ratty shawl was cast off in a far corner. A lonely lawn chair leaned against the wall.

Feeling defeated and unmoored—not just by the physical pain but by the anxiety and mental machinations that accompanied it—I plodded along, but now without the welcome distractions of cushion shopping. Following some new instructions from Goenka-ji, which I received from the televisions with reluctance, I began on the morning of day three to scan my body with my awareness, bringing my attention to each part of myself slowly, inch by inch. As often happened, I was soon off my breath. But then, something entirely unexpected and quite remarkable happened.

Several years flashed before my eyes. The best I could liken it to was watching a movie on super fast-forward. The years passed by in front of me in just a fraction of a second, yet every moment was rendered in great detail. And then it ended, just as unceremoniously as it had begun. It really was a flashback, and, once it was over, I opened my eyes and once again found myself sitting in the meditation hall, the televisions anchored at the front of the room, my co-retreatants with their cushion thrones all around me.

Just considering the mechanics of consciousness and memory that made the flashback possible made it nothing short of amazing. But what made the greatest impact on me was the content. In that very moment, I witnessed the years of my life from age twenty-one to age twenty-four like an impartial observer. And having lived through it already, I was surprised by how much of what had happened I saw anew and how much of it seemed, by virtue of this new perspective, pretty unsavory.

I had always thought of myself as an altruistic, generous, and emotionally aware person. I had dedicated my life thus far to the betterment of the world and humankind. I was the one who'd built a jungle school and raised awareness of the brutalities of Burma's military dictatorship. But in the flashback, I saw myself acting in ways that were selfish and hurtful. I saw that I took care of myself before I thought of others and that I put the movement and the perceived well-being of people thousands of miles away before the happiness of the people closest to me. I often ignored the feelings of my friends and family. I bypassed responsibility for the times that I caused harm to them—physically, mentally, and emotionally—and conducted myself in a way that could only be described as narcissistic, truly blind to my faults and the deleterious impacts of my actions. I had only been able to see the world through the lens of my own needs and desires. All of this was clear as day as I watched it play back at hyper speed. And yet I had previously been oblivious to it all. This was not exactly what I had come to this retreat for, but it changed my outlook going forward, beginning with how I approached the rest of my time on retreat.

Afterward, I returned to the cushion closet, but this time, it was to return all but one of the cushions and pillows that I had accumulated. I took a fresh look at all my indulgences and, for the rest of the time on the retreat, sat with a newfound determination to give things my all. As I continued to scan my body, my meditative concentration increased so that I, too, experienced moments of serenity and transcendence beyond my physical pain, which was otherwise extreme. I even began to think of the pain in my left knee as my most valuable teacher, appreciating it for the chance it gave me to practice deepening my concentration. I still wanted to outwork everybody on the retreat; that had not changed. But at least now it felt like it was coming from wanting to challenge and better myself rather than just wanting to be better than others.

After the retreat ended, the only way I could think to describe the clarity and insight I had gained was that it was like seeing something on the distant horizon. Like seeing El Dorado glittering on some far away mountaintop, I was propelled forward through the jungle by just having glimpsed it. However briefly I might have seen it, I knew that it was true. What I had experienced on the retreat felt like it landed with unquestionable confidence and finality, in my very bones. It left me with a feeling that there was more to life and more to me than I had previously known. Something was out there, just beyond my grasp. I knew that I had to keep reaching for it. Through hundreds of hours of meditation, retreats, and Buddhist study over the next twelve years, I would pursue more of this same feeling of waking up to the truth.

Shortly afterward, on the long plane ride to Bangkok, followed by overnight bus rides to the Thai-Burma border and then a short flight to Rangoon, I meditated in my seat. For the first time in seven years of making the same journey, I felt no pain. I thought to myself that, at the very least, I had taken from my retreat a mental protocol to fall back on if things went wrong inside Burma. I now knew how to sit, breathe, and focus my mind so that even pain was less of an obstacle.

But this was a small accomplishment in comparison to what I had truly learned, which was that there was a different way to see the world than how I had been seeing it for twenty-six years and a different way to be. Despite my dedicated activism and my good intentions, I was not the person I had thought I was or wanted to be. But I trusted the fact that I had now found a path forward so that, with a lot of practice, perhaps I could be.

3

INSIDE

Before I went inside Burma to meet with the leaders of the democracy movement, I spent a week in Bangkok and on the Thai-Burma border meeting with various NGOs, refugees, and exiles. After a week of this, I took the overnight bus back from the border to Bangkok and then departed for Rangoon. It was a short flight, only an hour and twenty minutes throughout which I did my best to pretend I was just an innocent backpacker on vacation. Upon arrival, I got into a taxi and rode to my hostel, a place I had chosen because of the large number of European backpackers who stayed there and for the fact that they offered an internet connection.

I had agreed to meet the next day with Min Ko Naing, Burma's second most prominent democracy activist after Nobel Peace Prize laureate and future prime minister Aung San Suu Kyi. We met at a small café frequented by expats, diplomats, and NGO employees—a place where the secret police were less brazen about their surveillance lest they cause an international incident. Min Ko Naing and I had been in touch in the months prior, and I had called him on his cell phone when I arrived to arrange our rendezvous.

Sitting in the café, I was reluctant to talk about my purpose for being in Rangoon, but Min Ko Naing spoke openly. I had heard about places like these being bugged by the secret police, so I wondered if the aloof café staff might be spies. But Min Ko Naing pressed me for the kinds of stories I was hoping to hear in my interviews. He did not quiet his voice around critical words like "protest," "revolution," or "political prisoner" or when mentioning the names of other activists.

Finally, Min Ko Naing was ready to leave, saying we would go meet some of his friends. In the cab, Min Ko Naing received call after call on his cell phone, and, not understanding much Burmese, I took the time to watch the city unfold, its dusty side streets and wide avenues baking under the bright, tropical sun. In many ways, Rangoon resembled the Thai cities with which I was more familiar. The big differences could be found, however, in the ways that the city and its citizens felt disjointed, out of sync. Glamorous K-pop stars were pictured on billboards advertising expensive face creams and cell phones. Their pale, made-up faces seemed to peer down at the men and women walking below and wearing traditional Burmese longyi and sandalwood paste, not expensive Korean creams, painted onto their darkly browned cheeks. When I caught a glimpse of a residential street from the taxi, I reflected on Burma's political, economic, and technological isolation and imagined that I could be looking upon a scene out of colonial times, the same as it might have looked a hundred years before.

At one point, Min Ko Naing said something curtly to the driver, and the cab lurched to a stop. After springing out, Min Ko Naing paid the driver through the window in what seemed like a terse and contentious exchange. The interaction was confusing, but there was nothing I could do but follow along.

"We'll walk a short way," Min Ko Naing said, and I did as told. Soon, he hailed another cab, and, as I sat down inside, I realized we were switching directions and cabs to avoid being followed by the secret police. The next time we switched cabs, though, it was because we were going quite far from downtown and the driver didn't want to take us all the way, but I guessed that suited Min Ko Naing fine.

When we finally arrived at our destination, I met the who's who of the Burmese pro-democracy movement. Like most educated, urban Burmese, they all had old-fashioned and literary senses of humor. They loved to laugh about puns and compare their real lives to the fictional works of Franz Kafka and George Orwell, whose famous book *1984* mirrored the disorienting doublespeak of Burma's military dictatorship. They were shrewd strategists but also incorrigible romantics whose stories contained a beautiful and absurdist quality alongside sharp political insights. Over the many hours I spent with them over the week, I was swept up in their nostalgic retellings of their teenaged years, tinged with the usual hormones and self-discovery but also by the excitement and danger of political revolution.

One moment, Min Ko Naing would be describing how economic hardship had sparked civil unrest in the mid- to late-1980s, leading to widespread protests inside Burma in 1987. The next, he would recount with delight how he and his friends spent their evenings serenading the girls they courted, climbing trees so they could sing to them from outside their bedroom windows. Min Ko Naing spoke of traversing the city standing on the back of friends' bicycles. With a guitar still slung across his back, they rode to underground meetings where they planned their next protest or political satire, a quintessentially Burmese approach to politics. One satirical show he told me about was *Goat's Eye*, a reference to the pervasive intelligence network of informants and secret police throughout Burma and also an allusion to the French philosopher Michel Foucault's Panopticon—itself a metaphor for a system of social control in which the fear of constant surveillance makes people docile and easy to control.

"If you look at a goat's eye," Min Ko Naing said to me, grinning widely, "you cannot tell which way it's looking, correct? It could be watching you ... "

He paused for dramatic effect and then shouted, "Watching everything!"

For many in Burma who came across *Goat's Eye* in the streets or, as it was later distributed, as a magazine, it riled up an incomparable sense of disgust for the ruling regime as well as the courage to stand up against it. Min Ko Naing was an activist, but he was also an artist who had used metaphor and humor to start no less than a revolution.

In between interviews, in long taxi rides, and as we often waited for his compatriots to arrive, Min Ko Naing asked about my life. I shared how I had recently completed a vipassana retreat and now meditated two hours a day, one hour in the morning and one hour in the evening. His response, to my surprise, was to say that I must be a saint. I knew Burmese culture to be very conservative, especially when it came to young women's behavior, so I squirmed while earnestly trying to convince him that, as a typical twenty-something living in a major American city, I was most definitely not.

When the conversation turned to my involvement in the Free Burma Movement, I tried to be strategic in what I shared. He knew that my interviews were not a part of any official campaign, just a personal project that I hoped would help the movement. But, in fact, my trip to Rangoon marked my departure from the advocacy organization where I'd worked with Aung Din for the past seven years. I had grown frustrated in the organization and in the movement, and with its internal politics. Too outspoken and idealistic, and insensitive to how others experienced my headstrong behavior and frequent confrontations, I earned at least one disparaging nickname: Mad Dog Moon. By the time I arrived in Rangoon, I was already becoming a lone wolf in the movement. And by myself, I had less support to manage the psychological and emotional toll of international human rights work. I may not have known it at the time, and certainly not enough so to share with Min Ko Naing, but my days working for a free Burma were numbered.

One day during my week in Rangoon, when there were no interviews arranged, Min Ko Naing took me on a tour of the city, beginning with a visit to his childhood home. A famous monk from Mandalay had been staying with a neighbor, and he thought I might like to meet him.

"He is an *arahant*," he said. "Do you know what arahant is?"

I did know what an arahant was: someone who was thought to have severed all their worldly attachments and could be considered enlightened. Though I knew what the word meant, I did not know what to expect of meeting an arahant in person. Perhaps, I thought, the monk would glow with the light of his realization, or I would feel awestruck in his presence. In actuality, I only encountered an old, skinny monk sitting on the floor, alone in an empty room. His white hair was shaved down to a short stubble, and he scratched like an idle child at the small rashes on his arms and chest. All he wore was a maroon robe slung across one shoulder and wrapped around his body. He smiled a sweet, toothless grin. I felt the marked absence of sagacity and awe in his presence. I was dismayed that all I really felt was my own nervousness.

Afterward, we walked through the backstreets of colonial neighborhoods that seemed untouched by time and which I ached to stop and explore. It was hot, and Min Ko Naing and I both sweated profusely. Much of the time, Min Ko Naing was punching text messages into his phone or talking on it while walking. Suddenly, he announced that we'd stop soon at a friend's house where we could shower. We arrived at a large and impressive home, and a beautiful, rail-thin woman opened the heavy wooden door, her face painted with yellow *thanaka* sandalwood paste, her long, black hair smooth and shining as it fell below her waist. We only chatted for a few minutes before Min Ko Naing stepped into the bathroom. He emerged a few minutes later, refreshed. I was sticky with sweat, my face slick, and I eagerly accepted the invitation to freshen up, as well.

In our host's bathroom, I hurriedly removed my clothes and then paused, suddenly self-conscious that I had not considered how exactly this shower was going to work. Instead of a tub or a shower in the bathroom, there was only a large, tiled cistern filled with water. A small plastic bucket with a handle, like a large ladle, floated there. I reached for it and began to pour big ladlefuls of water over myself and then poured some into a cupped hand so I could wash my face. It was then that I was struck by the curiousness of doing something so ordinary as taking a bath in a revolutionary's home.

When I came out, I was ushered into a side room by our host. She produced a sarong and matching traditional Burmese women's shirt for me to wear. Then, she handed me a tub of thanaka. I looked at it longingly but could only thank her and hand it back to her, admitting that I didn't know how to apply it. Taking it back from me, she proceeded to massage it into my arms and legs and then paint it onto my face with a firm and caring touch. As embarrassed as I was to be cared for in this way, like a child, I also luxuriated in how good it felt.

Finally, I saw myself in a mirror and saw a passing facsimile of a real Burmese girl. Lingering in front of the mirror, I stared not at myself but at the large poster of the Burmese democracy movement leader Aung San Suu Kyi on the wall just beyond my reflection. I knew that poster alone might be enough to get our host thrown in prison, and, as a bold act of defiance and love, it made me admire her even more.

When I emerged, Min Ko Naing clapped his hands and announced that he was going to sneak me into the famous Shwedagon Pagoda that night through the Burmese Only entrance.

"Please," he said apologetically, "don't talk."

We drove to Shwedagon, and I walked silently by his side past the guards at the Burmese Only entrance. There were no foreign tourists in sight. Once we had made it into the elevator, he expressed his delight at what felt like a small win against the regime.

Today, Shwedagon Pagoda is a cultural destination and tourist attraction, but in 1988, it was the site of mass protests, rallies, and the killings of pro-democracy demonstrators. As we walked around,

Min Ko Naing pointed out the places around the temple where he had camped for weeks during the protests and then to the spots where people he had known were gunned down. We stopped to ladle small cups of water onto statues for the minor gods watching over people born on each day of the week. I found the statue for the day of the week Min Ko Naing was born on and poured water over it, my heart breaking for all that he had lived through and wishing with all my might that at least his future might be safe and happy. Later, at a sidewalk food stall below the golden stupa, we sat on low plastic stools, eating pennywort salad and fried yellow lentils with onions, and I felt totally enveloped in the magic of the place as well as the epic stories of human struggle I had been hearing and recording all week.

When Min Ko Naing dropped me off at the airport, we exchanged a warm goodbye. We said that maybe we would meet again—next time, we said, in a free and democratic Burma. I had come to feel very close to Min Ko Naing and his colleagues and worried about what lay ahead for them. He didn't give me much time to dwell on it, though, ending our goodbyes by hopping back into the car and speeding away.

Alone now, I steeled myself for the last challenge of my journey. I had meditated for a long time that morning and reflected on how I had made it this far without getting anyone arrested or hurt. But my trip wasn't over. I went through my mental checklist: All of my notes were encrypted, compressed, and hidden on a thumb drive tucked into the travel pouch I wore beneath my clothes. I had stayed up all night transcribing the recordings of my interviews and then deleted the recordings. In the transcriptions, each of the people I had interviewed was identified using a fake name. The notes were also scrambled so that anybody aside from me would struggle to connect one paragraph to another. I had torn up any paper notes, burning some and flushing others down the toilet.

I walked through the airport and made it past the usual customs checkpoints and exit screening. I proceeded to walk toward my gate. No bag checks, no questions. As I neared the gate, I realized there was only one checkpoint left. The military officer there took my US passport and inspected it. For a moment, he held it up alongside my face and looked at me, comparing me to my image. As he did so, I felt a tinge of anxiety. Then, I remembered a kind of meditation I had learned on the Goenka retreat, called *metta*, or loving-kindness.

"May you be happy," I thought to myself, sending rays of warmth from my heart to the solider's, pushing all the warm feelings toward him that I could.

"May you be free from suffering. May you be at peace," I thought and smiled.

The officer made a note in my passport, looked up, and held it out to me. As I went to take it from his hand, I noticed that now he, too, was smiling. I looked him in the eye and smiled again. As he released my passport, he smiled even wider. And then he winked.

Six months later, in August 2007, everyone I had met in Rangoon, including Min Ko Naing, was arrested. Interview follow-up was shelved as I again turned my focus to advocating for their releases. Then, the work stayed on the shelf as I was swept up by another and then another urgent campaign. When I finally accepted a job offer outside of the Free Burma Movement the next year, working on the 2008 US Presidential election, Min Ko Naing and others remained in prison, and even the idea of reengaging the project felt like visiting a house full of ghosts. I couldn't bring myself to do it. It was at that time that I realized that I might never revisit those interviews and that I might never see Min Ko Naing and his colleagues ever again. I also admitted to myself that I might finally be leaving the Free Burma Movement for good.

Continuing to meditate seriously had helped me begin to see how much of a toll my Free Burma work had taken on me. I had mystery ailments and lingering symptoms from contracting typhoid twice on the Thai-Burma border. My adrenal glands were fried, and I had never had health insurance from my job, so what little knowledge of my health that I did have came from the occasional doctor's visit when I could afford to pay out of pocket. My relationships bore years of strain, caused by my always putting the movement before the people who cared most about me.

Over the following years, I moved from campaign to campaign and movement to movement. All along the way, I kept meditating and exploring Buddhism, finding relief from the traumas of my Free Burma work. But new questions about the meaning of life also began to arise, as what had been my greatest, singular purpose faded in the rearview mirror. I eventually found new purpose, broader and more effuse but also tempered by less egoism and judgment. In Buddhism, I found inspiration to accept and engage people as they were. This led me to San Francisco and Silicon Valley, working in social-change technology and then, eventually, to business school—something my brazen and antiestablishment younger self could never have imagined.

Curiously, business school ended up being the place that most encouraged me to pursue my passion for Buddhism and meditation. Of course, the means of doing so were limited to the kinds of ventures that made sense in Silicon Valley—corporate mindfulness, health trackers and stress-relief devices, and luxurious meditation retreats for startup CEOs and venture capitalists. It was when I was running marketing for one of these corporate mindfulness groups that I finally learned about Chozen-ji and decided to take some vacation time to check it out. Of that, we had plenty, as the organization I worked for gave us time each year to attend meditation retreats. I asked the head priest at Chozen-ji if I could come and train, agreeing that I would stay for one and then later three weeks.

It was a leap. Although I had been to Hawai'i on vacation before, I had never been to O'ahu and had never held an interest in Zen. I had also been a little nervous about being in heavily Japanese environments because of the bitter history of Japan's colonization of Korea, which spanned all the way from the late nineteenth century until the end of World War II. Almost every Korean family has stories from that time, their enduring grief and trauma passed down through the generations. But I was pushed past all this by my eagerness to explore what it was that Chozen-ji offered: approaching Zen through the body. And though I couldn't yet put a finger on it, it felt like something else mysterious but unmistakable was pulling me there.

4

"THIS IS NOT A DRILL."

On January 13, 2018, every person with a cell phone in the Hawaiian Islands received this text message:

> Emergency Alert—BALLISTIC MISSILE THREAT INBOUND TO HAWAII. SEEK IMMEDIATE SHELTER. THIS IS NOT A DRILL.

For months, US president Donald Trump and North Korean supreme leader Kim Jong Un had been trading diplomatic barbs across the Pacific Ocean. Beyond the belittling names they called each other—"rocketman," "dotard"—there were ballistic missile tests, war games, and even a hydrogen bomb test, or at least that's what North Korea said. So when the missile alert came in, millions of people in paradise really believed that this could be the end.

Videos instantly appeared on social media showing how people took the news: a father lowered his young daughter into an open sewer drain hoping beyond hope that it would protect her from a coming nuclear blast, tourists in swimsuits and shorts swarmed across the lawn of the Hilton Hawaiian Village, and whole families took shelter in their bathtubs. As he would later recount in an interview, the actor Jim Carrey was at his home in Hawaiʻi that day. After seeing the emergency alert, he declined to meet up with friends and colleagues on island; he didn't want to die in his car. Instead, he chose to sit out on his lanai and count his blessings. Soon, he was wrapped in a moment of grace, ready to close his eyes for the last time to the sight of a bright white flash.[2]

At Daihonzan Chozen-ji, a small Rinzai Zen temple in the back of Kalihi Valley on Oʻahu, a few people had been getting set up for an annual memorial service for the temple's founder, Tanouye Tenshin Rotaishi. They had driven up that morning from various points on the island, traveling along long and winding Kalihi Street. Their destination was almost at the very end of the road, at the terminus of a valley in the Koʻolau Mountain Range.

At the temple, simply called "The Dojo" by those who knew it, members set out snacks and arranged flowers. Inside the large martial arts hall, small, elegant tables stood in front of racks of practice swords. On top of the tables, flowers were being artfully arranged in large ceramic vases. Bright fluorescent lights recessed into the twenty-foot-high ceiling beams masked the fact that the winter morning light was only just filtering in. Walking softly but working quickly on the light green, rubberized tatami flooring for martial arts like Judo and Aikido, a Chozen-ji priest named Michael—tall, muscular, and with the lithe movement of a martial artist—was setting up rows of folding chairs.

"It was 8:11," he would later say about the moment his phone buzzed in his pocket. "It was bright and sunny with clouds that morning. It's hard to describe, but I looked at my phone and laughed: 'OK, this is how it goes down.'"

In contrast to the scenes playing out in the rest of the islands, there was no panic at Chozen-ji. Michael put in a call to the temple's abbot, Sayama Daian Roshi, to see what they should do. Should they cancel the memorial service? Maybe, Sayama Roshi said, but he was already on his way and wanted to continue on, missile alert or no.

After he hung up the phone, Michael did a quick mental assessment of how hard Chozen-ji might be hit, nestled as it is in the back of the valley and protected on all sides by mountains. Lush, wet, and green, Chozen-ji feels rural, but it's only fifteen minutes from Honolulu's international airport. And although many local people remark that they have never, in decades of living on O'ahu, come so far back in the valley, it's only five miles from downtown. Calculating it all, Michael decided that there would have to be a direct hit to the Kalihi neighborhood for the back of the valley to be wiped out. The likelihood of that was slim. But in case they were in the farther ranges of a nuclear blast, he did think about which buildings would be best to take cover in. He reconciled himself to the fact that Chozen-ji, with its rustic construction and thrifty materials, would probably be a complete loss.

"There was no sadness," he would later recall. "Just looking at the situation and recognizing it for what it was. And that really quick check-in, like, 'Ready to go?' Everyone I loved knew I loved them. I didn't have any loose ends. So yeah, I guess so."

Somewhere high above, as the missile alert came in, I was in the air, en route to Hawai'i but still waiting to touch down. By the time I landed, the governor had finally found his Twitter password, so he could tell the public that the missile alert was a false alarm, a technical error caused by the ancient computers down at Hawai'i's Department of Defense. From my window seat on the plane, everything outside looked as I thought Hawai'i must always look: bright, warm, and like paradise. It was only after we had begun to taxi that I saw a screenshot of the false missile alert on my phone and a text message that read, "It's been an exciting morning."

I waited at the curb to be picked up at the airport and was surprised that everything seemed to be operating as usual. Nobody seemed to pause on the fact that a missile alert had just happened. A small, white pickup truck arrived promptly, driven by someone sent by Chozen-ji, a Chinese Hawaiian man in his early fifties. My flight landed just as activities were wrapping up at the Dojo, but in keeping with local custom, my offers to find my own way by bus or taxi were graciously and firmly refused. I would be picked up, and there would be no further discussion about it.

Clearing a rise on our way to the main highway, the H-1, we came out of the shadows of access roads and emerged into the bright Hawai'i sun. Once we were on the elevated highway, it wasn't long before I could see the sweeping expanse of the island and the endless blue ocean around it. On one side of the highway were mostly short, one- and two-story industrial buildings, warehouses, factories, and the occasional strip mall. Emerald green mountains cascaded down from the other side toward the industrial flats, the highway bisecting the two landscapes. As the truck moved across several lanes of traffic, a huge half rainbow emerged from the mist in front of the mountains.

"Oh, wow. Look at that rainbow!" I remarked.

"Oh?" my driver replied. At first, he kept his eyes on the road. But later, he seemed to collect himself, remembering that I was brand new to Hawai'i and unused to such daily miracles.

"Oh shoot," he said with dramatic emphasis. "Sorry, yeah? Forgot to call in a full one."

Pulling off the H-1 and onto a smaller highway named after the Hawaiian princess Likelike, the working-class neighborhood of Kalihi Valley came into view. We made a quick turn into a shopping center to pick up some lunch to bring to the Dojo. Emerging from the truck, I looked around and saw so many brown, Asian faces that, had I not known better, I might have questioned whether I was still in America. Micronesian women walked by in flip-flops and long skirts with large flowers appliquéd near the hems. Their waist-length hair was pulled into loose braids and buns that sat atop their heads, and their flip-flops slapped the pavement as they walked with the slow, languorous gait of the developing world. A few white-haired Asian shoppers shuffled with groceries to their cars. Teenagers with dark, tawny skin, thick shocks of black hair, and scant mustaches walked by with skateboards under their arms. Three brawny young men loitered on the upper level of the parking structure, watching the comings and goings of the people down below with what I mistakenly interpreted as a menacing air.

After walking by a Korean BBQ takeout place, we entered a Vietnamese lunch counter. A Starbucks, GNC, and Jamba Juice just around the corner affirmed that, yes, we were still in America. But what I took from the stores and the people felt both like America and not at the same time. I felt as if I were standing at an unexpected intersection of . . . what? Southeast Asia and East Los Angeles, perhaps? The only comparisons I could think of were the Chinatowns and Little Hanois I'd been to in mainland cities or the small island community of Alameda in the San Francisco Bay Area, where almost every other face seems to be Asian.

My Korean face helped me blend in when I visited many of these Asian enclaves, but it was evident in my broad-shouldered, confident walk that I did not call such places home. I grew up mostly in Connecticut, in a suburb of Manhattan, but by the time I was twelve, I had also lived in Manila, Seoul, Hong Kong, and Mexico City. My parents' uniquely metropolitan outlook and these global experiences contributed to a watering down of our Koreanness. We eschewed the small diaspora community nearby. We stopped going to Korean church when I was ten. During my years in Connecticut, I was for the most part one of only a handful of Asian kids in my school. I adopted the boisterous defiance of the boys I played with after school, whose roots were Italian, Jewish, and Irish. Riding bikes and trampling through the woods, I bore little resemblance to the obedient and studious Korean girl many expected.

When I was in my early thirties, after living and working in half a dozen major American cities, I moved to the San Francisco Bay Area for work and, eventually, business school. It was on the suburban island of Alameda that I walked the streets and saw not just Asian faces but also Asian bodies that resembled my own. The Asian Americans who lived on Alameda were second-, third-, and sometimes even fourth- or fifth-generation Americans. The kids played basketball, softball, football, and tennis. I saw them streaming out of the public pool, loud with laughter, their straight black hair plastered to their heads, their bodies muscular and darkly tanned. They spoke perfect American English. Their shoulders were thrown back, and their heads held high. They were masters of their small island universe. Unlike in most Chinatowns, where the communities are mostly immigrants and often newer arrivals, these Asians were born of that land. In these youngsters, I saw myself and my own childhood outside of my own body and memory for the first time.

But the Kamehameha Shopping Center of Kalihi Valley was far different still. Here, I found a truly unprecedented mix of all sorts of different Asian peoples who all walked with the confidence and swagger of being of this place and at home. It did not seem like they had ever had to sacrifice their Asianness to belong. Even us East Coast and California Asians had had to do that, to some degree. But here, they did not code-switch, and they behaved as if they took it for granted to live surrounded by an eclectic and diverse mix of other Asians. First, second, third, and fourth generations blended with each other seamlessly, as well as with the shoppers whom I guessed to be Native Hawaiian.

Outside of Alameda, I had always felt an uncomfortable distance between myself and the insular enclaves of recent Asian immigrants. Not only was I very Americanized, but the differences between our ethnic backgrounds also separated us. Korean, Vietnamese, Chinese—we all shopped in different stores, ate different food, and spoke different languages, even, it seemed, when we were speaking English. But here, everyone was shopping at the same grocery store, where *pancit* and *mei fun* sat in one aisle, mochi and *kulolo* in another. The diner in the corner of the strip mall had everything on its menu from spaghetti and Hawaiian *lau lau* to oxtail soup and kimchi fried rice. Still recognizably distinct in where they came from and who their people were, everyone here shared space, regarding each other as neighbors and enjoying each other's cultures.

As we walked in to the lunch counter, my ride's voice took on the singsongy lilt of Hawaiian Pidgin, a creole language from Hawai'i's pineapple and sugar plantations, where Japanese, Korean, Chinese, Filipino, Native Hawaiian, and Portuguese laborers all worked and lived side by side. He greeted the woman behind the counter with a booming "Aloha" and let her know we'd be getting some lunch to go. Glass cases of banh mi, summer rolls, and sticky rice desserts gleamed under the fluorescent lights. I moved toward the refrigerator of coconut waters and tapioca puddings, surveying the flavors: coconut, taro, and chocolate. After ordering, the driver needed to run next door to the grocery store to grab something and asked me to wait for him. Sensing that I might try to pick up the tab while he stepped out, he joked loudly with the woman behind the counter that he was going to pay.

"Sistah," he said, addressing the woman and smiling broadly, "she just got in from da mainland. I wanna show her how we treat guests. So if she try pay, don't take her money, OK?

"OK?" he asked a second time. "Promise me now." He made sure she nodded in agreement before he stepped out of the store.

I made small talk with the woman behind the counter, who asked where I came from and talked about family she had on the mainland. Her smile was warm. Even though I had been outed as being an outsider just a moment before, she quickly made me feel welcome and at home. I would learn later how many of the people here in Hawai'i were outsiders—"transplants" and "settlers"—of one kind or another. But the earliest Asian settlers had recognized the importance of being fluent in ʻŌlelo Hawaiʻi, and everyone learned what it meant to treat each other with aloha. The driver of the pickup soon returned and invited me to pick out a few desserts. I pulled one of each flavor of tapioca pudding from the refrigerator.

It was another ten minutes in the truck to Chozen-ji. As we continued driving, the road began to narrow, and the densely packed houses gave way to more trees, greenery, and open spaces. After passing a giant tree, aerial roots descending from its branches, the road narrowed to only a little wider than one lane. At this point, everything all around was jungle. Wild chickens, myna birds, and the occasional white egret skittered across the road or pecked through the roadside litter. Finally, after a few more residential driveways and homes, we came up one last rise. Then, the view opened up suddenly, and an expanse of gray gravel and Japanese-style buildings unfolded beyond a chain-link fence, one ridge of the Koʻolau Mountains visible.

We pulled into the parking lot of Chozen-ji, and, as I exited the truck and fetched my large backpack from the truck bed, I could see that the property stretched back a ways. With my bag hanging off my shoulder, I walked down the gravel driveway, noticing Japanese-style buildings continuing down the path. The gravel finally ended at the edge of a green forest of trees and bamboo. To my right rose a small, steep hill. The side of the hill was covered with a stunning wall of ferns and wild orchids. Looking up to the top of the hillside, I recognized the setting as one I'd seen in a photo on the temple website of the founder Tanouye Rotaishi and Native Hawaiian spiritual leader Nana Veary. The photo had been captivating; I was taken by the thought of the respectful meeting of Japanese Zen and Native Hawaiian spirituality, and by the contents of the photo, too. In it, Tanouye Rotaishi's and Nana Veary's darkly tanned faces wore brilliant smiles, faces cheek to cheek against the bright sky.

We proceeded down the gravel driveway along a low rock wall. Several long stone and wooden steps led to what seemed to be the main hall. Above the hall's double doors hung a large wooden board bearing the characters 武道 (*Bu Do*), meaning "the Martial Way" or "martial arts," carved into it. At the top of the steps stood two of Chozen-ji's teachers waiting to greet me.

I was happy to see them, especially Michael, the head priest. Michael and I had met years before, prior to either of us taking up Buddhism and meditation seriously, he at Chozen-ji from the young age of twenty-two and me on my own, meandering path a little later on. Six months earlier, he had emailed me to say that he had been asked—after his decade and a half of serious training and after starting two other dojos—to move in full-time at Chozen-ji and bring up a new generation of Zen students. He knew that I had been meditating for a long time. If I ever found myself in Hawai'i, he'd written me, I'd be welcome to come for a visit. It just so happened that I had just then decided to plan a trip to Hawai'i. This made it a foregone conclusion that I would drop by Chozen-ji. We corresponded at length, and the duration of my visit expanded from a short visit to a one-week stay, then two, and finally what he described as a full cycle: three weeks of traditional "live-in," or residential, training.

Now here I was, my feet finally on the temple grounds. Both teachers did their best to wrap their arms around me and my massive pack. It was only after the hugs that I thought to unfasten my bag and drop it on the wooden walkway, and as I did so, I glimpsed Michael out of the corner of my eye, bending his tall frame down to turn my flip-flops (or in local parlance, slippers) around. The other teacher departed, leaving Michael and me to sit on the faded orange carpet of the kitchen surrounding several low tables. Sitting with our legs folded beneath us, Japanese style, we talked about what was to come: two quiet days as we rode out the weekend and then training beginning in earnest on Monday. I'd be getting a relatively gentle introduction to Zen training and ample time to settle in.

As we left the building, I realized that Michael's turning my slippers around was in anticipation of our eventual exit. Now I had only to step into them—I didn't have to turn around, first, slowing down my departure. I quickly saw the efficiency of being able to just step in and walk away.

A light rain had fallen while we were inside, and puddles of rainwater had collected in the deep indentations of my slippers. My feet sloshing in the puddles, I stepped from the top of the stairs, and just as I did, both feet slid straight out from under me.

Boom! I fell squarely on my behind on the wooden steps.

I jumped up quickly and said I was all right, finding Michael amused but unfazed. I straightened my short skirt, which I had just learned did not meet the Dojo's dress code.

"We sit on the floor a lot," Michael had said by way of explanation. And apparently, one sometimes also falls embarrassingly on her ass.

Thus began my introduction to Chozen-ji.

5

DAIHONZAN CHOZEN-JI

Near the front of Chozen-ji's property stands a rustic wooden sign with a shingled roof, a multilayered lintel cut at upward angles like a traditional Japanese gate. The kanji, Japanese writing using Chinese characters, that is carved and painted in calligraphy on the sign reads 超禪寺:

超 (*cho*)—beyond, transcendent, super
禪 (*zen*)—Zen
寺 (*ji*)—temple

This can be translated several ways—as "the temple of Zen transcending Zen" or "Zen temple transcending the form of a Zen temple." Tanouye Rotaishi liked a translation that was based on the colloquial use of 超 (cho) as "super"—that is, "super Zen."

Three additional smaller characters, 大本山, are inscribed above the temple's name:

大 (*dai*)—big, great

本 (*hon*)—central

山 (*zan*)—mountain, temple

A *daihonzan* is a central headquarters temple and the seat of its own new line of Zen. A daihonzan usually oversees a network of subtemples, which feed the daihonzan young people to train as monks and ordain as priests. The daihonzan also assigns priests to the subtemples every few years. But aside from Chozen-ji, no other daihonzan has ever been created outside of Japan. Even inside Japan, a new daihonzan has not been designated in more than four hundred years.

It is impossible to understand how this significant feat was accomplished without knowing who Chozen-ji's founders, Tanouye Tenshin Rotaishi and Omori Sogen Rotaishi, were. Tanouye Tenshin was born in 1938 in Honolulu, where he grew up and later studied music at the University of Hawai'i at Mānoa. There, he heard a lecture by the Japanese Zen scholar D. T. Suzuki about Zen and the martial arts that inspired him to commit himself to understanding the nature of reality through Buddhism. Upon graduation, he became a band teacher, teaching first at King David Kalākaua Middle School and later at Governor Wallace Rider Farrington High School.

Tanouye was a martial arts genius. Between the ages of twenty-two and thirty-two, he acquired sixth- and seventh-degree black belts in seven different Japanese martial arts, ranging from Judo ("the Gentle Way," or wrestling) to Kendo ("the Way of the Sword," or Japanese fencing). On his memorial at Chozen-ji, each of the seven arts are listed in the order in which he achieved his final ranking, with each of the Japanese schools in which he earned his ranking identified. As a teacher, Tanouye was able to travel to Japan each summer to train in various martial arts. I was told that he had trained in so many martial arts because he wasn't sure where he would ultimately find his teacher. Whether he turned out to be a Karate master or a Kendo master, he wanted to be ready to jump right in without wasting time on just the basics.

After years spent traveling between Hawaiʻi and Japan, however, Tanouye had yet to find his teacher. He was almost ready to give up and become a mountain hermit when someone recommended that he meet one last teacher, a highly respected Zen master, swordsman, and calligrapher. This man, Omori Sogen Rotaishi, was regarded by many as Japan's last real samurai. D. T. Suzuki, the Zen master and scholar Tanouye had heard speak at the university, had even recommended at one time that the emperor of Japan do *sanzen*, or Zen koan training, with Omori Rotaishi. Tanouye sought him out, and they agreed to meet. Upon meeting, he quickly upbraided Omori Rotaishi in the same way he did any new teacher he encountered, interrogating him about the poor state of martial arts in Japan, which had been hollowed out during the US occupation of postwar Japan.

Other Zen and martial arts masters that Tanouye had approached similarly became defensive or angry. But Omori Rotaishi, already an elegant old man, bowed and simply said, very politely, "I have no excuse." Later, he handed his soon-to-be student a copy of *Zen and Budo*, a book he had written ten years earlier with the same critique. He even specified in the book the very date on which he believed real Kendo had died.

Omori Rotaishi was a master of Kendo and of the *Hojo*, a five-hundred-year-old sword form that had come to its creator all at once, in a dream. Tanouye Rotaishi later recounted that, upon seeing the Hojo for the first time, he saw in it the secrets of all the martial arts. He immediately asked Omori Rotaishi if he could learn it. Hearing that he only had three days left in Japan, Omori Rotaishi laughed and said he should come back when he had three years. Tanouye asked to be allowed to at least begin, a request that was granted by Omori Rotaishi, and within those three days, Tanouye mastered the Hojo to the point that Omori Rotaishi authorized him to teach it.

Tanouye had finally found his teacher. In addition to being a

Zen and martial arts master, Omori Rotaishi was also a political strategist. In his biography, which I had read prior to my arrival, he described the most crucial period in his time as an adviser to the Japanese imperial court, when he was going every day to the home of the man expected to be the next chief adviser to the emperor, trying to prevent Japan's entrance into World War II.

"If I hadn't been so weak," he is quoted, "I might have been able to prevent the war. I deeply regret this."

With these words, Omori Rotaishi referred to not being able to convince the next chief adviser to seek an imperial order to designate a commander of the army who would not bring Japan into the war. The two candidates he had in mind would have had the wisdom and courage to prevent Japan from entering World War II, but neither met the technical requirements of the role. This could be overcome by an imperial order, which the adviser could request, but to ask for one would bring irreversible shame on the adviser and his family, as it would be seen as "hiding behind the emperor's skirt" and, possibly, treason.

"I said, 'Please hide behind the emperor's skirt. I know the extreme dilemma you are in . . . but please sacrifice your . . . family reputation for the sake of Japan. Hide behind the emperor's skirts and bear the dishonor of being called a traitor. Please crush your family and save Japan. Please, I beg of you.'"

At some point, no longer able to get an audience with the chief adviser to the emperor because he only repeated this same appeal every time, Omori Rotaishi gave up.

"When I think of it now," he is quoted saying in his biography, "I was weak of purpose. I should have persisted until the end. If one trains in Zen, one must do everything thoroughly and completely, but in this case, I neglected to do it. I should not have given up. I should have persevered and even used intimidation if necessary. This is the one thing that I regret deeply."[3]

Later, Omori Rotaishi served as the president of Hanazono

University in Kyoto and was a widely sought after mediator with the Tokyo Bar Association. In 1948, Omori Rotaishi took over as the priest of Koho-in, the temple of Yamaoka Tesshu, a legendary swordsman and samurai who was instrumental in the Meiji Restoration and later became a Zen priest. Although, before I had arrived, I had thought of the martial arts as secondary to Zen at Chozen-ji, it didn't take long for me to understand that the temple's samurai lineage is of equal importance to its formal Buddhist lineage. In some ways, I would later learn, this warrior ethos and spirit even trump some of the more institutionalized aspects of Japanese Zen.

It was in this Zen warrior spirit that, in 1972, Tanouye asked for five years of Omori Rotaishi's life to bring shugyo to the West. "Shugyo" is one of six words in the Japanese language that describe spiritual training. It lacks a direct English translation but can be roughly understood as the deepest possible spiritual discipline. Another way to understand it is, when one is doing shugyo, there is nothing in life that isn't training—that is, nothing that cannot be used as a way to approach one's True Self (a phrase which is synonymous in Zen with Enlightenment). But even this, too, is an incomplete understanding.

Despite a lot of talk in the 1960s and 1970s about Buddhism, selflessness, and compassion, Tanouye Rotaishi felt that many in the West were missing the means to not just *act* selfless and compassionate but *be* selfless and compassionate. Shugyo, he felt, was the missing link. It cultivated the kind of strength—physical, psychological, and spiritual—one would need to live up to the ancient meaning of the word "compassion," derived from the Latin for "with" and "to suffer." To *suffer with* somebody takes more than empathy or kindness. It takes strength, and it takes spiritual strength in particular. To describe this kind of spiritual strength, they used the Japanese word *kiai*, and kiai became a foundational element of what would come to be known as Chozen-ji Zen. Together, Omori Rotaishi and Tanouye Rotaishi defined Chozen-ji Zen as a psychophysical—or mind/body—approach. This innovation accelerated the maturity, strength, sensitivity, and transcendent insight already cultivated by monastery-style Zen training.

In 1972, Chozen-ji was officially founded in the line of Rinzai Zen coming down from Daihonzan Tenryu-ji, in Kyoto. At its founding, Chozen-ji did not yet exist as a physical temple. For a while, it existed physically as the contents of two trunks that were carried around to wherever people wanted to train, beginning with Tanouye's band classroom at Farrington High School. Farrington was known back then as a rough school. And according to an early student of Tanouye's, band was not yet an elite class with high-performing students as it would become in later decades. It was a place you were more apt to find "the criminals."[4] Many of Farrington's students and even some of the teachers turned out to be excellent students in Omori Rotaishi and Tanouye Rotaishi's style of warrior Zen.

Chozen-ji eventually outgrew the band room and moved, first into a retail space and then into a small house known as the Kokea Street Dojo. Until the Dojo found a permanent home, the intensive weeklong training held twice a year and called sesshin was held in the martial arts classroom that Tanouye Rotaishi had created at Farrington. Food was prepared at the Tanouyes' house and brought to the school, a makeshift sword rack was perched on the blackboard, and calligraphies by Omori Rotaishi were hung on the cinderblock walls.

In 1976, Chozen-ji finally broke ground on its permanent home on two and a half acres of what was then just eucalyptus grove in the back of Kalihi Valley. Tanouye Rotaishi had had a choice between this parcel and a smaller plot of land in nearby Mānoa, which was closer to town and the university and already had some buildings on it. But he reasoned that, with all the young, strong men he had training with him already, it was better to have a place where they could start from scratch and shape the land themselves. It would give the students plenty of exhausting work to do, which was perfect for entering Zen, as Tanouye Rotaishi would say, through the body.

In 1979, Omori Rotaishi designated Chozen-ji as a daihonzan, a central headquarters temple, in the Tenryu-ji line. In 1975, he had gone through the *kaido* ceremony at Tenryu-ji, which made him the archbishop of Tenryu-ji for a day—a way to formally recognize his stature and realization in Japanese Rinzai Zen. Completing the ceremony meant that Omori Rotaishi now had the authority to create new daihonzan. Despite the tension it created in Japan, where they struggled to accept the idea of laypeople and priests training in Zen together, Omori Rotaishi designated Chozen-ji as a daihonzan in 1979. In doing so, he encouraged Tanouye to shed as many of the Japanese aspects of Rinzai Zen as needed in order to establish what was essentially a totally new line of Zen in Hawai'i.

After meeting briefly with Michael after my arrival, I was given a tour of the temple grounds. We surveyed a variety of statuary—two large lanterns, each ten feet tall and which stood imposingly at the base of the hill; a large bell tower; and the fat, bare-chested monk named Hotei. Each had a meaning and story demonstrating not just some Zen principle but also the ingenuity and relationships of Chozen-ji. The lanterns, for example, had been carved by the first president of the board of Chozen-ji, whose auto body shop almost went out of business while he devoted himself to perfecting their design to meet Tanouye Rotaishi's vision. I rapped my knuckles on the side of one of them and was surprised by how it resounded, as if it were hollow. It was carved out of fiberglass, the same material used to shape surfboards. The Hotei statue had been bestowed as a gift to a local family by Syngman Rhee, the first democratically elected president of Korea, before it eventually made its way to the Dojo.

Leaving the statues behind, we walked up the steps carved into the hill, each one held in place by a three-foot-long, six-inch-wide rectangular stone. These were old curb stones from downtown Honolulu, chiseled by hand 150 years ago. Somehow, they had been rescued and brought here as the city replaced them with concrete. More curbstones lined the walkway to the top of the hill, each one sunk a foot or two down into the earth and weighing at least a hundred pounds.

At the top of the rise, we had a 360-degree view of the whole temple grounds. Down below, near the spot where I had been dropped off, were the Budo Dojo and the kitchen. The wooden walkway that wrapped around and led between the Budo Dojo, the kitchen, and the bathrooms was called the *engawa*, an iconic element of Japanese architecture that functions as an open-air hallway. Many of Chozen-ji's buildings have this quality of blurring the lines between outdoors and indoors. In addition to the engawa, many of the structures had plentiful windows and doors opening to the outside. The walls had no insulation that I could see, which was possible because of Hawai'i's pleasant year-round climate.

The more time we spent on the top of the hill, the more I felt an unmistakable energy. My whole body buzzed, and I felt heady. I learned that this small green rise that greeted visitors to Chozen-ji was considered a place of special spiritual energy, a place of great kiai and *mana*. All around us, the mountain ridges curved inward, creating the appearance not of a straight valley but of a bowl. The place felt protected and contained, somewhere the energy could collect. Pilahi Paki, the Native Hawaiian spiritual leader whose definition of the Aloha Spirit is enshrined in Hawai'i state law, had also spent time at Chozen-ji, I was told. She had determined that it was a *manawa*, a sacred energy mountain. In the same spirit, Tanouye Rotaishi had placed a large, black marble pillar with a calligraphy of an enso, or circle, at this spot. This was where he said one could best feel 浩然の気 (*Kozen No Ki*, or "universal energy").

We descended from the hill down another set of stone steps curving all the way down its side, returning us to the gravel driveway, which we followed toward the back of the grounds. On the left was another dojo that I was told was the first full-length range for Kyudo, traditional Japanese archery, built outside of Japan. Inside, I was shown how to remove the wooden panels that formed the dojo's far wall. Each one came out of a groove in the floor and ceiling, unlocking from the one next to it. In this way, the whole wall could be removed for shooting. Standing under the high-beamed ceiling of the dojo, I could see down to the target house thirty meters away. A small strip of brown dirt and sand was piled up against its long back wall. That was where the targets went, though beginners learned to shoot by first aiming at the *makiwara*, which was made of two hay bales in a five-foot-tall wooden stand on rollers.

Along one side of the Kyudo range stood a row of cypress trees, whose untrimmed tops grew into tapered tongues that licked the sky. Along the opposite side were several shrubs and small trees blocking the view to another building, the tea house. Just in front of these bushes and trees stood a large stone slab on a concrete platform, inscribed with another calligraphy, 一射絶命:

一 (*I*)—One
射 (*Sha*)—Shot, Archery
絶 (*Zetsu*)—Cease
命 (*Mei*)—Life

Issha Zetsumei, like the meaning of the name Chozen-ji, had several translations, such as "One Arrow, One Life." But not surprisingly, I was told that Tanouye Rotaishi favored the translation that was the most aggressive: "One Shot, Absolute Destruction." Read this way, the phrase spoke to how everything could ride on just one attempt, one shot. I thought of a soldier with one last opportunity to end the battle, everything hinging on her last round. And I thought of how our whole lives are our one shot. After they are over, everything we know and which makes up our understanding of reality will be destroyed. I let this meaning sink in as I looked beyond the Kyudo range at the forest and the Koʻolau Mountains, framed below by the target house and above by the bright blue sky.

The Kyudo Dojo was designed and built by one of Tanouye Rotaishi's early students, an artist, after he trained in Kyudo in Japan. This story mirrors many others belonging to students of Tanouye Rotaishi's. I was told that others, too, after learning the principles of Zen from Tanouye Rotaishi, had been sent to Japan and China to hone their different arts. Returning home, they established new schools of Kyudo, Tai Chi, flower arrangement, and ceramics under the guidance of true masters in those disciplines, while also imbuing their arts with the martial disposition and physical approach that were hallmarks of this new and unique line of Chozen-ji Zen.

Evidence of this tradition was visible in the ceramics studio. Each of the potters' wheels inside the studio had a large mirror standing in front of it. The mirrors help ceramics students maintain their posture while working on the wheel. Posture, breath, and concentration are all emphasized in *zazen* and throughout all the arts that make up Chozen-ji training.

The energetic nature of the training and the Dojo was contagious, and I was feeling giddy. Admiring the green environment, Japanese buildings, and martial arts training equipment, I felt like Beatrix Kiddo, the protagonist in Quentin Tarantino's martial arts revenge film, *Kill Bill*. Not yet able to predict the specific training I would be doing, I imagined myself as Kiddo, dressed in martial arts training clothes, carrying water and punching boards until my arms were limp.

The descriptions of the training I heard reinforced this fantasy. I was told there was often little explanation and that the crux of training—whether with a sword or with clay—was repetition, doing one thing over and over again. Training in ceramics, for example, resembled a traditional Japanese apprenticeship: cleaning the dojo, making and throwing away pieces while learning to hitch long breaths to each movement at the wheel, and then making five hundred, one thousand, or ten thousand of a single form, be it a tea bowl or a coffee mug.

In the workshop next door, where an extensive collection of tools and machinery lived, I saw a simple white sign mounted inside a wooden frame. It read, in all caps, KI'AI FIRST—THEN MA'AI. After reading Omori Rotaishi's biography, I had understood in a cursory way that "kiai" meant energy or spirit, and I felt that it had a slightly mystical connotation. "Ma'ai," I was told, meant form. Throughout my tour, the word "kiai" was also interchangeably used to suggest fierceness, energy, the electricity one could feel in a room, and a person's presence. It was something often borne out of intensity, a product of zazen (seated Zen meditation) and practicing the martial and fine arts. An idea I would hear many times in the coming days to describe Chozen-ji's approach was that it was one thing to feel calm and in control sitting on our meditation cushions, but could we do the same thing with swords at our throats? Or with brushes in our hands? Cultivating this ability to be the master of all circumstances out of the raw materials of breath, posture, and concentration were indelibly intertwined with embodying this kiai.

Even the outside work, I learned, was used for this end and was regarded as an important form of training. The idea of this hard, manual labor excited me. I looked forward to the long daily schedule of zazen, martial and fine arts, manual labor, and an overall culture of relentless vigor and sharp attention. I wanted it to push me right up to the edge of my self-imposed limitations and then, perhaps, beyond them. I was told that, in the days to come, I might be moving rocks and building a rock wall or cutting down trees. That work would be interspersed with hundreds of sword cuts, memorizing how to chant Buddhist sutras, and whatever other forms of training the teachers might recommend. It was all to be done with vigor, with "balls to the wall" energy.

This spirit characterized the grounds themselves as even the buildings had been built by Dojo members and Zen students as part of their training. Looking closely, I could see that they weren't fancy Japanese carpentry, just plywood topped with two colors of exterior paint chosen for their low price and easy availability. But taken collectively, it was all still stunning. The grounds had been personally shaped by Tanouye Rotaishi, and the way one would move about and experience the landscape and architectural elements had all been engineered to facilitate transformation and awakening. Everything around me took on an even more magical light now that I knew the blood, sweat, tears, and intention that had brought it into being.

On the ride from the airport to the Dojo, I had been asked why I was coming to train and what I hoped to do with the training. I gave my customary answer, which was usually received with appreciation and solemn nods in mainland Buddhist circles: I was looking for a spiritual home and a tradition in which I could teach the dharma.

I was surprised when I was asked what I meant by "teaching the dharma." I stuttered for a moment and then explained that dharma was the name for the body of Buddhist teaching. But then, I realized that it wasn't my meaning but my intent that was being questioned. In short, who was I to think that I had something to teach? I had never gotten this sort of reaction before, and I took it as a warning shot, straightening my spine and noting how the world I was stepping into clearly differed from the one from whence I came.

Although Chozen-ji was founded with a global purpose, I was told that, day to day, it operated as a local temple, filled with members from around O'ahu and few outsiders. In years past, Chozen-ji had also had subdojos around the world. If live-ins came from outside of Hawai'i, they arrived with a recommendation from a Chozen-ji priest or teacher or a martial arts teacher who reached out on the student's behalf. Most had some experience already with Chozen-ji's physical approach to Zen and local Hawai'i culture.

Only a minority of Chozen-ji's student body arrived to live in with no training background or relationship to the Dojo.

I initially assumed that my time at Chozen-ji would be like the times I had spent at silent meditation retreat centers around the United States over the years, first in the Goenka vipassana tradition and then later in the insight meditation tradition. Rotating casts of characters populated such centers, each week bringing a different Buddhist teacher and their acolytes, with professional staff managing the logistics and facilities. Recently, I had been frequenting the same center every year in rural Washington State. I sat with the same teachers and then kept in touch with them in between retreats through email, video calls, and mentorship programs.

Other than that, though, I had been relatively on my own. However, I thought of myself as part of a disparate and diverse web of people on the Path, following the dharma. And from what I had observed and experienced, what I had was as good as it was going to get. I assumed that I would eventually join a community-leader or teacher-training program. But until then, I believed that I was already engaged in the deepest spiritual practice possible short of fully ordaining as a Buddhist monk. Ordaining to me meant renunciation, eschewing my worldly possessions and ambitions, abandoning the hopes of ever having a family and career, and stepping away from global activism and an overall engagement with the world. I wasn't ready for that just yet, and I felt reservations about it really being the only way to go deeper. Instead of becoming a renunciant, I tried to find a path forward that would allow me to remain part of the world while still practicing deeply. That, to me, meant becoming some sort of lay Buddhist teacher, writing books, and giving talks, perhaps while offering coaching or running a mindfulness business at the same time. Indeed, those were the paths I had seen other people take and, thus, the extent of what I thought was possible.

Based on this particular—and I was soon to learn, limited—view, I found myself on my first night describing a path forward that was sorely out of place at Chozen-ji. I wish I could say that later, as I heard the same words emerge from other people's mouths, I responded with the same generosity and patience that I received. But, perhaps out of shame for my own ignorance and entitlement, I would usually cringe or scoff incredulously, pouncing on those who came after me as they echoed this same view of Buddhism, their accomplishments in it, and what their future path could entail.

"I'd really like to take what I learn here and combine it with my expertise in vipassana and insight to teach," I told Michael.

I had come across many teachers on the mainland and from Europe and Asia who syncretically combined traditions, teaching yoga alongside vipassana- and insight-style meditation, which they also combined with some of the formalities of Zen. It was also becoming more common for Western Buddhist teachers to quote Sufi and Native American teachers in their dharma talks, tying together Buddhism and different Indigenous practices like sage burning, and even New Age practices such as sound baths and tarot card reading. For quite a long time, the world of Western Buddhism had also overlapped deeply with Western psychotherapy, neuroscience, and clinical practices for dealing with chronic pain. So I didn't think that what I was describing was controversial. I naively assumed that everyone would be open to the spirit of creative spiritual fusion that had dominated the spiritual circles I'd known.

Instead, Michael paused thoughtfully and swallowed audibly. When he did finally respond, he did so kindly but firmly.

"The best thing you can do," he said "is approach the next three weeks as a totally blank slate. Throw away whatever other training you've done. It'll still be there when the three weeks are over, and if this doesn't end up being for you, that's fine. If anything, maybe you'll find a way to go deeper with what you've already been doing. But if you spend the next three weeks trying to pick and choose or trying to apply it to a framework you already have, you're not going to really get anything out of being here. It won't be worth your time and energy to have come all the way out here—and we don't want to waste our time, either. In all honesty, in three weeks, all you're going to get is a tongue-tip taste."

This was in line with how Michael had consistently described Zen training to me, which was, more than anything, like a very powerful and refined technology. He had emphasized that here, there were no religious tenets that students were asked to believe in or to which they were expected to pledge faith. Instead, they were expected to just do as they were told. In the course of doing just that—whether it was zazen and martial arts or simply changing one's posture—each person would arrive at their own insight and understanding.

Of course, the particular forms at Chozen-ji, beginning with zazen and the daily schedule, had been tested and iterated upon for hundreds if not thousands of years. In sum, Michael said, they produced relatively reliable and specific results that were perhaps best encapsulated in Omori Sogen Rotaishi's definition of Zen in Chozen-ji's canon: "Zen is to transcend life and death (all dualism) to truly realize that the entire universe is the 'True Human Body' through the discipline of 'mind and body in oneness.'"[5]

The building blocks of this mind and body in oneness were universal and simple: breath, posture, and concentration. Noticeably absent from that list was anything that had to do with esoteric religious knowledge or belief. That was why even Catholic priests and nuns had trained over the years at Chozen-ji. Likening religious ideology like Catholicism to computer software, he emphasized that what they focused on at Chozen-ji was more like hardware.

"If you can get all this working optimally," he said, motioning to his head and his body, "then any software you're running on it is going to run better, whether it's being a baker or being a nun. And that's available to everybody. But it takes time and it's much harder work than people expect."

By the time we finished talking, I was heady with anticipation.

But it was also late, time for me to get some rest and prepare for my real introduction to Zen training the following day. I took what I'd need for the night out of my backpack and laid a few meditation cushions on the floor to sleep. The grounds were peaceful and quiet, tree frogs chirping softly in the distance.

Almost as soon as I lay down on my makeshift bed, I was asleep. I did not dream at all. I slept in fits and starts, my body sore from sleeping on the floor. I pulled at my sleeping bag as the temperature fell. When I got up to close the windows, the clock read 3:30 a.m. Looking briefly outside, I could see that everything was now black, silent, and still. When I woke up again and then a few more times after that, the early morning had progressed only slightly. But each time I fell back asleep, it was with the anticipation of the imminent beginning of my training.

6

THE VIBRATION OF PEACE

Sundays, I had been told, were quiet at the Dojo. There would be no evening training, only a sitting and some classes in the morning, and then a whole day for outside work and free training. Knowing this, my alarm went off at a leisurely 6:00 a.m. I had agreed to be up and ready to begin the day at 6:30 a.m., starting with ringing the huge Peace Bell on the hill. I had tried hard to be a good student the night before, standing by and watching closely as to how it was rung. I noted the instructions on how to use the massive striker, a skinny tree trunk suspended by ropes, and how to count the seven rings with the fingers of my left hand pressing against my thigh. After ringing the bell, there was a long list of tasks to learn so that I could take responsibility for opening the dojo each morning. I would be shown how to do this today and be expected to memorize it quickly so that I'd be ready to jump in and take care of things, anticipating needs wherever they arose.

Before leaving my room, I changed into the clothes that I had been told to bring: a navy-blue *samue*, a pajama-like outfit that serves as Japanese monks' and priests' casual wear. In the women's bathroom adjacent to the kitchen, I washed my face and brushed my teeth. I removed my earrings and rings and clucked at myself for not thinking to remove the polish on my fingernails before I'd arrived. Unable to find any nail polish remover in the cabinets beneath the sink, I reconciled myself to the fact that I'd be wearing this sparkly golden varnish for a while, which was very unbecoming of a Zen monk, even a temporary one. I closed the door and made sure to shut off the light, remembering how I had been brusquely corrected the night before for absentmindedly leaving it on. I walked along the engawa, hearing and feeling the reverberations in the wood each time my heels came down, each board giving slightly under my weight.

I checked the clock in the kitchen: 6:28 a.m. It was time to go ring the bell. On the main steps in front of the Budo Dojo, I put on my slippers a bit on guard this time after my earlier fall at this same spot.

As I walked up the narrow stone steps that led from the gravel driveway to the bell tower, I heard the crowing of roosters nearby. The very tops of the mountains all around were still draped in mist. Once at the tower, I looked back toward the buildings and just then saw the lights illuminating the engawa and the main buildings flick off. A *senpai*, or senior student, appeared from the direction of the women's bathroom, next to which was a panel of switches for the exterior lights. He walked along the engawa and entered the kitchen. Standing in front of the statue of the Medicine Buddha, Yakushi Nyorai, I put my hands together and bowed. Turning around, I then bowed to the bell tower. Finally, keeping my hands clasped, I walked up the stone steps of the bell tower and crouched to pass between the upper and lower railings. Once inside, I bowed one last time to the four-foot-wide metal bell.

At the top of the Peace Bell were cast two doves. Their embrace formed the loop where the whole bell was winched by a huge metal hook bolted to the underside of the tower. On the side of the bell read an inscription, "Praying for the eternal peace of the world and the everlasting friendship between Honolulu and Kyoto.

1st February 1966." On the other side, carvings of Benzaiten—the patron goddess of water, knowledge, femininity, and culture—adorned the bell. Underneath her beatific face and flowing robes was carved her mythological husband, a terrifying sea dragon. Well-worn and directly opposite the skinny tree trunk that served as the bell's striker was the raised image of a lotus flower. This was the target. I was to hit it seven times, each time sending the vibration of the massive Peace Bell out into the world.

I stood with one foot forward and one foot back, my right hand grasping the knot in the rope that dangled from the striker. I pulled it all the way forward up to the bell and then relaxed my arm so that it swung backward, my hand still on the rope. I followed the striker's arc as it traveled backward and then again forward toward the bell. I added just a little more power at the end, and there was a soft ring as the striker gently hit its mark. It was a pleasant sound but a rather muted invocation for world peace, I thought. I resolved to make the next ring louder and added more power. This time, the bell clanged sharply, setting off a cacophony of crowing among the roosters in the neighborhood. It felt right for the bell to be rung loudly and boldly, and I thought that rousing the chickens must be a sign that I was doing it right. I kept count with my left hand, touching my leg with one fingertip each time the bell had been rung until all five fingers rested there. Then, I double backed for rings six and seven. After the final ring, I put my hands back together and bowed again, came out of the bell tower, and bowed twice more, to the bell tower and finally to Yakushi Nyorai.

After coming down from the hill, my thorough instruction on how to open the Dojo began, starting with opening the temple gate. Two of us did it in tandem. I spun the combination on the lock and undid the chain that kept the two chain-link panels stretched out through the night. But before I was ready with my hands on the end of the gate, it was already moving. As it began to accordion shut, my end scraped the concrete loudly.

"Don't drag the gate like that!" I was scolded sharply. "The gate is old! If you treat it like that, it'll fall apart!"

The words sent a small shock through me as they landed, and I took care to finish closing the gate quietly, rattling the chain with the lock as little as I could as I secured it to keep the gate open. I strung the skinny chain through the loops of the chain link and then closed the clip on the end.

I had been warned that such corrections, or scoldings, would be part of Zen training. It was as much a facet of local Hawai'i culture as a practical means of maintaining a sharp air, keeping Zen students on their toes. There was value, I'd been told, in learning to take what was useful out of the verbal reproaches and then let the rest go, but I had never taken well to such feedback. I'd always been sensitive and cried easily as a child, especially when I received criticism from my characteristically blunt Korean immigrant parents, and even when I simply struggled to do something and felt helpless as to how to get it right. Somehow though, I still maintained a self-image of toughness. I had even convinced myself that I relished a feedback-rich environment and responded, upon hearing about the scoldings, that I would be ready for them and take them on the chin.

I was told that the scoldings, as well as the myriad tasks and rules, all had one fundamental purpose: to teach people how to pay attention. And, indeed, there were a lot of things to pay attention to. After ringing the bell and opening the gate, a sequence of events were executed with rapid efficiency in the kitchen: opening the sliding glass doors, filling the hot water boiler, checking the trash, making the coffee, and preparing a breakfast of granola and yogurt. The coffee was made with two pieces of industrial equipment that sat on the kitchen island and, although I said that I had worked as a waitress in a place with the same grinder and coffeemaker years earlier, I was still given detailed instructions on how to use them. The level of beans in the grinder had to be checked regularly, I was told; extra coffee beans could be found in the freezer outside. The temperature of the hot water reservoir in the coffeemaker also had to be checked each morning. If the circuit had tripped or for some other reason the water wasn't hot, it would ruin the coffee, leaving people with something more golden than black and only lukewarm.

"Tanouye Roshi said we couldn't offer people much in the old days," I was told. "The Dojo didn't have money for fancy foods, and most of what the live-ins ate was donated, expired cans of food from a local supermarket. But he said we could at least give people good coffee."

I was assured that, after weeks of exhaustion and under the microscopic lens of Zen training, it wouldn't be hard to forget important details and make mistakes. If the basket wasn't in the coffeemaker when the water was poured in, hot water would spray all over the counter, the machines, and the thin, industrial carpet covering the linoleum floor. To put it simply and in local slang, there were a lot of ways that the coffee could turn out "junk."

"So," I was told, "just follow along and pay attention."

Breakfast was eaten quickly and with minimal talking, everyone kneeling on the carpeted kitchen floor at the low tables. I noticed that the others ate quickly, taking large mouthfuls, but I assumed it was just their personal preference. Halfway through my bowl of granola, however, everyone rose to start soaping, rinsing, and drying dishes. As someone returned with a rag in hand to wipe down the table, I lifted my bowl and moved out of the way, trying to eat faster with my bowl in midair while the tables were wiped briskly and in long strokes. Nobody scolded me, hoping perhaps that I was already getting the message.

"We eat pretty fast here," I was told later. "Same with the cleanup. If it's done right, it should feel like a NASCAR pit stop."

It did.

After all the dishes had been dried and put away, we left the main building and walked toward the back of the grounds. Just beyond was the tea house, which had been built as a place for Omori

Rotaishi to stay when he was visiting from Japan. It was the most Japanese building on the premises. At the entrance stood two stone lanterns, and inside the high front step was a *genkan*, a stone entryway complete with a large rectangular stone that could be used as a step up to the hardwood foyer. Many of the rooms had tatami floors—and, aside from the front and back doors, there were no other swinging doors in the building, only sliding pocket doors, architectural echoes of the traditional sliding shoji screens around the main room, the tea room.

Before we could begin zazen or the Chado (Way of Tea) class, the whole tea house had to be cleaned. I was given the job of sweeping. I was only a few seconds into it before I was corrected and shown how to sweep along the grain of each tatami mat rather than against it. As I finished sweeping the kitchen, foyer, and engawa, someone followed quickly behind with a sponge mop and a large, rolling bucket full of hot water and Pine-Sol. The only room that did not get mopped was the tea room. The proper way to clean the tatami in there was on one's hands and knees, with one small, wet towel in each hand used only for this purpose. Moving backward, I wiped along the grain of the tatami, back and forth and back and forth until each mat had been rid of dust and hair.

All together, the class also cleaned the bathrooms and cast open all the curtains, sliding glass doors, and shoji screens, bringing the fresh air and the sounds of the outdoors in. Someone lit two sticks of incense, putting one into a cone-shaped vase on a black pillar in the foyer under a massive calligraphy by Omori Rotaishi. The other went into a similarly shaped incense bowl inside the tea room.

As we finished cleaning, I heard the crunch of gravel and watched as a small, white SUV whipped down the gravel path and then around the back of the grounds. It finally parked facing a row of cypress trees in front of the two founders' memorials adjacent to the tea house. A beautiful, older Japanese woman emerged from the car dressed in traditional kimono. Her black hair was pulled back into a low bun, elegant bangs sweeping to one side of her forehead. She looked like a movie star, with perfect features and a long neck accentuated by the broad neckline of her kimono, which started at a tight V below the notch in her throat and ended in a wide arch in the back, exposing the nape of her neck.

"Hello, good morning!" she called out as she came to the door of the tea house. This was Yumiko Sayama, the teacher of the Chado class and the wife of Chozen-ji's abbot. She was warm and welcoming, and her alacrity brightened what had otherwise been a morning of tense instruction. Yumiko surveyed the tea house, leaving dry footprints as she walked from room to room across the freshly mopped floors in white split-toe socks, or tabi. With surprising energy, she then went about pulling things out of the refrigerator and various kitchen drawers and set a giant kettle onto the stove to boil. After leaving the tea house with a pair of patinated garden shears in hand, she returned with several long stems of the yellow irises that grew plentifully around the Dojo. Snipping away the extra leaves and dead flowers, she deftly made an elegant arrangement and placed it in the alcove of the tea room, next to a calligraphy scroll hanging on the back wall.

All the cleaning and setup for class happened quickly and with almost no talking, like an ensemble cast of characters playing out well-rehearsed roles. Teacher and students moved with clarity and purpose from room to room. After I was done wiping the tatami, it was all I could do to stand back, watch, and try not to get in the way.

Once the tea house was clean, it was time for zazen. We arranged several *zabuton* (large, square meditation pads) on the tatami in the tea room, each with a few small, rectangular *zafu*, or small meditation cushions, on top. Ever since I had first begun attending meditation sittings, dharma talks, and silent meditation retreats, I had counted my breaths in quiet rooms, more than a year of my life spent meditating overall. I assumed now that whatever was to come next would be old hat.

Quickly and without ceremony, the meditation instruction began. First, I was to find a sitting posture from among a few options: tailor, with each leg fully on the floor; calf or quarter lotus, with the top of one foot resting on the opposite calf; half lotus, with the foot on the thigh; or full lotus. I opted for calf lotus. Over the years, I had become used to sitting this way, usually alternating between calf lotus and tailor as my legs became sore. I had been told by various Buddhist teachers over the years that it was excessively willful to muscle through the pain that accompanied sitting on the floor, and I had been encouraged to shift my posture when needed. There had been times when I achieved a deep meditative concentration and could sit without moving for long periods. I had also found myself sitting just a few times without any sense of the time passing or any discomfort. On those occasions, it was only when the meditation period was over that I would realize that my foot, leg, or hip hurt, meditative absorption having allowed me to bypass that pain for a time. But this was usually on long retreats, and, for regular sitting, I had been encouraged to adjust my body whenever and however I wanted. In these other settings, pain had been regarded as having the power to distract, to make one clench and tighten when the goal was release and surrender. Pushing through physical pain was usually seen as unnecessary and a sign of the ego striving for some badge of achievement or competition.

Again and again, the Buddhist teachers I had encountered instead emphasized the Middle Path and how the historical Buddha had cast aside ascetic rigors and pain. I had been encouraged to do the same. It did not take long for me to learn that this was not the case at Chozen-ji.

I watched with surprise as the senpai, or senior student, giving the meditation instructions pulled his right foot up onto his left thigh in half lotus. I wasn't sure if I had ever even attempted to sit that way, and I was shocked by how matter-of-fact he was in doing it, tendons clicking and popping as he set his right foot high up near his left hip. Afterward, he demonstrated the way to hold my hands, grasping my left thumb, my right hand balled into a fist. The fingers of my left hand were to cradle my right fist, both hands resting in my lap or held against my body, an inch or two below my belly button. In other places, I had seen many different hand positions during meditation, usually with the hands resting on the thighs or with the tips of the thumbs lightly touching. This was the first time I'd ever seen someone holding a fist.

I was told to push the back of my head up toward the ceiling, tucking my chin just slightly. My back should be straight, my shoulders back but relaxed. These kinds of instructions were familiar, and furthermore, I had always been complimented on my good posture, so I felt confident in how I sat. But as I settled in, the senpai leading the sitting walked over to me and, without a word, placed both hands on either side of my face until he was cradling my whole head in his hands. Then, he pulled straight up, straightening my spine so that I sat a full inch or two taller. After twelve years of what had been to me very serious Buddhist meditation, this was the first time that my posture had ever been corrected and one of few times that, in a meditation setting, I had ever even been touched.

My chest felt puffed out and my body more upright than I had known it could be. As I put intention and effort toward maintaining this new, very upright posture, the instructions continued. I was instructed to count my breaths one to ten, then one to ten, over and over again. I tried to match the senpai as he demonstrated the breathing, each of his exhales spanning ten to twenty seconds. With some effort, I squeezed the air out of my lungs to make my exhales long and slow, as instructed. But my body rebelled, signaling through strong twitches in my diaphragm the need to breathe in. I knew, though, that there was more air left in my lungs. So I plowed ahead, continuing to squeeze out every drop of air I could in my long exhale and fighting the urge to gulp in air like a fish.

Both physically and in terms of where I was to focus my mind, the instructions emphasized the trunk of the body beneath the belly button, which was called the *hara* in Japanese. That was the part of the body, rather than my chest, that should rise and fall with each breath. I was to let all the tension in my upper body melt toward my hara on every exhale and then sit up even taller. The overarching feeling was not, as I had been instructed so many times before, to surrender or let the body fade away. Instead, the instruction was to "be big," taking up the space of the whole room and sitting as if I were a giant mountain.

With its clean, minimalist architecture, natural materials, and the way that the inside blended with the outside world, our environment was the epitome of what one might think of as Zen. Yet the air in the tea room was taut as a drum skin. It was unlike the sort of soft, allowing feeling of the retreat centers and meditation centers I had been to over the years. Here, I felt tension—my every move, even in meditation, observed and judged. What contributed to this most of all during the zazen was the fact that the eyes were kept open and everyone sat facing the center of the room. This meant I could see how straight and tall—and how still—everyone else was sitting. Their faces were slack and serious, concentrated on their breathing and their posture, and yet they also took in every feature of the room. And I was acutely aware that, in the same way that I observed them now, they were all able to see everything I did, too.

"A good analogy for zazen," the senior student said to sum up his instructions, "is early man hunting. Totally silent, totally still. Seeing everything. Hearing everything. Feeling everything . . . And ready to jump up and kill something."

My ears pricked up at hearing this. *Ready to kill something?*

I knew that I had come to the temple of Super Zen, of samurai and sword fighting, but I had still never imagined hearing hunting, killing, and meditation mentioned in the same breath. Not that I couldn't see the analogy, however, once I gave it some thought. I had never hunted in my life, but I had stalked birds and deer in the suburbs throughout my childhood—to admire them, though, not kill them. I remembered how it felt in those moments to be so silent, still, and attentive to everything inside of and around me. Breathing slowly and seeing, hearing, and feeling everything now felt similarly familiar and right, while it also unfolded anew in every moment.

"And the last thing," the senior student concluded as he sat with his fist in his lap, his back impossibly straight, "is don't move. Even if your knee is on fire," he continued. "Even if a mosquito lands right here," he said, his index finger alighting briefly on the bridge of his nose. "Don't move."

With that warning, he picked up the *taku*, two wooden blocks lying on the floor beside him, and struck them together with a loud *crack!* Putting them back down, he picked up the meditation bell, which resembled a small brass singing bowl affixed to the top of a brightly colored cushion mounted in turn to a small staff. Using a matching metal striker, he struck the bell four times. The intervals between each ring grew longer and longer as they went on. I made my vision wide, seeing the whole room, even out through the open doors to the cypress trees and the founders' memorials. I felt a slight breeze and the temperature of the air on my skin. The wind sometimes rustled in the trees, and I could hear the sounds of different birds, either as they flitted by the tea house or as their songs echoed in the forest nearby. I counted my breaths, one to ten, as many times as I could, lengthening each breath with effort. I tried my best to push each and every breath right up to the edge of strain. And for forty-five minutes, save for sitting up even straighter when the melting tension in my shoulders allowed, I did not move.

7

CHADO

It was not long before I regretted how I had chosen to sit during my first zazen at Chozen-ji. My left foot fell asleep (not for a lack of circulation, I would later be told, but because of the nerves being pinched). My right knee and ankle began to hurt, as well. I felt the familiar urge to shift position. I almost did move until I remembered the instructions not to do so, it seemed, at any cost. My legs hurt more. I tried to put more of my attention into counting my breaths and pushing the crown of my head up toward the ceiling, but the pain only grew worse. The periphery of the room darkened as my vision closed in, anxiety creeping in at the edges of my mind. My body tightened. I found scant refuge in counting my breaths, and then pursued it with more and more vigor trying to drown out the pain in my legs. I felt my face flush as my quiet counting began to sound in my head more like yelling at the top of my lungs.

When the bell was finally rung and the taku were hit again, I was instructed to put my hands together and bow, which I did in unison with everyone else. Afterward, I gingerly pulled my right foot onto the floor and then waited for things to equalize, pain subsiding in some parts, feeling returning in others. Everyone else stood up immediately. Even Yumiko rose quickly, even though she had been sitting with her legs folded beneath her in a position I'd always known as "Japanese style" but which I learned was called *seiza*. Without any trace of discomfort, everyone bowed and started putting their meditation cushions away. Everyone, of course, but me.

Someone came over and said that the one time I could get hurt doing zazen was now, if I were to get up too quickly before I could feel my feet.

"Take your time!" Yumiko chirped cheerfully. I appreciated the permission and encouragement but was also unhappy at being the slowest in the group to recover from the sitting. In fact, I resented the notion of having to recover from the sitting at all. I had always been a good meditator, the most physically capable among as many as one hundred other people on a retreat. Before the pins and needles and pain in my feet had subsided completely, I pushed myself to stand up, bow, and put my cushion away in the next room.

The Chado class began as promptly as the meditation had ended. Expecting a short bathroom break and a chance to transition to what came next, I instead followed the other students right back into the tea room. Looking to my left and right, I saw with disappointment that everyone was sitting down seiza. I did the same, kneeling with both knees, shins, and the tops of both feet on the tatami. My right ankle screamed in protest, and before I could bring my weight fully down to sit on my heels, I had to brace my weight with my hands.

"Please," Yumiko said, seeing me strain. "It doesn't matter sitting seiza. Just be comfortable." I nodded and gave a halfhearted smile but didn't move.

After teacher and students bowed to one another, I was invited to be the guest. The student serving as host rose and walked to the entrance to the tea room. There, he sat down again and produced a square of bright purple cloth from inside his gi. After folding it into a triangle, he took it with his left hand and tucked it under the straps of his hakama, a more serious and expensive kind of training clothes. Picking up a small plate with several sweets of pressed sugar molded into the shapes of different flower and leaves, he walked over to me, sat down again, and presented the plate. After placing it on the tatami between us, he slid backward a few inches and looked me in the eye. His face, which had evinced the relaxed seriousness of zazen all morning, suddenly brightened. Touching his fingers to the floor in front of him, he smiled and bowed.

"Please enjoy the sweets," he said. Each word was relaxed and warm, such a pleasant departure in tone from the rest of the morning. For the briefest of moments, my preoccupation with the discomfort in my feet disappeared. I made a cautious attempt to return the bow, touching both hands to the tatami and then lowering my head toward the ground. As awkward and, most likely, incorrect as it was, no scolding or correction followed. I watched the host's face set, once again, into the relaxed expression of zazen. Then, he stood, turned, and walked slowly back to the entrance.

It wasn't long before I took the permission I had been given earlier to sit comfortably. Various tea utensils were brought into the room, ferried from a few small *dai*, small wooden stands set by the entrance. Meanwhile, I adjusted myself to sit cross-legged and watched. I had never seen Chado before, so I did not know what to expect next or the meaning of the host's actions as he wiped the tea bowl or as he took the small bamboo whisk and dipped it into hot water before raising it up, his eyes gazing upon the bristles. If I had expected anything, it might have been that Chado was something ceremonial and that it was something very dainty done by women. But what I was seeing now held strength and precision. There were no extraneous movements and no flourishes. The room was without conversation, only a feeling of quiet attentiveness and steady equipoise and effort.

After a while, the tea bowl was set down on the tatami, a thin veil of steam rising from the emerald green matcha inside it. Yumiko invited me to advance toward the tea bowl. The proper way was to slide myself along the tatami, she demonstrated, my hands balled into fists and taking my weight so I could slide my knees and shins along the floor. To do so, though, I first had to uncross my legs and roll forward back to seiza. Once there, I attempted to slide forward as instructed but only managed to half scoot and half walk on my knees across the floor. I retrieved the tea bowl and scooted backward just as awkwardly. As I approached my seat again, I finally began to feel like I was getting the hang of this sliding across the tatami. But my self-satisfaction was quickly interrupted when I clipped the edge of my big toenail sharply on the edge of the last tatami mat. Pain shot up my foot, and I winced, pausing for a moment. When I forced myself to continue sliding, I felt anxious that I'd ripped part of the nail off and might be bleeding onto the tatami. It was that painful, but nobody paid attention in the least. Everything continued on, and Yumiko began to instruct me on the proper way to drink the tea I'd been served. She pantomimed picking up the tea bowl with her right hand and placing it on her left palm, and I did the same. I paid attention very hard to her continuing instructions to override the distraction of my hurt toe, following along closely to first bow to the tea, then turn the tea bowl twice, and then, finally, drink out of the bowl in long sips until it was all gone.

"At the end, make a sound," Yumiko said. She pursed her lips together and made a slight slurping sound. "That means, 'Thank you, I liked the tea.'"

I inhaled the last of the green foam left in my bowl and then scooted forward to return it. Coming back, I paid close attention to the gaps between the tatami, cautiously walking my feet over the black fabric piping running along the edge of each mat this time. I was relieved to see no crimson trail.

As the class continued, each student took a turn at being the host. Yumiko lifted and adjusted their arms, manipulating their limbs. Her constant reminder was to hold one's arms out in front of oneself as if "hugging the big tree." It impressed me that she could be so sharp and direct yet also warm and refined at the same time. She had a commanding and magnetic presence. When class ended after an hour and a half, she effortlessly returned to the bright, warm, and reassuring manner she had had when she'd first arrived. The feeling she gave was of being teacher, mother, big sister, and friend all in one.

After class, the tea house was closed up, all the preparatory tasks now performed in reverse so that the curtains, glass doors, and shoji were all shut, and the utensils put away. Earlier in the morning, every dish had been removed from the drying rack in the kitchen and then dried and put back in the kitchen cabinets. This way, at a moment's notice, it could accommodate any event. Likewise, the tea house was returned to a state of quiet readiness. As the lights were turned off and the building emptied, it still radiated with the sharpness that had permeated zazen and Chado class. I held on to this energy as I proceeded to the next activity and found that the whole of the temple grounds lent itself to this same feeling. I noticed for the first time how every wooden beam and fretwork felt crisp, with a clean and strong line. The buildings and the terrain themselves seemed to see, hear, and feel everything.

8

ZEN AND THE ART OF MOVING ROCKS

As morning arrives in the back of Kalihi Valley, crowing roosters interrupt the steady, undulating soundscape of chirping birds and Kalihi Stream. Looking around Chozen-ji, one sees towering trees and jungle, but the 2.5-acre property also has a cluster of houses abutting it on two sides. Some are only yards from the back of the Budo Dojo, their windows often open to the comfortable, tropical air—and vulnerable to the strange sounds of Zen training. At such a close distance, the neighbors are able to hear all of the ceremonies, chanting, yelling, and the other sounds of martial arts quite clearly.

I initially thought, *I hope they knew what they were signing up for by being neighbors to a Zen temple and martial arts dojo.* But it seems that Tanouye Rotaishi's stature in the community and the work of the Dojo to shape local leaders earned it not only respect in the early days but a wide latitude to be as noisy and strange as it would ever need to be. For some of the neighbors, the Dojo can simply do no wrong. If others have a less emphatic view, their behavior is still governed by aloha.

Sometimes, the neighbors even become members. This was famously the case for Pierce B. Rillamas, who owned the nursery at the very end of Kalihi Street. Driving by after the Dojo had purchased the land on Kalihi Street, Pierce would see Tanouye Rotaishi and a coterie of young men shaping the grounds with pickaxes and shovels. Knowing that this was a monumental task with such primitive equipment, Pierce drove over on his backhoe one day to lend it to the Dojo. In old photos, Pierce can be seen sitting on the base of one of the *toro*, the large lanterns, at the bottom of the hill, a handsome man with a mustache and an afro dressed in pants so flared they're almost bell-bottoms. Eventually, Pierce became a student of Tanouye Rotaishi's and even lived in like me. Many of the curbstones that line the pathway to the top of the hill today came from his nursery, as did the Hotei statue. Because of his pivotal role in the founding of the Dojo, Pierce's name is still enshrined in the *okyo*, or chanting, done here. His enduring presence is a reminder of Chozen-ji's deep and intertwining connections to the local community, as well as the value placed on earning trust not through knowledge of fancy, esoteric Buddhist principles but rather through the simple knowledge of how to do hard work.

After the Tea class, I changed into a boxy, faded blue jumpsuit pulled for me from a small collection in the kitchen closet. It must have dated from the 1980s—it was polyester, well-worn, and still bore a tag on the inside from Sears. A past live-in's name was scrawled in red marker on the inside, big letters in all caps taking up the whole height of the waistband. Despite the jumpsuit's wide girth, the sleeves and pant legs were just the right length for me, and wearing it made me feel ready for anything. The jumpsuits were a rite of passage, a take on the traditional samue worn in Japanese temples but better matched to the rugged landscape and down-to-earth nature of local Hawai'i culture. I was beginning to understand just how much this Hawai'i differed from the postcard Hawai'i I had imagined before, the latter an exoticized landscape of beaches and resorts divorced from the practical, hardworking people who have for generations made Hawai'i home.

Dressed in my jumpsuit, I made my way to my next assigned task. The chain-link gate to the empty lot across the street from the temple grounds bore a tattered No Parking sign. I could see tall grass running up the sloping acre and a half. A huge boulder sat in the middle of the property, and rocks were strewn all around. One of Chozen-ji's many priests was going to be coming by to weed whack the lot later in the week. To make his job easier, I'd be helping move many of the rocks scattered amid the grass and weeds. I was offered a pair of gloves and told to start picking up the rocks and moving them to a large pile behind the boulder.

There were a lot of rocks. Some of them were light lava rock, perhaps sixteen inches in diameter and only twenty pounds. But some of the rocks, dense and heavy blue stone, weighed fifty or sixty pounds.

Real work! I thought to myself. *Real Zen training!*

I was excited to jump in and attacked the rocks with enthusiasm, chuckling to myself at how surprised my friends back home would be to see me doing such vigorous work as part of Buddhist training. The first rocks I tackled were small or medium sized, as I was encouraged to take it easy at first, and I was monitored closely for my form and posture, and to make sure I didn't hurt myself.

"Don't stick your butt out," someone called out. "Lift with your legs and from your hara," he said, slapping his abdomen.

I soon watched him lower down into a wide squat, his legs bending in half until he nearly sat on the ground. He wrapped his arms around a huge rock that could easily have weighed fifty pounds. Then, he stood up with a loud grunt, his back straight and upper body upright as he rose. His mouth clamped shut, and the corners of his lips turned downward. He let out a loud, long, and low exhale and then walked determinedly to the pile. There, he squatted again before dropping the rock from just a foot or two off the ground. As I picked up more rocks, I tried my best to follow suit, focusing my attention on my hara and on the flexing of my legs. Emulating him, I was free with my grunting and sounds.

"*Yosho*!" I heard this Japanese expression, which often accompanies physical effort, uttered from around the lot. I tried it myself, then repeated it with each rock I lifted, my consonants disappearing until they were a whisper between my teeth, my vowels becoming more and more guttural. Soon I was lifting each rock with an audible exclamation of enjoyable exertion.

Aside from some gardening, moving apartments, and the occasional volunteer work, I had never really done manual labor like this before. It was not very intellectually stimulating, but it felt deeply gratifying in a fundamental, almost primal, way. Soon, my thighs, back, and arms warmed up and became loose. My mind settled. It was just one rock, then another rock, and another—a refreshingly simple task that could take up most of my attention if I let it. As I picked up rocks and moved them over to the pile, I pushed my mind down below my belly button and tried to see 180 degrees in every direction, just like zazen. I took in all there was to see, smell, hear, and feel around me, watchful and intent. I breathed out long and slow.

My senses must have been wide open because, all of a sudden, a mysterious sadness and longing welled up from inside me. It wasn't acute, and I couldn't tie any of it to a specific event or memory. It was more like the feeling I'd sometimes get when a smell brought me back to a moment in the past, reliving more than remembering. I did not cry. The only outward evidence would have been the brief appearance of a thought out of place across my face.

I took this experience to mean that the Zen of moving rocks was working. Here, I thought, was some subconscious psychological or emotional material being brought to the surface, ostensibly to be let go. I had experienced this before, usually while exercising. Feelings would just come out of nowhere, sometimes attached to memories or sometimes free floating, and my jogs, swims, and bicycle rides could end up racked with sobs.

I kept moving rock after rock. I challenged myself to keep my attention in my hara, noticing that, if I did that, the feelings would move through me and eventually dissipate into the trade winds blowing through the valley. It felt good. Not with every new rock but with most of them came an accompanying upswell in emotions. It felt cathartic, and I welcomed it wholeheartedly. I was here to let things go, I thought to myself—my baggage, my traumas, my habits, my small self—and I started seeking out bigger rocks to move, hoping for bigger and bigger releases.

Some of the rocks were huge. As I started inspecting one such rock, my senpai came over and explained that it was more appropriate to roll such a rock than lift it. He pointed out which side of the rock was the front and which way it wanted to move. It was important to pay attention to what the combination of the rock's facets and the terrain would allow. I might not be able to go straight to my destination, but maybe I could zigzag my way to the line of rocks forming by the fence.

As I tired, my spirit filled in where my physical energy waned. I was intent on matching the steady driving energy I could see in the senior students around me—nobody complained or lagged, and there was no small talk. The work felt serious and purposeful. There was also a sense of enjoyment—in being outside, in using our bodies, and in training. After an hour or so, a bucket of water bottles appeared. I was happy to have a break and quickly downed one bottle and then another. Then, the work resumed quickly—we had only made a small dent in the many rocks strewn around the lot.

Squatting and grunting, feeling the trembling and burning setting into my thighs and my arms, I tried to do the work and take in all that I could with my senses wide open. *This is Zen training*, I thought. So was ringing the bell, eating breakfast, cleaning the

kitchen, zazen, and Tea, all of which had already happened today—
and it wasn't even noon yet. In fact, it felt like I had already been
at the Dojo for days, and when I voiced this later, I learned that it
was a common experience dubbed the "Dojo time warp." All the
day's events had been wonderfully varied and stimulating, and so
far, it had all been relatively fun, as well. I had been told many times
that, if done right, the training was going to make me want to quit.
I had expected things to be hard, harder than anything else I'd ever
done. But what I had experienced so far was great. I felt tired in a
good way and, frankly, exhilarated, already a little more "free." I felt
the training working on me, and this drove me to keep going, only
wanting more.

By the time we were called for lunch, I noticed with satisfaction
that my hands were shaking. I responded with aplomb to orders to
pick up the empty water bottles and cast-off gloves, and I strode
back across the street, feeling happy with myself. I hoped that I had
impressed my senpai with my work. Five feet five inches and 125
pounds, I felt that I had kept up with the bigger, stronger men without complaint. When I arrived back at the workshop, I met eyes
with one of them who smiled approvingly.

"Moving rocks is great Zen training," he said. I nodded vigorously.

"You can't think about moving a rock and have it move, right?"
he continued. He took the gloves from me to put them away. "You
just have to do it."

Sitting on the engawa in our dirty jumpsuits, we enjoyed generous plates of rice, stew, and potato chips for lunch. We also shared
some friendly conversation, as it seemed that lunch was one time
when talking casually was allowed and even encouraged. I was asked
how things were going and what I thought of my experience so far.
How did it differ from all the Buddhist training I had done before?

There was so much to say. As new and sometimes overwhelming

as all the routines, activities, and expectations were, I had enjoyed everything so far and genuinely felt game for all of it. Looking for something more specific to share, I mentioned how I had noticed that, at Chozen-ji, they used the word "training" a lot and how much I liked this. In other places, I had always heard the word "practice" regarding spiritual activities. Having gotten just a taste of training this morning, I could already see that, beyond just semantics, there was a real difference in feeling and intensity when one approached such activities as either practice or training.

"Have you ever seen the Allen Iverson meme where he's talking about practice?" someone asked. I had not. Nor did I know who Allen Iverson— NBA All-Star, star point guard, Rookie of the Year, and Most Valuable Player—was. The senpai who brought it up began to explain, and as he spoke, I appreciated that this place was not so divorced from the world that someone couldn't reference an internet meme as a means to explain Zen.

In a 2002 video, Iverson goes on and on in response to a question he finds offensive in a postgame press conference. He was known to give outstanding performances in every game, but in the video, he's being asked about missing practices.

"If I can't practice, I can't practice," he says, exasperated. "If I'm hurt, I'm hurt. Simple as that. It's not about that at all."

Indeed, the point of the press conference had been to celebrate the fact that Iverson, as one of the Philadelphia 76ers' star players, would be remaining with the team for another year. Instead, it would come to be known for this moment of conflict and the visible tension between Iverson and his head coach, who liked to complain about Iverson's absences at regular practices.

"I'm supposed to be the franchise player," he complained, getting more and more frustrated, "and we're in here talking about practice. I mean, listen, we're talking about practice. Not a game! Not a game! Not a game! We're talking about practice. Not a game; not the game that I go out there and die for and play every game like it's my last, not the game, we're talking about practice, man. I mean, how silly is that? We're talking about *practice*."[6]

Before the video ends, Iverson says the word "practice" twenty-two times.

Hearing Iverson's story resonated with my own experiences in Buddhist circles, and I appreciated how well it illustrated this issue of practice versus training. For years, I now shared, I had heard spiritual and religious activities ubiquitously described as practice. The word was often accompanied by encouragement to be measured and patient, to have acceptance—particularly self-acceptance—and to not be so hard on oneself.

"It's a practice," I had heard again and again. "That's why they call it practice," people would say.

For fourteen years, from age four until I was in college, I played the piano, and that meant practicing piano exercises and pieces almost every day. The word "practice" thus evoked for me repetition, drills, and memorization. Eventually, as I got older and better, practicing the piano could also mean playing in the currents of musicality and enjoying the fact that I could create music with my own two hands. But mostly, it meant methodically rehearsing a piece over and over until it was ready for performance, competition, or just to add to my repertoire. This type of practice seemed to me an inadequate metaphor for deep spiritual work.

Another common use of the word "practice" refers to an occupation, like having a law practice or a dental practice. This fits just as poorly. Ever since my first vipassana retreat, I had always felt that what I was getting after was something big, universal, and transcendently true. I could never put it to words in a satisfactory way or even really put my finger on it. I only knew that meditation had afforded me glimpses of something profound, beginning with a new perspective on myself and who I wanted to be and then extending as far out as how I perceived reality. Such experiences often didn't feel of my own making. Sometimes, I reflected, it wasn't so much me doing the meditating as the meditation seemed to be doing me. "Practice" again fell woefully short of describing what I'd experienced.

In the previous few years, the meaning of practice had also evolved to include not just a single practice, like that of meditation, or what you'd think of as religious practice, hewing to the forms and traditions of an established tradition. If anything, it now seemed more common for people to use it to refer to a bricolage of different religions, beliefs, and activities they collected liberally and freely. This syncretic spirituality was also often referred to in the possessive: "my practice." Something felt off about this. There was an implied dichotomy to "my practice." The person was on one side, and the spiritual activity on the other, and in that relationship of possession and ownership, the person was clearly more important. This couldn't feel farther from my own experience.

Looking around me at lunch, I saw nods of agreement. It occurred to me that, despite our faded blue jumpsuits, each of the people sitting on the engawa that day was quite accomplished, with multiple graduate-level degrees and professional successes represented among us. But here we were, knocking ourselves down to something more plain and pure—paying attention and matching those around us, learning new art forms, and all wearing the same navy-blue training clothes and jumpsuits. The formalities of Chado and the physical realities of moving rocks had been refreshing opportunities to abandon how I wanted to do things. Individual self-expression and desires—in other words, my practice—were being thrown away here, through every Chado procedure executed and every rock moved.

It all added up to something bigger than practice: it was training. And it came with the sense that training had a goal or an end, a moment when the training would come to bear. The inevitable moment for each and every one of us would be facing death—our own or the deaths of the people we loved. I felt determined to abandon any notions of Buddhism as endless practice and to stop using it as an excuse to not wake up right here, right now. I was tired of being that person who used "it's a practice" as an excuse for my own faults and misbehaviors. I wanted to do everything in life the same way that Allen Iverson said he played every game: like it was his last. And I didn't want to wait patiently for some future lifetime to become the person I wanted to be. For myself, for the people I loved, and for the world, I wanted to do everything I could to become that person now. And in the same mysterious way that I had glimpsed something on the horizon during my first meditation retreat, I thought I saw in front of me now a method to make progress toward becoming that person.

9

"WAKE UP!"

For years, much of my experience with Buddhism was colored by the persistent belief that Americans are too hard on ourselves and that our most salient quality is that we ignore or violate healthy boundaries in pursuit of our own egoistic goals. I heard many Buddhist teachers say that we have to recognize and interrupt this same impulse in how we approach meditation rather than blindly pushing for some enlightening realization. They often summed up this individual and collective trait in one word: striving.

Striving was roundly discouraged wherever I went. The consistent response it prompted was to be told to stop, surrender, and let go of chasing goals, even spiritual ones. This was never easy for me. Much of what had made me successful in life was that I threw myself into whatever I did. By nature, I was hard charging, an enthusiastic and focused person. I liked to see my labors culminate in achievement and found enjoyment in tackling tough problems. I possessed the intensity and drive shared by many Koreans, as we are the descendants of tough-as-nails (if also impetuous and emotional) survivors—of colonization, poverty, and war. We always persist and often out of sheer, ferocious will. So I was by default a striver, through and through.

For years, I tried my best to follow what was presented to me as the teachings of Buddhism, recognizing and squelching my tendency for striving and my overall intensity. It had some positive effects; it was a good way to put my ego in check. I recognized that, out of callousness and solipsism, I sometimes leaped before looking, and I often pushed my own agenda too hard. Countering striving became a mantra I heard in my own head and in Buddhist conversations all around me. I came to accept this overall discouragement of striving as a given. It must, I figured, be a part of what made Buddhism what it was. One time, however, I met a Buddhist teacher who took a different tack.

It was 2008 when, facing a hall full of silent retreatants, Buddhist teacher Rodney Smith extolled some forty of us on retreat to "wake up!" He had just finished explaining how the word "buddha" in ancient Pali meant "one who is awakened." That, he said, was the simple, elegant, and yet hard-to-attain goal of all of Buddhism: to wake up. It was also our call to action as Buddhist meditators: *Wake up!*

It was this spirit of radical, total awakening that had initially drawn me to Buddhism. The forcefulness of this call to wake up also matched my first experience on retreat when I had charged into meditative practice with the seriousness required by my circumstances— heading into Burma to meet with political dissidents and possibly arrest and torture. But I had never heard a Western teacher sharing this kind of bold call to action: to go for it and to go all the way.

To be fair, the story of the historical Buddha's enlightenment reads like fantasy—that he sat with immoveable determination for six days under the Bodhi Tree, having resolved not to move until he was enlightened; that he dove into the earth as if it were water to avoid prowling tigers; that a giant king cobra spread its hooded neck over him as he sat in meditation so he'd be sheltered from the rain. As a rule, the Western teachers I had come across treated this story the same way many modern Christians treat the stories in the Bible—most useful as metaphor. They certainly did not prescribe sitting for days on end to their students. As laypeople, they said,

Buddhist practice had to be woven into our daily lives with yielding, gentleness, and patience and with the acceptance of the fact that sometimes we will feel like we are making progress by leaps and bounds and at other times like we aren't going anywhere at all. This prevailing sentiment could be recognized in a unique lexicon that many different meditation teachers seemed to adopt in unison in the 2010s, liberally using words like "heartbreak," "tenderness," "refuge," "rest," and "surrender."

Rodney, who at the time of this retreat was in his early sixties, recounted what it was like to be a young monk in Asia in the 1970s and 1980s. He had gone to Burma, then India, and finally Thailand to live as a monk with some of the great Buddhist teachers of the day: Mahasi Sayadaw, Nisargadatta Maharaj, and Ajahn Buddhadasa. Rodney described how he and his fellow monks walked their morning alms rounds at dawn, each with their head shaved, wearing monk's robes, barefooted and carrying a wooden bowl to beg for food. The living conditions were very poor.

"Some days," he said, "you'd get some rice or curry in your bowl. You go back and share that. Some days, you might only get a scoop of buffalo fat and some rice. If that was all you received, that was what you would eat. That was it."

Rodney also described himself as stubborn and how his stubbornness ultimately proved to be a great gift. Despite the hardships of monastic life, Rodney never gave up. He persisted to the point that something eventually opened up in him, leading him to have a realization, which later led to him becoming a well-known and beloved Buddhist teacher.

Rodney's stories sounded amazing. As I listened, the world of my imagination in which Rodney lived as a monk expanded rapidly, populated by details from the times I myself had lived, studied, and worked in Asia. The hot, dusty air of the dry season. Stepping briskly on umber earth, clouds of dust kicked up by well-worn sandals. The sounds of distant tuk-tuks and calls to mosque projected over loudspeakers in the Muslim quarters of town. The smells of freshly boiled rice, incense, mosquito coils, and sweat. I couldn't imagine the monks' exhaustion, sleeping only four hours a night, or the monotony of monastery life. But I imagined all the other aspects of Rodney's stories so vividly that I almost felt as if I were there in line with the other monks, making the morning alms rounds.

Pointing out the ample food, electricity, heat, and private rooms at our retreat center, Rodney continued his talk by suggesting that we had everything we needed to break through our attachments and have our own realization. If he had done it in such bare conditions, certainly we could figure something out here. We had all journeyed so far and set aside time in our lives to practice deeply. With everything taken care of and in the company of a *sangha*—a community of people committed to meditating and being mindful—perhaps we had even better conditions for a breakthrough than he had had in the monastery.

"Stay and sit as late as you want," he said, gesturing to the meditation hall. "Go all night, even. The hall will stay open. This time is precious. Why not go for it? Right now. Why wait? Why not go all the way? Why not wake up?" Hearing this, my heart swelled. It sang! I wanted to go all the way. I wanted to wake up! I felt that Rodney had given me permission and shown me the path. Having been told it was here before me, I was ready not just to walk it but to run.

Rodney ended his talk with that exhortation, and I did run—but first to the dining hall to down a cup of coffee. I would need fuel, I thought, to sit through the night. I looked forward to the prospect of sitting in meditation until the sun rose. The idea excited me, and I thought that I did, indeed, have in front of me the ideal conditions for a realization, surrounded by more than forty other people who had all signed up for this retreat and who, I deduced, must be really serious Buddhists.

Rodney rang a bell at 9:00 p.m. to start the last formal sitting of the night. I settled into my cushion and wrapped a blanket around my shoulders, closing my eyes. At first, I just felt the air pass in and out below my nostrils. I counted my breaths, one to ten, over and over again. When I was able to sustain my concentration for a while, I stopped counting and felt myself just breathing, heard the sounds in the meditation hall, and cultivated the sense of all-allowing mindful awareness as Rodney had instructed us in earlier. When a thought arose, I regarded it like a cloud passing through a clear blue sky. Then, I labeled the thought, noting "thinking," and returned my attention to the full, wide expanse of my perception. Other metaphorical clouds were labeled: "hearing," "ruminating," "tension," and so on. When my mind became agitated or unfocused, I returned to counting my breaths to restore my concentration.

After forty-five minutes, Rodney rang the meditation bell three times to end the sitting. After the third bell, everyone opened their eyes, put their palms together, and bowed. As Rodney exited, I roused myself.

More sitting! I thought. As I left the hall for a quick bathroom break, I saw other people continuing to sit.

I'll be back soon! my heart called out to them.

Just a few minutes later, I returned to the meditation hall and saw that, to my surprise, most of the meditation cushions in the hall were empty. Only ten or so of us were left. What had happened? I thought maybe some people had also gone to the bathroom or to the dining hall and would be back soon. No doubt everyone had heard Rodney's call to action and was planning to sit through the night. I cast aside my doubts, and still optimistic about the prospect of having a realization, I sat back down and again began to meditate.

As I sat through my usual bedtime, I found myself drifting away from mindful awareness. Soon, I was nodding off. In my more lucid moments, I willed myself to think rousing thoughts. Still, I found myself losing track of my breaths and my counting. I opened my eyes once in a while to try to urge myself awake, but soon, my eyelids drooped and closed. At one point, I couldn't tell if I was just think-ing or dreaming. As the minutes went by, I floated along, trying to wake up over and over again. Eventually, I opened my eyes, put my palms together, and bowed. I looked at the clock on the wall. It read 11:00 p.m.

I wasn't sure what to do. I was tired. My brain felt like molasses. Going back to my room and going to sleep suddenly sounded very attractive! Wanting to keep going, instead, I closed my eyes and re-sumed meditating. But again, I drifted in and out, unable to stay awake. At around midnight, I got up and did some pushups and then swung my arms back and forth in a corner of the hall to get my blood flowing. By that time, I was the only person left.

For another thirty or forty minutes, I didn't really meditate; I only drifted in and out of sleep. Opening my eyes, I looked around the empty meditation hall. Alone in the cavernous space in the middle of the night, I felt lonely and small. Most of all, I felt dis-appointed. I tasted a sourness in my mouth, the bite of defeat and loneliness.

Resignedly, I took the blanket from around my shoulders and folded it, placing it on top of my meditation cushion. I picked up my notebook and pen and put them on top of my folded blanket. Slowly, I walked back out of the hall and toward my room. When I saw one of the retreat participants closer to my age walking in on my way out, I thought for a moment about turning around and trying again, buoyed by his presence. But it was already too late. Even if I could stay awake just a little longer, my spirit had failed me. I had given up.

The next morning, I learned that I hadn't just been fighting my own lack of resolve to sit through the night but also a quiet consensus among some of the retreatants that this was not the time or the place to go all the way. When Rodney got up on the dais in the morning, he shared that he had heard from several people that his invocation had prompted them to feel that this wasn't where they belonged.

"You belong here," Rodney reassured them, apologizing profusely. "I'm sorry. You absolutely belong here." He had not meant to imply that anyone was out of place here, he went on, only that the conditions were right to go as far as any of us had wanted. Then, he encouraged all of us to forget what he had said about going all the way. We all had to train in the way each of us felt appropriate and to figure out what was right for ourselves. From where I sat, I could see the grandfatherly smile on Rodney's face, but I wondered if I didn't see some sadness behind it, too. For my own part, I felt discouraged and confused, and that sourness lingered on my tongue.

For perhaps a decade after that retreat with Rodney, I took what seemed to be the prevailing message from the sangha to heart: that I should be more measured in my spiritual pursuits and that the foremost enemy of spiritual progress was this delusive thinking called striving. Who was I to think I could have a realization, anyway? Trying to be what I thought was a good Buddhist, I tempered my enthusiasm and tamped down the energy with which I approached life. I gave up capoeira, the martial art I had trained in all through college, because it felt too aggressive and at odds with the placid demeanor I was trying to cultivate through meditation and Buddhist study. I took up yoga, instead. I tried to be more aware of times when I came across as too brash, loud, or bossy for those around me, and I took jobs doing work that seemed more respectable and less radical. As a headstrong young woman, I tried hard to be quieter, softer, more calm and measured, and to take up less space.

Throughout my teen years and young adulthood, I had not flagged in my motivation to be an activist and, later, to help free Burma. I had felt that it was my life's purpose to advocate for democracy and human rights there and to be a voice for the voiceless. But after I began to meditate and study Buddhism seriously, I beat a slow retreat from the movement. I was driven in part by a budding awareness of the physical and psychological toll that the work was taking on me through vicarious and direct trauma. But I also with-drew because I had come to think that my intensity and the strength of my convictions—about Burma, yes, but also about everything else—were more destructive than helpful. These traits did not line up with my new ideals of quiet Buddhist restraint and softness. To me, this meant that they were, obviously and inherently, bad. And by extension, so was I.

I was too big, too loud, too sharp. Throwing away my ego, I decided, meant chipping away at myself until I was so small that I disappeared. One teacher I later sat retreats with talked about a "thinning of the me" and likened it to dissolving into something bigger and more universal. Another teacher I encountered likened it to being porous. I leaned into this approach so much that, at one point, a strong wind could've blown right through me. Over time, it became second nature to stop, breathe, and identify my thoughts as just thoughts and not "me" until my sense of self faded down to a whisper. For a decade or so, I focused on diminishing myself in this way and on practices like loving-kindness meditation, which involved flooding myself with feelings of love and softness to negate the sharp and forceful person that I was. Never again during that time did I try to sit up all night in meditation; nor did I want to anymore. That was so obviously striving.

In the weeks and months leading up to my arrival at Chozen-ji, it did not occur to me that I was about to encounter such a differ-ent approach to developing the spirit. I felt exhilarated by every-thing I heard about the history of Rinzai Zen and the role of the martial arts in Chozen-ji training. This combined with the kismet of the timing—Michael happening to reach out just as I was al-ready planning a trip to Hawai'i—made it so that I never even gave it a second thought. And once I was here, I embraced everything that this samurai Zen had to offer, easily shedding the albatross of struggling not to strive. I guess it had really been an unnatural fit; I had been forcing things all along by trying not to be so forceful.

Within moments of arriving at Chozen-ji, it was as if the ever-present critique of striving had disappeared from my mind. However, the habits I'd accumulated over years of making myself quiet and small—hesitation, freezing, and flinching—remained and needed to be addressed.

Not long after my arrival, Michael told me he'd scheduled something that happened not infrequently at Chozen-ji: an all-night training. Capping off my three-week live-in, the all-night training would include zazen, martial arts, and fine arts. He challenged me to work on the sword cuts I was learning so that I could do several hundred, maybe even one thousand, that night. And to figure out how to sit zazen through the night without falling asleep. The all-night training would be a time to challenge myself to do things I couldn't ordinarily or otherwise do.

I didn't remember at first that I had tried—and failed—at training through the night once before. When I did remember, it was with a chuckle. How different this was, I thought, from any sort of Buddhism I had ever done before. And yet, it felt so good, so natural. This sort of intensity and vigor was the perfect fit for my personality. It challenged me, of course—it was designed to. But within the challenge and every moment of training was the feeling of coming home, as if this kind of "balls to the wall" approach to life was the way I had always been meant to live; I just hadn't known it.

Every day, I was feeling stronger, my senses more astute, and lighter. Whether it was for the psychological burdens I was letting go or just my improving musculature and posture, I felt amazing. I embraced the upcoming all-night training as another sign that I was finally where I belonged and that I had finally found my kin—the kind of people whose idea of fun was to do crazy things like staying up all night sitting zazen and swinging swords. Every day from that day forward until the end of my first three weeks at Chozen-ji, I thought about the upcoming all-night training, looking forward to it and counting down the days.

10

"DON'T MOVE!"

One of the things that was new and challenging to me at Chozen-ji was also the most basic and fundamental: sitting zazen for forty-five minutes without moving. With the exception of just a few hour-long sittings on the Goenka vipassana retreats, where we were encouraged not to move our hands or legs or open our eyes in "Sittings of Strong Determination," I had never before sat without moving. But now, the daily schedule required me to do this for forty-five minutes at a time, three times a day.

Each sitting was accompanied by a crescendo of pain. My left foot reliably fell asleep when I sat—not just a little numb with pins and needles but to the point that it became completely inert and unfeeling, like a block of wood. Meanwhile, my right ankle and the tendons along the outside of my right shin screamed. Even after the sittings were over, it would take several minutes before all the pain fully disappeared and before I could feel my feet enough to stand or walk.

None of this was improved by changing my sitting position or changing the arrangement of my cushions. Not that this stopped me from trying! I found myself spending much of the first evening sittings scheming about how I could relieve some of the pressure on my legs in the second. Perhaps, I thought, by switching from calf lotus to tailor or from tailor to calf lotus, I'd find some relief. But then, after twenty or thirty minutes, pain just sprang up anew.

The instructions in zazen were clear: don't move. I had been warned that the *jiki* who ran the sittings would scold me if I moved or fell asleep. And if I were a repeat offender, he could even eject me from the dojo and make me sit outside on the engawa. During the formal sittings—the sitting in the morning and the second evening sitting, which began at 6:45 p.m. at night—the jiki bowed at his cushion and then rose to walk over to the butsudan, the shrine at the front of the room. There, he bowed and picked up the *keisaku*, a long, flat stick the length of a practice sword. He walked slowly from one end of the line of meditators to the other with the keisaku on his shoulder. During that first formal evening sitting, he would often stop in front of me to adjust my posture, again lifting me up by the head, tilting me forward, and pushing down on my shoulders. But I had also been told that he might stop in front of me to hit me with the keisaku, three times on either side of the spine, to help me stay awake or to help steady my mind. It was a few days before I saw people bring their palms together in gassho as the jiki passed. Seeing them raise their hands, he would stop and return the gesture, and then, together in unison, they would bow. After bowing, the person sitting leaned over, one hand down on the tatami and the other wrapped under their body, and the jiki would bring the keisaku swiftly down.

Whack! Whack! Whack!

Switching sides, three more strikes would be delivered, each breaking the silence of the room and rendering it more still. Finally, the jiki and the person sitting would bow to one another again, and the jiki would continue down the line.

Each time the jiki approached me, I sat up a little straighter, paid attention a little harder, and wondered if he could sense how much

my legs burned. I wished for some special dispensation to shift position, to be able to reach down, pick up my right leg, and move it.
But no such signal ever came. By the end of evening zazen, I was
shaking, twitching, and trembling. Any muscle with tension, which
I realized with dismay might be every muscle in my body, spasmed
from time to time. As I worked myself into a state of overwhelm,
my blood pressure rose, and my vision went red and then black. Especially in the last few minutes of the sitting, before the bell would
ring, I felt as if I were about to fall off the edge of a cliff. But then,
the sitting would end, my body and mind would return to normal,
and I would invariably become full of energy and enthusiasm for
training again.

At first, it seemed to me like the training was designed to pro-
voke these kinds of extreme states. Okyo, or sutra chanting, during
which everyone sat seiza, did this especially well. Sitting seiza was
the best way to ensure correct posture, opening space in our bodies
for the chanting to become louder, fuller, and more resonant. This
resonance was the goal. So much so that I was instructed to chant
as loudly as I could, almost yelling. To loosen up our throats and
chests, we actually did yell one of the chants at the top of our lungs
once, shaking the room: "*Na! Mu! Sa! Man! Da!*"

It was better to be loud and a mess, giving it all I had, than to be
soft and accurate. If I lost the rhythm, rather than searching silently
for my place on the page, I was told to say "Ahhhh" at full volume
until I found my place again. To aid our posture, we were to hold
the okyo books high up in front of our faces rather than down in
our laps. While some Western Zen centers chant the sutras in English, we chanted in Japanese. Some of the chants, which were not
translated in the back of the book, are Japanese transliterations of
ancient Pali or Sanskrit, which means that they are, essentially, gib-
berish, just sounds. Their conceptual meaning has been lost over
the past two thousand years. However, their vibration—the actual
crests and valleys of the sound waves as each consonant and vowel

is sounded out—has been preserved and can be experienced in the body. And at Chozen-ji, that was what mattered.

On the mornings we did okyo, I navigated its alien sounds with sharp attention, pushed forward by the fast beating of the *mokugyo*, a big, red, wooden drum carved in the shape of a fish. It was possible to sit with a few zafu, perhaps under the ankles or in the crook of my legs, but I knew that I should sit straight on the zabuton. That was what everybody else did unless they had serious injuries or were very old. On just the second day of my okyo training, with my left hand holding the sutra book, I reached with my right hand at an opportune moment to pull my zafu forward beneath my legs. Several minutes later, at another such interval, I realized I had made a mistake, the zafu were better where they had started out, and I reached down to move them back.

"Stop moving!" one of the senior students yelled sharply from across the room. I froze and then, a few seconds later, put both hands back on the okyo book. Soon, not just my ankles but the whole of my legs felt like they were on fire. I tried to shift my weight to one side to give the other leg a break. It didn't work. Before long, I was spasming and trembling again, my voice rattling as I tried to enunciate the words.

Finally, after thirty-five minutes, the okyo was over. The student leading and striking the bells hit the small bell once. Nobody moved. He hit it again with two hits in quick succession. Now everyone stood up. As soon as I could feel my feet enough to not topple over, I forced myself up and joined the rest of the group in sampai, bowing from the waist and then going down to our knees to bow again, forehead and elbows on the floor, palms rising up to the ceiling, three times. At the moment all of our hands came up above our heads, the bell was stopped, and the slight rattling sound cued us to stand up again.

As everyone sat back down in seiza after the bows, worry was no doubt evident on my face. I could not help but telegraph the smallness and doubt I felt inside, wincing as I sat back down. We sat in silence for a moment, the okyo leader at the bells smiling and looking at each of us as he surveyed the room.

"Any questions?" he finally asked. Finding no response, he turned his attention to me.

"So, did all that squirming help?" His question, asked so directly and in front of an audience, pinned me to my cushion. I had so little self-awareness at this early juncture that my instinct under pressure like this was to become defensive, and to dig in. In my head, I sniped back, *Of course it helped. Why else would I have done it?* Sure, it had not been long before the pain returned, but for a precious moment, moving did offer relief. No doubt, struggling to maintain one's composure in the midst of terrible pain was a normal, human response! *What the hell did he expect?!* I thought.

But I didn't say that. As soon as the thoughts materialized in my head, as justified and appropriate as I thought they were, I knew better than to invite what would have invariably been a pointed scolding. So, had all that squirming helped me?

"No," I finally said. "It didn't help. It just hurt again somewhere else." And that was, I realized, the truth.

While I sat there, I still smoldered at being singled out. Meanwhile, the senior student started to speak at some length about what all of this—the okyo, sitting seiza—had to do with Zen. And all the while, we kept sitting seiza.

"It's worth taking a deep look at that impulse to squirm around. Why do you want to move? Why do you think it's OK for you to move when nobody else is? It's a habit, usually from when we're children. When you're a kid, you cry or find a way to show that you don't like something, so people will feel bad for you, and then you don't have to be uncomfortable anymore."

He looked straight at me while he spoke, his piercing eyes contrasting against his relaxed face and body. It was then that I realized that he had been sitting seiza this whole time. Because he had had the responsibility of ringing the bells while we got up and bowed, he had not had even that brief chance to stretch his legs. Yet here he was, totally relaxed.

"That's essentially what you're doing, trying to get people to feel bad for you and let you move," he continued. "Isn't that childish?

"There are definitely people in the room in more pain than you are," he said. He motioned to the students with actual injuries: torn tendons, recent surgeries, and degenerated joints. "When you move around like that, only thinking about your own pain, it makes it harder for everyone else. That hardly seems fair."

This cut right through me. I squirmed with the feeling of being so small, petty, and, most of all, selfish. I found it worse than the pain in my knees or struggling to understand the Dojo's many rules and procedures. I felt cornered, with nowhere to hide. More demoralizing than being singled out was realizing that he was right and that I had been acting like a child. I recognized that I often wanted someone to come along and give me special permission to take it easy or be an exception to the rules. In contrast, none of the other students evinced that they were running away from whatever needed to be done, whether it was sitting zazen without moving, going all out in the okyo, or any one of the myriad other responsibilities they performed to keep the Dojo and the training going.

"Do you guys have any advice?" he finally asked the room. He turned to the student at the drum, encouraging him to speak.

"You just do it," he said, shrugging his shoulders cheerfully. A young man in his mid-twenties, his speech was peppered with Hawaiian Pidgin, and he spoke with a characteristic directness that I was fast becoming used to here. "You gotta relax, just like zazen. Whatever you feeling, jus gotta put in da okyo. Go loudah. Sounds nuts, yeah? But you take up all da space, try hard, then no more room for be scared or think, 'Oh, my foot hurts, like, *so* much.'"

"Yeah, you have the keys already," the okyo leader jumped in again, newly enthusiastic. "You just have to be like, 'I'm going to unlock whatever this is. I'm going to figure it out no matter what.' You're here. This is what this place is for, so experiment. You can sit seiza on your own, do more okyo. Sit more zazen. Just be determined to figure it out.

"I can promise you one thing," he concluded, taking in my collapsed posture and the look of defeat plastered across my face. "Definitely none of this is going to work if you give up and feel sorry for yourself."

"Sayama Roshi," he continued, referring to Chozen-ji's abbot, "always says, 'Don't be a victim.' Don't indulge in the pain or in feeling sorry for yourself. You have to go for it. Be relentless. It really all comes back to breath and posture. Everyone can do it."

And then, after a brief pause, he concluded, "But you have to want to."

As much as I wanted all the messages of challenge and encouragement to sink in, I just couldn't wrap my head around how to do any of what was being recommended to me. How could breath and posture solve so much? Could I really just decide not to be defeated, going forward against what felt like unsurpassable discomfort? It felt hard to believe that everybody else's legs hurt, too. They all seemed so calm and collected. As for me, my feet hurt so badly that my whole body was tense. Even as I listened, I was pushing down into the zabuton with my hands to try to take some of the weight off my feet and legs. Meanwhile, everyone else continued to sit in seiza, backs straight, faces calm, eyes bright.

The next time we sat in meditation, which was the following morning, I thought about what I had been told in okyo class. I wasn't ready, though, to figure out how to put it into practice. So, instead, like hitting snooze on my morning alarm, I fell back on an old practice I had learned on a silent meditation retreat and later had seen used everywhere from yoga classes to workplace team-bonding retreats. As I meditated, I visualized the strength that I felt that I lacked, feeling the energy of that strength in my body, in my heart, and all around me. It helped relieve some of the inner pangs I felt from my own lack of willpower in comparison to the other students, and I soon became swept up in my own vision.

"I closed my eyes, and I could see it, this outline of a warrior," I later told one of my senpai, hoping that he would see this as a sign that I really was trying and had the potential for progress. "It was a little bigger than me. So, like, me but also around me." After describing more of how it looked, an androgynous, exotic warrior, I concluded that it made me feel like I could grow into being the spiritual warrior this training was trying to get me to be.

For a moment, he was quiet. Then, he asked, "So, you imagined this?"

"I saw it," I responded, not quite sure how to respond. And then, hesitantly, I said, "Yes, I guess you could say I imagined it."

"Well," he started, then took a long pause. "That sounds like a waste of a good zazen."

His last words, yet to be delivered, had the same tenor and tone as the instructions I'd received on eating fast, doing okyo, and moving rocks. They would stay with me long after our conversation had ended, embodying as they did the directness and no-nonsense approach with which I was so enamored here at Chozen-ji and which also still left me completely dumbfounded. There was something to it that I knew was real and true. Yet it also felt out of reach.

Looking me straight in the eye, he said, "Don't *imagine* being anything. Just *be* it."

11

ALL OF MY HABITS SINCE THE DAY I WAS BORN

The inside of the Kyudo, or archery, dojo felt too dim to see comfortably. It was only just past 7:30 p.m., but the winter night was already an impenetrable, inky blank. I had survived the night's double sittings, and at the end of my third full day of live-in training at Chozen-ji, I had moved rocks, cleaned the bathrooms, pulled weeds, done two hours and fifteen minutes of zazen, practiced okyo, and eaten three remarkably hearty meals. I had been awake since before 5:00 a.m., throwing myself into each activity of the day from before sunrise to after sunset, and now it was time for my first experience of martial arts: learning the Hojo.

After zazen ended, we put away the cushions and quickly cleared out so as to not disrupt the Tai Chi class that was about to start in the Budo Dojo. I followed along down the steps of the building and across the gravel path. Once we arrived at the Kyudo Dojo, we latched the front doors open and removed the wall panels on the opposite side so that a breeze moved through the building. I could see the target house a few dozen yards away. Directly behind was the ceramics studio. Somewhere beyond were the mountains, rising up toward the starry night.

Along with zazen and sesshin, the weeklong intensive training done twice a year, the Hojo was one of the pillars of Chozen-ji training. Some five hundred years old, the Hojo is a foundational means of instruction used in the Jikishinkage-ryu school of fencing. I was enamored with the idea that the Hojo had come to its creator all at once, in its entirety, in a dream. And, of course, I was impressed by the fact that it was not just a prescribed set of martial arts movements but a spiritual vehicle. Throughout the Hojo, there are references to various aspects of Buddhist, Zen, and Taoist philosophy, as well as Japanese arts and culture. The overarching purpose of the Hojo is to help one get rid of all her habits since the day she was born.

As a kata, or a prescribed set of movements, the Hojo is performed by two partners, one called the *shin* (mind-heart) and the other, *kage* (shadow). There are four parts to the kata, each with the feeling or the kiai of the four seasons: spring, summer, fall, and winter. Tanouye Rotaishi said that he'd seen the secrets of all the martial arts in the Hojo. The Hojo thus became a core component of Chozen-ji's training, not to teach the technicalities of the martial arts but their true spirit.

"Do you remember the statues in the kitchen, the *nio*?" I was asked. The senpai giving me my first lesson in the Hojo was referring to the foot-tall metal sculptures with heavily muscled bodies and swords sitting in the *tokonoma*, or alcove, in the kitchen. I nodded.

"In Zen temples in Japan, there are usually giant nio standing at the entrance. They're there to ward off bad energy but also as a warning to anyone who wants to enter. One of them has its mouth open, the other closed, doing this ah-um breathing." He demonstrated, opening his mouth into a wide grimace and inhaling in a loud "aaahhh." His right hand was clenched in a fist and he pulled it up along his side, inhaling. The other he held flat, parallel to the floor. Having taken a full breath, he clamped his lips into a frown and let out a loud "ummmm" as his right fist descended slowly back down toward the floor. As he demonstrated, his eyes bulged reflexively, his face fierce.

I was impressed by his lack of self-consciousness, his face so vividly contorted and his countenance so aggressive. He seemed willing to fully inhabit his role in this moment. This was a trait I had begun to recognize in all the teachers, priests, and senior students at Chozen-ji—that they seemed unhindered by embarrassment or timidity. They embodied the appropriate energy of their training at every moment, the dial turned up to ten, even eleven, and in those moments seemed to even grow in size and stature. At some moments with a sharp glance and at others with a booming voice, they skillfully wielded the ability to shock, interrupt, and redirect a wayward mind. And then at the drop of a hat, they could return to calmness as if nothing had ever happened.

Now, as I witnessed this demonstration of the ah-um breathing, my senpai took on the appearance of a real live nio in front of me. A thick tension filled the room, and I knew that, soon, it would be my turn. When it came, I tried to approach the ah-um breathing with the same vigor. But I was totally hamstrung by self-consciousness. What else was holding me back I couldn't quite understand, but I felt suddenly less capable and then embarrassed. Looking at my reflection in the full-length mirror at the far end of the dojo, I saw a comically distorted face trying to breathe in, "ah," and breathe out, "um." I fumbled opening my mouth wide enough to inhale, even though I knew that physically, I could open it wider than I was. My brain signaled one thing, but my face seemed to have missed the instruction. I also saw that I was exaggerating the downturn at the corners of my mouth. The result was that the face I saw in the mirror was that of a sad, pathetic clown.

I was told to open my mouth wider and swallow the air; the sound

ALL OF MY HABITS SINCE THE DAY I WAS BORN   105

should've been like a loud wind. I was successful on some attempts, but on others I just sounded like I was imitating the sucking sound of a draining sink. I did not feel like a large and powerful nio—I felt small. Yet I kept trying, just standing and breathing ah-um for what was just several minutes but felt like an eternity.

Despite my fumbling at such a basic task, we soon moved on, and I began to learn the foundation of the Hojo, the Hojo Walk. The Hojo Walk has four basic principles:

1. The belly button always faces straight forward, without going side to side.
2. The shoulders stay level.
3. The feet always maintain contact with the floor.
4. Every movement is coordinated with the breath.

I bent my knees slightly and put my hands flat, all the fingers and thumbs touching, on the fronts of my hip points, mimicking my senpai. As I breathed in, ah, I stepped forward, my foot touching down on the wooden floor and rolling heel to toe. As I exhaled, um, I dragged the ball of the back foot until it caught up with the other. Then I began the next inhale, stepping forward with the opposite foot.

For some reason, whenever I bent my knees, my back would arch, and my butt would stick out. This was repeatedly corrected. Each time, I would fix it. And then, in short order, I became lost in the other mechanics of the walk, and my low back would collapse again causing my rear to stick out behind me. I also could not maintain a grasp on the coordination between breath and movement and was unable to hitch the two together. For ten or fifteen minutes, I walked back and forth trying to keep track of all the small adjustments needed in my body while still seeing 180 degrees in every direction and breathing ah and um in time with each step. It was a terrible lot to keep track of, but I was reassured that the walk was intentionally unnatural. The awkward unfamiliarity was apparently a big part of what helped to surface and correct one's habits.

Whenever the coordination of my breath and movement fell apart, my senpai would stop me and tell me to start again.

"Feet together," he would say as soon as he caught me. "Start again."

"Keep your back heel down." He pushed my heel down several inches with his own foot. "Start again."

"Don't lean forward." He pushed my shoulders back several inches so that I was standing up straight.

"Look straight ahead. . . . Don't lead with your head. . . . Finish one movement before you start the next. . . . Don't stop in the middle, step all the way through."

"Push from your hara." He slapped his own abdomen. "Start again."

Finally, we stopped walking back and forth for just a moment. It was long enough for him to say the closest thing to a reassuring word I'd heard all night.

"There are plenty of people who've spent, like, three months here just doing the Hojo Walk," he said. He picked up a bamboo *shinai*, the practice sword used in Kendo, and held one end out to me.

"Put your end underneath your belly button," he said, standing three feet in front of me and doing the same on his side.

"This is me setting my hara," he said.

I did not see his body move, not even an inch. Yet the force of his setting his hara suddenly pushed me backward. The shinai fell from its perch between us and clattered against the wooden floor. We picked up the shinai and when he demonstrated again, I could only vaguely make out a slight thrust or upturn of his pelvis. He seemed to be able to make his lower abdomen bulge outwards by flexing some muscles that, at this point, I could not discern but, I guessed, must have been his hara. I flexed my own abdominal muscles in search of mine.

"Don't lean forward," he corrected.

On the third or fourth try, I managed to eke out just a little strength from my hara. It might have lasted one or two seconds. That seemed to be enough, and we promptly began doing the Hojo Walk, facing each other and with the shinai suspended between us. My senpai snapped into posture, his hands on his hip points, his back straight, and his feet gripping the floor with each step. He looked me straight in the eyes, breathing loudly and with the same menacing nio look on his face. With each step, I felt less and less like I was moving backward by the power of my own steps and more and more like I was skewered on the end of the sword and being slowly propelled across the room. Judging how much to move backward and how much to push forward was a tense negotiation with the guardian demon across from me. All the while, I struggled to keep my feet on the ground and keep seeing 180 degrees. My ankles wobbled. I hesitated. And then everything fell apart as I stumbled and my senpai continued forward. The shinai fell again.

"Feet together. Start again."

We kept going and going, and through it all, I was seized by the strong desire to run away and hide. It wasn't that I didn't want to be here learning the Hojo Walk. I was here for it, for all the Zen training and all the ways it pushed me. It was just that, at the same time, those parts of me that the training challenged wanted desperately to hide and disappear. My gaze fell to my senpai's feet, as if I had to be staring at them to match their steps forward.

"Look at my eyes," I was promptly told.

Another time, against my own conviction and effort, I found myself looking past him or to the sides of the room.

"Look at my eyes," he ordered.

Feeling conflicted but also unable to look anywhere else, I finally forced my self-consciousness out of the way. I looked straight at his face, seeing it all—the grimacing mouth, the wide and terrifying eyes. And then finally, something clicked. I realized all of a sudden that I could now see the whole room. I saw my senpai's eyes. We breathed together and moved together. And I took in everything between and around us—our coordinated movement, the dimensions of the Kyudo Dojo, the cool air, and the dark night outside.

The secret, it seemed, was the opposite of what I had been attempting to do by staring at his feet, mentally running through the four principles of the Hojo Walk, or looking around the room. To make the Hojo Walk work, what I actually had to do was stop thinking. I felt my face settle into the same slack and relaxed expression I had seen on my senpai's and teacher's faces during Chado and okyo, as if, now freed from conscious effort, my features naturally fell into place. Now I could look straight on at my senpai's face, simply seeing it for what it was. No longer were fear and discomfort automatically elicited from that seeing. His visage was terrifying, eyes open so wide that I could see the whole of his pupils sitting in bright pools of white, his mouth wide. But now I made the same face back. When it was my time to walk forward, pushing him backward, I matched his kiai—the ferocity, vigorous presence, and energy that he emanated—and the walk progressed smoothly, almost effortlessly. More equally matched in both sensitivity and now strength, we could move easily backward and forward. I had only to let go of any feeling that we were two, separate people on either end of the shinai. I had only to stop thinking at all, and we moved as one.

Realizing this was one thing. Sustaining it, however, was another. As I began to lose steam, this flow between us waned as did my concentration. When I hesitated or let up on the pressure between us, the shinai again fell. But we just picked it up and kept going.

Feet together. Start again.

After fifteen minutes or so of this, the shinai was finally put aside, and a wooden practice sword was placed in my hands. Standing at a slightly further distance, we still faced each other, our left hands at the base of our respective swords and our right hands riding the top. Inhaling ah, we raised the swords up until they were up over our heads. Then, stepping forward and bringing the swords down at the same time, we each let out a yell, "Yaaaahh-eh!" as loud as we could. The tip of each sword came to a stop at a height that, if we had been within striking range, would have cut three inches into the tops of each other's heads. We repeated this, doing the Hojo Walk, now with accompanying sword cuts, crossing the Kyudo Dojo almost a dozen times.

A little before nine o'clock, we finally stopped. Mirroring my senpai, I pulled the hilt of my sword away from me and then slid it into an imaginary sheath on my left side. And then, facing each other, we bowed. This simple bow marked the end of the night's training. Without speaking, we put all the wall panels back and shut the doors to the Kyudo Dojo. Senpai went to close the kitchen—and seeing that no cars were left in the parking lot, I shut and locked the gate. In six and a half hours, I would again be running the gauntlet of a schedule that I had just completed. I breathed in the cool night air, everything around me still and shrouded in darkness.

In the days to come, I would receive only one or two more one-on-one lessons like this. Instead of personal instruction, I'd soon be thrown into the Hojo and Kendo class to learn amid the din of other students and teachers breathing loudly, swallowing the air and grunting, a room full of guardian demons come to life. Within a week, I would be showing the Hojo Walk to a new student whose more recent arrival automatically made me *her* senpai. I would get used to correcting the same habits that I had seen come out in myself—averting my eyes, shrinking away, pulling back, and wanting to hide. Over time, I watched others shed these habits, and they also began to fade away in me with more, regular practice of the Hojo—all my habits since the day I was born, ripe for throwing away.

12

SWORD AT MY THROAT

I was scheduled to meet Chozen-ji's abbot, Sayama Daian Roshi, on the afternoon of my fourth day at the temple. Throughout the day, I religiously watched the clock to stay on a schedule of one hour of activity separated by short water and bathroom breaks. I was expected to follow through on it by myself in the same way that countless other Zen students before me had cycled through their arts and disciplines and contributed to Dojo projects like building rock walls and painting buildings. There was no overseer or enforcer, no one to whom to delegate my shugyo. I desired to understand shugyo more than just intellectually, by entraining myself to the temple's methods and high expectations. Although I did have senpai and teachers, at the end of the day, what I got out of the training would be entirely up to me.

I was looking forward to meeting Sayama Roshi on this sunny, perfect Hawai'i day. I had found myself nothing short of smitten with the training—even the scoldings, the painful zazen, and the unnerving instruction in the Hojo Walk—and had listened with fascination to many of Sayama Roshi's sayings and stories told

secondhand. One of the more magical ones was about Tanouye Rotaishi cutting the rain.

Several decades earlier, when Sayama Roshi had been a live-in
like me, he had watched Tanouye Rotaishi use a metal sword to cut
the rain, the sword moving in one clean motion through a curtain
of water coming off the roof. Standing on the engawa in front of
the kitchen, Tanouye Rotaishi wielded the sword with such other-
worldly expertise that, afterward, not a single drop of rain remained
on the blade. When he repeated the act, one or two drops were visible, but they were whole and intact, like pearls. Sayama tried, but
when he cut the rain, the blade came out splattered with water. The
story was so popular because it was such an effective illustration of
Tanouye Rotaishi's abilities—his perception of a universal rhythm
that governed even the pattern of the rain and his ability to act in
accord, cutting through the sheets with just the right speed and at
just the right interval to avoid all but a few drops. It also conveyed
to me how close Sayama Roshi, having spent the previous forty years
training in the method Tanouye Rotaishi had created, had been to
the source of Chozen-ji's genius.

After living in as a twenty-two-year-old, Sayama Roshi trained
in Kendo, earned a PhD in clinical psychology, became a health
care executive, and wrote and published several books. Few, if any,
of the other Buddhist teachers I had met over the years had been
executives. They were often monks, or if they were employed, they
usually worked as coaches and psychotherapists. None of them, as
far as I had known, had been martial artists. I hoped that Sayama
Roshi was going to be a different kind of Buddhist teacher—harder
charging and shrewder. Out of the many Western Buddhist teachers
I had encountered over the years, I had also only ever met one other
Asian American teacher before.

I sat seiza on the cushioned wall-to-wall carpet in the kitchen
and waited for Sayama Roshi to arrive. Around three o'clock, I

heard his silver Acura TL, a zippy sports sedan with a spoiler on the back, driving over the gravel as he peeled through the gate. When he walked into the kitchen, my eyes were drawn to Sayama Roshi's all-white hair, styled in a short, almost military haircut. It gleamed on his head. He was dressed casually, in a polo shirt and jeans, and I wondered if I would have recognized him as a Zen master if I'd seen him on the street, the only giveaway being the intense way in which his eyes sparkled. Sitting down on the floor opposite me at the kitchen tables, he smiled broadly in a way that felt welcoming and engaging, but I could also sense that he was already sizing me up.

"So, how are you liking it?" he asked. Rather than waste time on the usual pleasantries, I decided that here, sitting in front of the abbot of this amazing temple, was my chance to get right to business.

"I like it a lot," I replied. "I want to stay. I heard that the usual periods for longer live-ins are three months, one year, and three years. I'd like to start with a year."

Sayama Roshi looked at me for a moment and then burst into laughter. It was such an honest, spontaneous laugh that I found my own studied manner falling apart and was soon laughing with him. Before we could discuss the possibility of my living in long-term, though, he shifted the conversation to other topics. What had I been doing with my time so far, and what had brought me to Chozen-ji? I explained the long and winding path that had brought me here, beginning with my first meditation retreat and later spending more than a decade sitting with various teachers and groups in different Buddhist traditions. As I rattled off the names of the meditation centers and schools I had practiced in over the years, I did not see any recognition in his expression. Like the other priests and senior students I had met so far at Chozen-ji, it seemed that Sayama Roshi had been happily cloistered here in the middle of the Pacific Ocean and was ignorant to spiritual trends on the mainland. More than four decades had passed since he'd met Tanouye Rotaishi and begun his training, and apparently he'd never even thought to look anywhere else.

Eventually, I brought the conversation back to the topic of my living in and emphatically described Chozen-ji as everything I had been looking for my whole life. Of course, I had not actually been searching for a Zen dojo. I had not even known that such a thing existed. But now that I was here, I felt an irresistible desire to dive into the training and to go as deep as I could. Never had I experienced a spiritual method so direct, straightforward, or effective. The temple itself was magical, and the people I had encountered were among the most impressive I had ever met—genuine, unconflicted, and unapologetically themselves. It felt, in a way that I could not explain, like home.

Sayama Roshi was much more interested, however, to hear that I had started learning the Hojo Walk and how to do sword cuts than about how Chozen-ji compared to other kinds of spiritual training. Most of all, he was looking ahead to tonight's Kendo class, which would be my first. Ending our conversation, Sayama Roshi perfunctorily excused himself to check on some plants he was caring for on the grounds. As I watched him go, I saw Michael catch up and then walk with him in stride. Seeing the two of them side by side on the gravel path, I held a strong suspicion that they were talking about me and the sort of impression I had given. I returned to the Budo Dojo to practice the Hojo Walk some more, hoping that perhaps my request to stay had not fallen on deaf ears, only that it required further discussion.

Following that night's zazen, I was able to stand up faster than before, though I still needed the help of my hands to push up from the floor. As I stood, I dangled one leg in midair and kept it there until it was no longer asleep. It was not the elegant rise upward that the other students executed, hands already held in gassho as they stood without any hint of discomfort or numbness in their legs. But it was an improvement, and that gave me a sense of accomplishment and progress. As I laid my cushions on the perfect stacks in the corner of the Budo Dojo, the overhead fluorescents clicked on. Without any time to spare, as quickly as the Chado class had begun following zazen what now felt like weeks but was actually just two days before, it was time for Kendo. Most of those present for the night's zazen sat seiza in a straight line facing the front of the dojo. This included Sayama Roshi and two Japanese gentlemen who looked to be in their sixties. One, I knew, was Dick "Deku" Teshima, or Teshima Sensei. As one of Hawaii's few *nana dan*, or seventh-degree black belts, in Kendo, Teshima Sensei's presence elevated the stature and rigor of the Kendo class, and I had already heard at length what a true privilege it was to be able to train with him. The other gentleman was Terushi Ueno, also an excellent teacher, *roku dan*, or sixth degree, and the former president of the Hawai'i Kendo Federation.

At the front of the room, a student sat in seiza facing us and, after scanning the lineup of teachers and students, spun quickly on his knees to turn and face the butsudan. We all bowed in unison. He turned back to us, and we bowed again. Then began about twenty minutes of vigorous breathing, stretches, and warm-ups. He counted off every stretch and exercise loudly in Japanese: "*Ichi! Ni! San! Shi! Go! Roku! Shichi! Hachi!*" Working from the head down, we twisted and turned our bodies. We swiveled our heads back and forth and circled our necks. We did pushups, we struck the backs of our necks with the knife edge of each hand, and we sat seiza while lying back as far as we could, stretching our arms up overhead. When it came time to stretch the calves, Sayama Roshi came up behind me and, reaching down, picked up my back foot with his hands and set it back down so it was pointing to twelve o'clock. I realized that I was getting used to these brusque physical adjustments, but I chuckled to myself imagining how alarmed my old yoga instructors would have been, as they never touched their students without asking first.

"Hojo Walk! Put up your hakama!" Sayama Roshi announced

after the exercises had ended. I was still only wearing a samue, so I watched as everyone else began to methodically pull up and tuck the fabric of their hakama. Having done the Hojo Walk several times, I also joined the line with my hands flat on the front points of my hips.

Finally, something I know how to do, I thought to myself, sure that the sensei and other students would be impressed that I could follow along with the Hojo Walk in my very first class.

As Teshima Sensei led us all in a line, moving forward across the room, I breathed ah and um and moved in sync with everyone else. Though my thighs trembled and my balance faltered, I remembered to keep looking straight ahead. Sayama Roshi came up behind me and told me to lower my back heel, pushing it down with his own foot. He also pulled my shoulders back and took my face and head in his hands to tuck my chin in, so I was not going into each step chin out and face first. Time and again, I was told to stand up straight, to "be big, stand tall," even though I had been sure that I was already doing so.

The Hojo Walk quickened, taking on the kiai of each of the seasons of the year. From the spring kata, with the energy of the first green shoots breaking upward through the snow, we moved on to summer, the kiai of which was compared to a burning, hot wind. Next was autumn, with the *sara-sara* of falling leaves cutting back and forth through the air. Finally, energy returned to the roots in winter. After that, everyone picked up *bokken* and *bokuto*, the wooden practice swords on the wall. In pairs, we did the Hojo Walk back and forth across the short end of the dojo, sword cuts now accompanying each step. The dojo was filled with a dozen voices now, men and women all yelling at full volume. Curiously, I deduced from the instructions given that this, too, was called kiai. The same word was used to describe one's presence, a feeling, or, more esoterically, the signature of one's vital energy, and it was also the Japanese word for a yell that accompanies a strike in martial arts.

"Yaaaahhh-eh!" we kiai'd in unison, swords cutting down to the height of three inches into our partners' heads. During summer, the pace quickened, and the yells became louder, longer, and more aggressive. During autumn, the kiai was "Eh!" and my arms already burned with the weight of the skinny bokken I had been handed, even though I guessed it to be only half the weight of the fatter bokuto the other students used.

As the Hojo Walk with bokken concluded, Sayama Roshi called me over to the side of the room, where he told me to continue doing the Hojo Walk by myself in front of the mirror. He then left to observe the other students practicing the kata, the set sequence of movements that made up the full Hojo. When he returned, he told me to stand in front of the mirror with him. He showed me how to plant both feet on the ground and curl my left hand into a fist, holding it at my waist. He told me to make a big circle with my right arm, sweeping my right hand, also clenched into a fist, first in front of my thighs while breathing in, ah. Once my hand reached the height of my left shoulder, I was to finish the circle with extra force and let out the same kiai we had done earlier, "Yaaaaah-eh!"

He demonstrated first. Sayama Roshi's yell was loud, clear, and rose above the raucous din of people yelling and wooden swords striking each other. The sound emerged without restriction, no tension at all, his voice both resonant and gravelly. Next, it was my turn. I turned down the corners of my lips, breathed in, and brought my arm around in a half circle. Having reached the top, I easily brought my arm down to complete the circle, but my voice got stuck mid yell, caught in my throat. Surprised, I choked and stood there, coughing, for several seconds.

"Try it again," Sayama Roshi instructed me. "Relax your body and let it all out." He let out a short "Yah!" to illustrate, his shoulders thrown back and relaxed.

Again, I breathed in and traced the top half of a circle with my arm. As I brought it down this time, a louder yell came out, but it was painfully shrill and high-pitched.

"Let the sound come from down here," Sayama Roshi said, patting his hara. "You can hear it right? It's too up in your head."

I yelled again, and then again and again for several minutes while Sayama Roshi shared his assessment of the quality of my voice and all that it revealed—where I had stuck points, the balance of tension and relaxation in my body, my ability to bring out my power, my concentration and focus, and more. Some of the kiai sounded good to me, more resonant than when I had started, but several also sounded tight and tense. By the time we were done, I was red in the face and sweating, and my throat was sore.

"Keep practicing," Sayama Roshi said as he again walked away to observe the rest of the class. I remained in front of the mirror, looking at what was fast becoming a pitiful reflection: sweaty and red-faced, both body and face contorting. Same as the previous night, I bore a strong resemblance to a gasping, sad clown.

After a few minutes, I was called to line up again with the other students, who were again sitting seiza at the back of the Budo Dojo. They each had lying next to them a shinai, the same kind of bamboo sword I had used to learn the Hojo Walk. Various pieces of their *bogu*, the Kendo armor, were laid out in front of them. Sayama Roshi and Teshima Sensei also sat in the back and began first by putting on their *tare*, the placketed apron that was one part of the Kendo armor. Following that, they put on their *do*, the chest protectors made of bamboo and lacquer, securing the long indigo-dyed straps at the backs of their waists and at the fronts of each shoulder. When they had finished with these two pieces, they picked up the shinai at their sides, their gloves, and their helmets and made for the front of the room. As they walked, all the students rose, moved up in unison, and sat down again.

Teshima Sensei surveyed the line from one end to the other, his eyes wide and a soft grin on his face. Then, his back straightened, and his face snapped into a hardened expression. With great seriousness, he brought the tips of his fingers together in front of his knees and bowed. The line of students returned the bow.

"*Onegaishimasu*," Teshima Sensei said, greeting us, and we responded in unison with the same.

Everyone then began affixing the rest of their bogu: the *tenegui*, a long, thin cloth that wraps around the head; the *men*, helmets, complete with metal grates across the face; and the *kote*, gloves. The first person to finish rose quickly and stood opposite Teshima Sensei, who was the first among the sensei to be dressed and standing. The two bowed to one another, and then walked forward before coming down to the floor in a low squat. Finally, each removed their bamboo swords from imaginary sheaths and rose. In what seemed like less than an instant, the student was lunging toward Teshima Sensei, screaming "Mennn!" and trying to land a strike. Teshima Sensei deftly moved out of the way and landed a strike with lightning-fast speed on the student's helmet, instead.

Sayama Roshi again motioned me to the side of the room. He handed me a shinai. Removing his gloves, he showed me the proper way to hold the sword and the proper stance for my feet in Kendo. Synchronized with both the sword cut and my step forward should be my kiai, "Men," he said. He held out a shorter shinai for me to use as my target, holding it at about the height of his own head. I tried to leap forward at first and stumbled. Still, I managed to strike the shinai at the last minute and yell out, "Mennn!" I passed him and moved across the room in an awkward gallop, as he had also instructed.

"The right foot has to come down at the same time as the sword," Sayama Roshi said, demonstrating. My feet wanted to shuffle before my sword came down, and over my next few attempts, I tried to synchronize my leap forward and the landing of the shinai.

Several pairs of students and sensei had taken up their positions spanning the length of the dojo. Now they fought each other, yelling, striking, and colliding again and again. Whenever the shinai struck their targets, they made whip-cracking sounds. The younger men in particular attacked each other at full speed and with dizzyingly fast strikes, sometimes several in quick succession. Occasionally, they would crash into one another and lock up. For a few seconds, they would push against one another until, finally, they exploded backward, sometimes only coming to a stop dangerously close to the sword racks on the wall or the large taiko drum in the corner. And then after one or two seconds, they would rush back in for another hit and do it all over again. The room was loud, filled with yelling, the sounds of feet striking the tatami, and the high, whip-cracking sounds of the shinai.

Although I had done some martial arts before, this experience approached being overwhelming for me. Rather than focus on drills and technique for the start of the class, everyone had just begun sparring immediately. They seemed to attack each other with full force, holding nothing back. Each match also seemed like it could easily tip over into a real fight, coming to blows at any moment. This all made it difficult to focus on Sayama Roshi's instructions. I strained to keep my attention on him when it felt like not just one real fight but multiple were happening right next to us.

Over and over, I leaped toward him, cutting with my sword and yelling. He yelled that I should follow through on my cuts by running all the way to the far end of the room, only turning around once I'd reached the opposite wall. Yelling at full volume, leaping, and now running across the whole width of the dojo, I was soon out of breath. As I became more tired, what little form my movements had had fell apart, inviting more corrections. Focusing on the physical movements, for example, my voice would falter. "Mennn!" Sayama Roshi would remind me. If I struggled to time my feet and the shinai together, he repeated his earlier correction, demonstrating the coordination of the forward leap and the sword cut. As I slowed further, I began to feel Sayama Roshi's shinai tapping me on the low back, a warning that I was not running fast enough and was within striking distance. I pushed myself to go faster. My legs became tired and wobbly until, finally, I tripped over my own feet and fell to the floor. I hit the tatami with a hard thud.

If the activity in the room stopped at all, it was only for a moment. I quickly stood up, a smile on my face to show that everything was fine, and the class continued. Perhaps out of concern that I would find other ways of hurting myself—or maybe just disappointed by my clumsiness, I suspected—Sayama Roshi quickly showed me how to close out our practice. We bowed to one another and took three steps back, sheathing our swords. There would be no more partner drills for me tonight it seemed, and I was told again to practice by myself in front of the mirror.

It wasn't long, though, before I stopped cutting and yelling on my own—half pretending to catch my breath—so that I could watch the matches happening around the room. I marveled at everyone's energy and focus. No one seemed to be giving anything short of their all. They were so fast and so strong. They also seemed remarkably focused and collected. This was despite the intensity of the Kendo and the feeling in the room of being on the edge of falling into chaos. I wondered if I'd ever be able to match them and felt impatient to put on my own bogu and join the *keiko*, or practice.

When keiko finally ended, everyone came to sit again in seiza, students and sensei facing each other. Breathing heavily and drenched with sweat, everyone removed their gloves and placed them to their right. The straps tied at the back of their helmets were undone and then folded and held in one hand while everyone waited until all the sensei had removed theirs. The tenegui, the cloths underneath everyone's helmets, were so wet that many of them were shades darker now than they had been at the beginning of class. After being removed, each one was folded and placed neatly inside everyone's helmets.

"*Mokuso!*" Teshima Sensei snapped. Everyone immediately put their hands in zazen position, cradling their right fist in their left hand, both hands in their laps, and began to meditate. With adrenaline still pumping through my veins, I was aware of every movement and sound in the room. I could hear quickened breaths around me, and soon they began to lengthen and slow. In my peripheral vision, I saw a single bead of sweat drip slowly down Sayama Roshi's flushed face. My whole body buzzed, so invigorated by the class that it was now surprisingly easy to overlook the pain I felt in my feet from sitting seiza.

"*Yame!*" Teshima Sensei snapped again after just a minute or so. We bowed to each other and to the butsudan, and then everyone was up on their feet again, moving in a line toward the back of the room. I followed and watched as the senior students arranged their gloves, helmets, and shinai on the floor. As soon as these were put down, they were running to the far corner of the room, forming a line, so they could each take turns bowing to Teshima Sensei. I joined the back of the line, moving closer and closer toward Teshima Sensei as each student bowed and then departed to sweep the dojo or clean the kitchen. When it came my turn, I knelt in front of him and was surprised to find a gentle, grandfatherly look on his face.

"How was your first class?" he asked.

"Great!" I responded brightly.

It *had* been great. Even tripping over my own feet and falling down had only made my first experience in Kendo more exciting.

"Oh!" Teshima Sensei replied with mock surprise. Then, he joked, "We'll have to take care of that."

He smiled and brought his hands together, arms straight and fingertips touching on the floor in front of him. Then, he bowed. I returned the bow, thanking him with an "*Arigatou gozaimashita*," as I had heard the other students say. As I rose and walked away, I heard my name being called once again.

"Cristina!" Sayama Roshi yelled, pointing at Ueno Sensei, who was briskly sweeping the tatami, one row at a time. "Take that broom from him!"

Smirking, he continued, "You shouldn't let an old man do something you can do." I nodded and ran over, my hands timidly reaching for the broom. Ueno Sensei, however, wouldn't give it up.

"No, no. It's OK," he said politely, continuing to sweep and leaving me standing at a loss as to what to do.

Finally, one of the senpai approached.

"You have to insist," he told me, demonstrating how to ask, this time with kiai.

"Ueno Sensei, I'll take that," he said.

His voice was polite and friendly but left no room for disagreement. It was clear that he wasn't going to take no for an answer. Ueno Sensei stopped in his tracks and relinquished the broom. Before he walked away, he bowed and my senpai did, too. Taking hold of the broom, I began to sweep as Ueno Sensei had, from one end of the tatami to the other.

"Stand up straight!" I heard from across the room. "Be big. Your sweeping should give everyone energy!"

I straightened my back and picked up the pace of my sweeping so that the broom made a brisk "swish" sound as it traversed the tatami. I also made sure I could see the whole room. It was a new experience to apply the same disciplined focus from zazen and Kendo to something as mundane as sweeping, but I understood that the lessons at the Dojo about posture, breathing, and kiai really were meant to be applied everywhere. Everything, even sweeping, was Zen training.

As I swept, I remembered Michael telling me how one of the outcomes of training in Zen was to be able to possess the same clarity and control I felt on the meditation cushion even with a sword at my throat. Not having put on the Kendo armor yet, I did not understand fully what this meant, though I had just gotten a very small taste of just how heightened the full experience would be. I really did want to be that person who could walk into any situation and be a force for good, not just another person freaking out. I could see how much hard, hard work it would take to get there, though, and had a newfound respect for the stories of arduous training I had heard over the past several days.

After class, I thought I could sense the lingering kiai of all the blood, sweat, and tears that had been shed at the Dojo. My new understanding seemed to add dimension to every cushion, floorboard, and wooden beam. Having survived my first Kendo class, I thought, there was surely no question about whether I could stay.

"You'd better think twice," Tanouye Rotaishi had told Sayama when he had asked about training under him forty years before. Though I didn't recognize it as such at the time, my naive enthusiasm to begin my own Zen training stood in contrast to how Sayama had responded.

"I already have," Sayama had said then, his saving grace. In his shoes, I would not have known to muster up this kind of determination or sincere commitment to do whatever it would take to develop myself. I was still just leaping headfirst, moving forward without a clear plan for what came next, thinking that I'd have the chance to work out the details later. But at least I wasn't giving it a look back.

13

LIVE BLADE: THE WAY OF THE SWORD

Before my second Kendo class, I learned the spring and summer movements of the kage, or shadow, side of the Hojo kata. A kata is a set sequence of movements, the same as the ones I had learned as a kid doing Tae Kwon Do. But instead of punches, kicks, and blocks, the Hojo kata consists of advancing and retreating sword cuts choreographed between two roles, one being the kage side and the other being shin, which means mind-heart, as well as spirit. Shin and kage—the mind and its shadow. Most of the time, kage felt like just that, a shadow. But I saw moments when kage pushed shin backward, almost all the way up against the wall, until, like a wave retreating back into the ocean, it sped back from whence it came.

Between my first and second Kendo classes, I practiced the Hojo Walk, both on its own and combined with sword cuts and yells. Then, in the evenings, one of the senpai would teach me parts of the kata. The teaching was mostly wordless, the few verbal instructions being just to do as he did. That was the best way to learn, I soon understood, without the pesky interference of my overthinking mind.

Better that I learn to trust my body, mirroring what I saw in front of me and letting my limbs do the work. When he raised his arms, I raised mine. When he stepped forward, I followed, step by step and cut by cut. In the moments when our movements felt really connected, that was when I began to really recognize the promise of the Hojo to erase all my habits from the day I was born. The movements became no longer just my own.

When we broke from practicing the Hojo, the senpai also taught me how to put on the bogu, the Kendo armor. I'd be expected to know how to put it on and wear it in my second class, coming up only three days after my first. No longer would I just be allowed to dole out sword cuts and hits during the Kendo portion of class. I'd also be getting hit myself.

For the most part, the bogu was straightforward. My fingers had always been deft with knots, and I tied the straps of the tare and do easily. But I struggled with the tenegui. The long, rectangular piece of thin cotton slid around on my straight hair and bangs and came loose whenever I tried to tuck the corners behind my ears. Once I had the bogu on, including the men, or helmet, I took a cruise around the Budo Dojo. The armor was bulky, especially around my middle. The helmet blocked my peripheral vision and made it difficult to turn my head from side to side. My senpai pulled a shinai from the wooden bin next to a stand of wooden cubbies housing various students' bogu, each cubby labeled with a piece of blue tape bearing a student's name written in permanent marker. He came to stand in front of me at a distance of a few feet, holding the shinai in both hands and pointing the tip in the direction of my throat.

"This is what it feels like to get hit," he said. And with that, his sword flew upward and struck me on the top of the head.

The padding of the men did little to dull the impact, as it was only made of layered cotton. I had been caught by surprise, and now my head stung.

"Don't put your head down like that," my senpai said. The pain on my head confirmed that I had flinched and put my head down before the hit. It had all happened so fast that I only recognized after the fact that ducking down and getting small had been my first instinct.

"What you want is to face the hit," he explained. "If you take it face forward, the shinai's going to land here, where there's metal." He rapped the shinai lightly on the front of my men, at the very top of the metal grate protecting my face. He was right. I could only feel the reverberations of the hit, not the hit itself, and it didn't hurt.

"But if you duck . . . Put your head down again." I bowed my head obediently and was hit again in the same spot as I had been hit before. "There's basically no protection there."

I couldn't tell what made me sorer: the growing lump on my head, how pedantic and obvious the instruction was, or how I had stupidly followed along, allowing myself to get hit a second time. All of it smarted.

"Face the hit," he continued flatly. "You can also fold your tenegui on the top for a little extra cushion. Oh, and really get your tenegui on tight. It can fall down inside the men and cover your eyes. That's always fun." And with that, he walked away, leaving me to continue practicing tying my tenegui and putting on the bogu.

As my first week of training approached its end, I practiced putting on the armor—especially tying on the tenegui until I felt that it would stay on my head long enough to get through a round of Kendo keiko. I also filled my days after 5:30 a.m. morning zazen and before evening training with practicing the Hojo, moving rocks, pulling weeds, cleaning up around the Dojo, and memorizing chants from the okyo. And I began racking up more and more sword cuts, doing several hundred a day with the lightest wooden bokken on the racks in the Budo Dojo. Once in a while, I also swung the heavier bokuto until my arms burned and I had to retreat back to the bokken. By the time Sayama Roshi joined us for dinner on Friday night, my shoulders and arms felt like lead. Sayama Roshi took it as a sign that I was training hard and commented that I had already put on muscle. Then, with a mischievous smile, he suggested that maybe I didn't want *too* many muscles.

I immediately interpreted this to suggest that the Roshi felt it wasn't attractive for a woman to be too muscley. I suspected that he was just playing with me, but I also couldn't help but take offense. After all, hadn't I come to Chozen-ji for warrior training? Why shouldn't I be big and strong like the men? Did Sayama Roshi prefer I was slender and waiflike? Did he want me to be . . . *ladylike*?!

Sayama Roshi, who had been sitting back watching the gears spinning in my head, saw his opening. He pounced on it immediately and with glee.

"Oh, Cristina," he said, eyes sparkling and now smiling wide, "don't worry. You're strong enough—"

Then, his voice lilted churlishly as he delivered the punch line.

"For a girl."

His eyes widened expectantly.

"*For a girl*?!" I exclaimed, taking the bait hook, line, and sinker.

Sayama Roshi doubled over with laughter, fully self-satisfied.

"It's OK. It's OK," he said after getting his fill. It would take some time for me to appreciate this version of his agility, intuition, and precision. Only a few minutes before, Sayama Roshi had been the sage roshi, the calm and cool senior executive. Now, in a moment of true freedom and play, he had transformed into the rascally old grandfather.

He patted the air as if he were reassuringly patting me on the head, and my indignation slowly faded. An unfamiliar contentment settled over me, and I realized that I was quite happy. Happy like I had been as a child when I was finally allowed into the grownups' conversation—in on the joke, even if it was at my own expense. Happy to be here training and in the company of a very adept teacher who could see my weakest links and give them a good, playful yank.

Later that night, I donned the bogu and joined the lineup for the Kendo portion of the Kendo class. I tied my tenegui with a little bit of cushion on the top of my head. I was given a shinai from the bin, which I placed at my side as I lined up with the other students on the tatami. And once my men was on, it was time to fight.

I was relieved to find my first experience with actual Kendo keiko to be well-paced and instructive, very unlike what I had witnessed a few nights before. While they did take some of the many openings I inadvertently gave to hit my men, the sensei and senpai also gave me openings to hit them. Tilting their shinai downward meant I should try to hit their men, and to the side meant I should hit their kote, or wrists. After a while, they also raised their shinai up above their heads to signal that I should hit their do, as if I were slicing open their bellies. Each cut was delivered as I galloped across the dojo, landing my front foot on the tatami, cutting, and yelling at the same time. The sensei pushed me to run faster and faster, first tapping and then later smacking me on the back with their shinai as I slowed. Careful this time to keep my feet under me, I was confident that, tonight, I would not fall, at least not of my own accord.

When I made the beginner's mistake of going around Teshima Sensei—politely, I thought—he instructed me in what I would learn was one of the fundamentals of Kendo.

"Straight through!" he said, his voice ringing over the other matches happening around us. "In Kendo, you don't go around your problems. You cut straight through! If I don't move, you better go *right through me!*"

OK, I thought, and prepared myself for a head-on collision. On my next run, Teshima Sensei gave the opening to strike his men. I raised my shinai up over my head and flung the tip out, aiming for the top of his head. I let out the cry, "Mennn!" and leaped forward, my right foot sounding on the tatami as it landed. Pulled forward by my own momentum, I kept going, straight forward just as Teshima Sensei had instructed. And then, just when I thought we were going to slam into one another, he stepped out of the way and only our shoulders bumped roughly as I went by. And then by the time I had turned around, he was already in position again, ready for the next attack.

In addition to always cutting straight, I learned that there are no defensive maneuvers in Kendo, or at least not in Chozen-ji Kendo, anyway. The proper response to an attack is only to attack back. This is because the purpose of Kendo is not actually getting good at the techniques of swordsmanship, which is merely *Kenjutsu*. "Kendo" on the other hand means the *Way* of the Sword, a way to perfect a human being through swordsmanship in the same way that Chado, or the Way of Tea, is a way to perfect a human being through tea. Kendo is really taught at Chozen-ji to help students develop a fighting spirit, the energy and disposition to always be ready to attack a problem and move forward. The bare minimum of attention is given to the basics of form, etiquette, and technique. But, like me in only my second class, students are put into the bogu as soon as possible, so we can experience what it is like to really fight. At one point, in response to my describing all the meditation retreats I had done in the past, one of the other students joked that Chozen-ji never held retreats.

"No retreat. Only attack!" was the running joke.

I naturally improved at Kendo over the following days and weeks as my habits came to the surface. Remarkably, my training was helping me to not just surface them but also to let them go—sometimes slowly, but sometimes with surprising ease and speed. I came to see that each of my habits had both a psychological and a physical side, and as I continued fighting through welling emotions or as I overcame momentary hesitation in the middle of keiko, I each day began to feel lighter, livelier, and freer. I could feel this even in my first few classes, and I became excited about keeping on with my training and with Kendo. But first, I had to stop freezing, putting my head down, and getting small whenever I saw a hit coming! As a beginner, I was reminded that every other student was going to be faster than me, as they had years more experience under their belts. No matter what came at me, my job was to put everything I had into moving straight forward and cutting with full conviction, even if I was terrible at it. This was what made it not just Kendo but Zen training, not just about swordsmanship but about character.

It all brought to mind an allegory in the *Hagakure*, the seventeenth-century samurai manual that I had picked up in anticipation of my arrival. In it, a samurai stands on a bridge. With rushing waters below and the enemy behind and ahead, the *Hagakure* describes only one option for the samurai: to go forward.

For the samurai in the *Hagakure*, being slaughtered did not mean failure. Like Tanouye Rotaishi's favored translation of the calligraphy in the Kyudo range, "One Shot, Absolute Destruction," the lesson of the allegory was that if I could learn to commit fully and go for something completely, whatever happened next didn't matter. It would mean living or dying with the confidence that I had done everything I could and that I had left nothing on the table. So survival wasn't the goal, but moving forward—always forward—was. This seemed like a superhuman ability that I reasoned might take a whole lifetime to realize. Yet I also felt myself making a little bit of progress each day, developing nominally more technical skill in Kendo as well as some semblance of understanding in the Zen lessons Kendo offered.

14

KOTONK

On the official training schedule, Kendo class ended at 9:00 p.m., just like every other evening class, but that was really only the end of *formal* training. The spirit of Kendo continued, sometimes until ten thirty or eleven o'clock at night. After making a last bow to Teshima Sensei and removing my bogu, still dripping with sweat and red in the face, I rushed into the kitchen to start cleaning. Over the weeks, I began to arrive fast on the heels of my senpai rather than after cleanup was well underway. If I did, I could clear the coffee and all its accompaniments—sugars, creamers, disposable cups, a tray of mugs made in the ceramics studio—off the table, so it could be wiped down. Just as one of us finished wiping the six tables, they were then stood on their sides and moved to make way for vacuuming the carpet. When I was the one who vacuumed, I moved the machine in long strokes so that, after the first pass, the first row of kitchen tables could be put back in place. Meanwhile, someone else wiped down the counters and emptied the coffee pot for the night.

One night during my second week, I found myself vacuuming like a madwoman—for all intents and purposes, my body felt as though it was still in the middle of Kendo keiko. There had been moments in class when my body balked against whatever safety and assuredness my mind told it there was. Though I knew none of these people were out to hurt me, it still felt in my body like I was on the edge of fighting for my life. Even after class ended, my breathing remained fast and shallow, my heart pounding, and my sight tunnel-visioned. As I vacuumed, my brow was knitted, and my hair was wild.

"Cristina!" my senpai called out from the other side of the kitchen island. I looked up quickly, braced for the scolding that was surely coming.

"Even now," he said in a disarmingly friendly voice, "still see the whole room." And then as our eyes locked, he gave me an encouraging wink. A smile broadened across his face, and in its brief appearance, I recognized something resembling the smile of a proud parent or older sibling. It said, *We can all see you're training hard. Don't be discouraged. You're doing good, keep going.*

I smiled back, surprised and touched. Minutes earlier, this same person had been clobbering me in Kendo, yelling at me to cut straight and stand tall. One moment, when I had thrown my full weight against him and our swords had locked up, he had even pushed me back until I had crashed into the dojo closet. I had been on the brink of tears for much of the time. And now, here he was, compassionate with my disarray and how I was still caught in fight or flight. It began to dawn on me that the training here was more than just learning to be a warrior always charging into battle. It was to be able to perceive what was called for in *any* moment. This meant discerning in a diversity of situations how to best keep the training alive. In Kendo, that meant pushing me into the wall. In Chado, it was quite the opposite. When cleaning the kitchen, it meant a reminder to see 180 degrees, so I might notice a reassuring smile.

Very soon, the tables were back where they had been, and everything in the kitchen was in order. We went our separate ways, walking briskly toward the showers. I rinsed off, changed into fresh clothes, and then went as quickly as I could back to the tea house for the post-Kendo *pau hana*. When I arrived, the sensei, head priest

Michael, and Sayama Roshi were already settling in around a table made from a long plank of monkeypod.

"Cristina," I was greeted warmly. "Here, do you want some snacks?"

Bags of potato chips and Japanese rice crackers made their ways down the table. Sitting next to me, Teshima Sensei handed me a plastic tray of dried cuttlefish, its cellophane wrapper ripped haphazardly and the strong smell of the sea emanating from within. I looked up at him with surprise. I had never seen anyone outside of my own family eat dried cuttlefish before. It was a Korean snack that I devoured as a kid in front of the TV or while sitting and talking at the kitchen table. I noticed that the others at the table—Japanese, Chinese, Hawaiian, and *haole*, or White—had already taken some and were gnawing on it as if it was something that they, too, ate all the time. Teshima Sensei nodded encouragingly and, interpreting my pause as hesitation, explained what it was.

"It's dried squid. It's pretty chewy, but I bet your teeth are strong enough." He laughed.

I happily piled up the napkin in front of me with several strips of cuttlefish and a handful of potato chips and then accepted a tall glass of water with both hands. More glasses arrived at the table, and Sayama Roshi left and then reappeared a few seconds later with a stick of incense in hand. He set it into a large bowl filled with ash in the corner of the room, and fragrant smoke began to waft upward in front of a beautifully painted folding screen depicting carps and dragons.

Just as Sayama Roshi sat down, one of the senpai appeared as if on cue to hand him a glass and some snacks. This popped a certain bubble of illusion; Now was not the time, I realized, to relax and enjoy myself. I should not have so easily accepted my generous and warm welcome. Instead, I should've been up on my feet helping to prepare the space and serve the teachers. Still on the lowest rung of the ladder in the temple's hierarchy, I should be getting the drinks and snacks, not letting myself be served. Nobody had said anything, and no scolding was forthcoming. Perhaps they knew that they didn't need to as, two weeks into my training, I was finally becoming aware enough to scold myself.

From my first days at the Dojo, I had heard that one of the desired outcomes of training was to intuitively and automatically help others before helping myself. It was drilled into me at every opportunity, and I had found the most mundane examples of it, rather than the religious and romantic ones, to be the most powerful, like eating only after everyone else had been served. I found that ordinariness refreshing. Rather than taking esoteric vows, serious students were simply pushed to pay attention to others and jump in wherever help was needed. Progress was not in being able to give an eloquent lecture about the Buddhist principle of saving all beings from suffering. Instead, the training was to learn to anticipate when someone's glass needed refilling and to be able to lay a snack on the table just as someone realized they were hungry. I saw my teachers and senpai do just this every day in various ways, seemingly without conscious thought and never asking for an ounce of recognition.

I learned that this was what was called "sensitivity." Sensitivity encompasses the ability, on the simpler end of things, to just notice things, from peoples' conditions to how the cushions are stacked—a basic sharpening of the senses. On the more subtle end of the spectrum of sensitivity is being able to sense the vibe in a room or to diagnose someone's physical condition just through their kiai. At the most developed of stages, sensitivity is to perceive Kozen no Ki, the universal rhythm governing all phenomena. Sensitivity is also the ability to willingly match the object of one's perception, like being in accord with that universal energy, which I more commonly heard referred to at Chozen-ji as, simply, the Tao.

Rather than being treated as a principle unique to Zen or Japanese culture, I repeatedly heard sensitivity described as an innately human ability that is both primitive and transcendent. It is also universal. This universality was underscored by the fact that sensitivity was not only taught here through a Japanese lens but a Native Hawaiian one, as well.

Before she was overthrown by American plantation owners in 1893, Hawai'i's last ruling monarch, Queen Lili'uokalani, famously said: "To gain the kingdom of heaven is to hear what is not said, to see what cannot be seen, and to know the unknowable. This is Aloha." The first time I heard this definition was during my first few days at the Dojo, and I had heard it several times more in the following few weeks.

A poster bearing Native Hawaiian spiritual leader Pilahi Paki's definition of the Aloha Spirit also hung prominently in the kitchen. It was one of many that had been printed in a public awareness campaign spearheaded by Tanouye Rotaishi. Later on, I would meet many local people who were able to recite from memory each of the words in 'Ōlelo Hawai'i that made up Aunty Pilahi's rendering:

A—stands for AKAHAI, meaning kindness, to be expressed with tenderness.

L—stands for LOKAHI, meaning unity, to be expressed with harmony.

O—stands for OLU'OLU, meaning agreeable, to be expressed with pleasantness.

H—stands for HA'AHA'A, meaning humility, to be expressed with modesty.

A—stands for AHONUI, meaning patience, to be expressed with perseverance.

Cultivating my ability to hear what was unspoken and see what could not be seen would make me more sensitive to the existing flow of any situation. Then, I could see the ways in which I might be interrupting that flow, as well as how to be in accord with it. I had to cultivate humility—casting away my ego, individual desires, and small self—to just match my surroundings, not sticking out and not seeking attention or praise. And I had to be patient and persevere, knowing that all this self-cultivation would take years, if not an entire lifetime.

Though I had thought and talked about ideas of no-self or selflessness for many years, putting it into practice in the small, practical ways I saw demonstrated by my sensei and senpai was deeply challenging. Not only did it conflict with my sense of individual self-worth and my habits of attention seeking; it also abraded some of my political and social ideals. Rationally, I knew that my being a woman was not why I was expected to serve snacks to the sensei. I held the same charge expected of everyone else when they were the newest and most inexperienced student. But doubt and defiance were like stubborn splinters in my mind. This was baggage that weighed down my ability to see the room and just respond to what was in front of me, an obstacle to being in accord by just going with the flow. It interrupted my efforts to act intuitively and immediately in the spirit of a charming Japanese saying I had also been introduced to: "If you see a weed, pull it."

Indeed, no job for a true student of Zen was too small. The sensei exemplified this to the nth degree. So much so that I began to wonder if their humility and self-deprecating tendencies weren't more than just modesty. The sensei almost insisted on putting themselves down and doing the humblest of tasks, like serving drinks and snacks, doing dishes, and sweeping up. And, at the same time, it was the responsibilities of those of us who ranked lower in age and regard to refuse to let the sensei do such menial tasks. In fact, the more they put themselves down, the more respectfully and graciously they were treated.

Perhaps my greatest obstacle to cultivating my own sensitivity, I learned, came from the fact that I had grown up, for the most part, on the mainland. Not long after my arrival, Chozen-ji's archbishop, who was also Korean, sat me down to learn about my background and what I thought of Zen training. We talked about many things, including how he had come to train at the Dojo decades before and what it was like in the old days. In the intervening years, he had become one of Hawaiʻi's most successful businessmen, and I wanted to know how his training had contributed to his achievements. At one point, the conversation touched on the differences between how we had grown up—me as a Korean American on the mainland and him as a Korean American in Hawaiʻi.

"Do you know the word *kotonk*?" he asked enthusiastically. A mischievous smile spread across his face, reminding me of Sayama Roshi. I replied that no, I did not.

"Kotonk is what we call you—Asian Americans from the mainland. You guys have a chip on your shoulder." He might have seen the now familiar look of shellshock that came over me whenever I was being scolded, because he quickly qualified, "It's not your fault. It's because you grew up as a minority. It's kind of traumatic."

I had never met an Asian American person who had not grown up with the indelible traumas of being a minority—if not an overtly oppressed and discriminated against minority, then at least feeling at some point like they had been hoodwinked into assimilating, giving up their culture and sense of wholeness only to realize that they'd been sold a bill of goods. I had never imagined that a person of Asian descent could grow up in America without a chip on her shoulder. The clarity and insight of the archbishop's perspective, as someone so similar and yet so different from me, felt particularly piercing because it seemed purely due to the fact that he had been lucky enough to be born in Hawaiʻi.

"It makes you numb. Kind of, you know . . . stupid. The word 'kotonk' comes from the sound that it makes when you knock on your head," he said, rapping his knuckles on his own skull, "'cause it's empty."

I searched for the proper response and found none. Was I being insulted? Throughout our meeting, he had been so sympathetic and nice. He had even praised me, saying that, because of my global experience, I would bring a broader perspective to the Dojo. But still, I could not help but wonder if, by offering up an explanation of the word "kotonk," he was bringing home my shortcomings, delivering another of the innumerable and sometimes veiled scoldings that felt in such high supply at the Dojo. Perhaps he could already sense something, I thought, some deeper flaw in me I couldn't yet see. Or maybe I had betrayed my lack of sensitivity over the course of our conversation. Or maybe I really was just a little stupid.

Stupid! I said to myself, and at this thought, I found myself magically broken out of my spell of self-doubt. I even laughed a little. What a luxury it was, I realized, to be in a place where I could be stupid. I could falter and be out of sync here and screw things up, and yet, there weren't any real consequences. How fun, I thought, to be able to recognize and fully engage with the grating parts of myself that people had never had the courage to tell me about but that I had always suspected they felt. Moreover, what a privilege it was to know that everyone here was approaching their own limitations in their own ways, which meant I was, as far as I was concerned, in the best of company.

While sitting around the monkeypod table after Kendo, I realized how right the archbishop had been. I was, indeed, a numb kotonk. I did eventually absorb the priceless lessons in sensitivity; Japanese, Native Hawaiian, and local culture; and Zen on offer after Kendo class. But I did so slowly that they often had to be repeated. For several weeks or months, I only managed to jump up to serve the sensei maybe half of the time, often beat out by someone senior to me or, worse, by Michael or Sayama Roshi themselves. I was awkward in conversation, finding myself compulsively driving it to topics about which I could seem charming and smart. It proved hard not to chase what would otherwise be thought of as normal impulses, wanting to fall back into what was familiar and comfortable without the discipline and constant attention that Zen training demanded.

I had been warned that living in at Chozen-ji would allow no quarter for my mind, that everything would be on the table. I had wanted that at the time but now found that it was more than I bargained for. This felt especially so as days at the Dojo turned into weeks and then, after I had secured permission to stay long-term, as weeks turned into an indeterminate stretch of time unfolding in front of me. Slowly, I learned to regard the time in the tea house after Kendo as a continuation of class, a kind of social Kendo, and thus, to take it less personally. Until I was much more skilled and sensitive, my role, like in the formal Kendo class, was not to pursue the spotlight but to let the sensei give the openings. They directed the flow of the conversation and revealed gems of wisdom that had been polished by decades of life experience and Zen training.

I could, if I was fast enough and sensitive enough, get my own point from time to time, landing a zinger or being the first to get to a punch line. I learned that it worked especially well when I made myself the butt of the joke. But still, there were grating moments when my voice rose out of harmony, or I tried to push conversation in my preferred direction. At other times, I cringed as I realized that I was imposing my own needs and expectations or trying to make myself the center of attention.

The sensei were kind. They teased me and made light of my bumbling, as if nothing was of any consequence and everything was just a game. And yet, I knew that learning not to be numb and developing sensitivity were serious pursuits at Chozen-ji. It was a deeply rooted principle that much of our training hinged on.

One night around the monkeypod table, Teshima Sensei suggested that Michael, who taught the *Hitsuzendo*, or calligraphy, class should write the phrase 真剣—*Shin Ken*. Michael had recently started writing long, beautiful scrolls that he sent to Japan to be mounted on silk and that were later sold at Chozen-ji's annual art show. Teshima Sensei thought it a fitting phrase for Michael, who was not only a Zen priest but who had trained in Kendo for more than a decade and a half now.

"Many people translate 'Shin Ken' as 'real sword,'" Teshima Sensei explained, "but the real meaning is 'live blade.' In Japanese language, 'Shin Ken' is another way of saying 'sincerity.'"

I had been told that sincerity was the only real requirement of any prospective student requesting to come train at Chozen-ji. One did not have to have previous experience with Zen or martial arts. In fact, it was often better if one didn't. Better to just be blank slates rather than come in with habits that would only need to be unlearned. Somewhat as an expression of the teachers' and the Dojo's own sincerity but also as a way to better ensure the sincerity of its students, people were never charged money for Zen training. This helped ensure that nobody would be barred from training for lack of means. It also encouraged students not to feel entitled. This would never be a place where people could pay money for a certificate of some Zen realization. Real insight could only be earned through one's own shugyo. Similarly, Chozen-ji did not participate in the usual money-making activities of a temple, like funerals and blessings for hire. There were even stories of Tanouye Rotaishi turning down large donations, knowing that it would create some kind of expectation or come with strings attached. Training and training alone was prized above all else.

In English, sincerity simply means honesty, maybe earnestness. But neither was sufficient or deep enough to encompass its full meaning in Japanese as I came to understand it. Shin Ken, I inferred from Teshima Sensei, meant treating something as a matter of life and death, as if one were holding a live blade in her hands.

"A live blade means it's sharp enough to kill," he said. "But in Zen and Kendo, the Way of the Sword, it's also the sword that gives life."

This was a reference to something that lay at the heart of

Chozen-ji's Zen and samurai lineages—the philosophy that, by training deeply, one could learn to transcend life and death, all dualism, to go beyond the illusion of a separate self. This was also the definition of Zen captured in the Chozen-ji canon, rendering the word Zen as a verb: to transcend life and death, all dualism.

As the end of my initial three-week live-in period approached, I found that I still had as many questions as answers. I had received approval from Michael and Sayama Roshi to continue my stay and live in long-term, beginning with one year. But I never thought, after that year ended, that I would actually leave. Even only a few weeks in, I felt tied to the place, to the community, and to the training method in a way that I could neither explain nor refute.

I absorbed the lessons of Chozen-ji through my eyes, ears, nose, and mouth, even through the pores of my skin. Sensitivity and sincerity were but two of the lessons that I could put names to. In the same way that the scent of the incense that burned during zazen stayed on my clothes and skin for hours afterward, the training was leaving an indelible mark on me that would only saturate more deeply the longer I stayed.

Later on, reading the works of Zen scholars like D. T. Suzuki, I would come across a story that encapsulated the ways in which I was learning from every moment at the Dojo, especially the more mundane ones. In the seventh century, a student came to Zen Master Dogo seeking Zen training. After spending several weeks sweeping up and serving the master tea, the student expressed frustration to the master, asking when his training would begin. Dogo responded with a question: "When have I not instructed you in the essentials of Zen?

"Ever since you came to me," he continued, "I have always been pointing to how to study mind. . . . When you brought me a cup of tea, did I not accept it? When you served me with food, did I not partake of it? When you made bows to me, did I not return them?

"If you want to see," he concluded to his now remorseful student, "see directly into it; but when you try to think about it, it is altogether missed."[7]

Not a moment had passed in my first three weeks when I had not been offered some gem of insight—insights that seemed bigger than just Zen and that dug into the depth of who I was and how I might live in the world. As a recovering kotonk, I just needed to learn how to get out of my own way to receive them.

15

ALL-NIGHT
TRAINING

My first all-night training began on what was originally scheduled to be my last night at Chozen-ji. It was a Friday night, Kendo night, and all the Kendo sensei and students turned out. They arrived silently at the 6:00 p.m. sitting, filing in and then sitting like statues on a line of zabuton, the large square meditation cushions, on one side of the Budo Dojo. Because it was still winter and the light faded early, the large globe lights inside the dojo had been turned on. They cast a romantic, orange glow on the room. The racks of practice swords cast slight shadows on the wall, and the butsudan glowed as light reflected off the red felt tablecloth and the calligraphy on wood by Omori Rotaishi along the back wall. Outside, the migratory *kōlea* sounded off as they jockeyed for spots on the roofline.

Inside, the Budo Dojo was silent—save for my crying.

The crying came in long, weeping exhales that I tried to keep as quiet as I could. But the emotional release held a strong charge, as it had all been such a long time coming. For the past three weeks, I had felt upswells of emotion at various times, especially in zazen, Kendo, and while moving rocks. I was often on the verge of tears as what felt like a lifetime's worth of emotional baggage strained to break through. I had not been aware that I was carrying all this around with me, although it had apparently been obvious to the teachers at Chozen-ji since the moment I arrived.

"You're a warrior," Michael had said, and I thought I saw his eyes redden slightly, a sheen of tears forming in sympathy. "It makes me sad to think of you thinking that you had to be quiet or small," he said, referring to what I had voiced about my past approach to Buddhism.

Another time, he likened me to a lychee tree he had once encountered. From far away, it had looked like a beautiful lychee tree, perfectly proportioned and well watered. But at some point, it had stopped bearing fruit, and some of its leaves and branches had started to wither and fall. The owner, a friend of Michael's, had shown him the places where he had recently had to saw off dead growth—something he and especially his grandpa had been loath to do.

Inspecting the branches, Michael noticed something peculiar: something thick and rubbery enmeshed in the tree's flesh. He then noticed that the bark of the branches bore deep grooves, and what looked like rubber hoses protruded from the tree's skin. Michael then realized that, for decades, his friend's grandpa had been propping up and shaping his lychee tree with wires and irrigation hoses strung all around its branches. Over time, the tree had surrounded them, embedding them into its own flesh. Rather than cutting and pruning it, the grandpa had managed to hold on to every branch through his elaborate web of supports and irrigation. But later, as the tree was dying, it was clear that what had been most needed was what the grandpa had wanted to do least of all: to trim the excess branches so that the tree could grow freely.

I longed for a release. Every day at the Dojo and often for years before that, I had wished I could break down, cry, and feel more free. I wanted to prune the dead growth that were my attachments

and traumas. I wanted to cast off the supports of habits long held
and that had ceased being helpful. Now, past their usefulness and
corroded by time, they served only to eat away at me and hold me
back.

In just the past three weeks, I had already made great strides. Already, the work of building strength and muscle, of changing my
posture and the set of my bones, of deepening my breath and concentration, had delivered much more than any past spiritual work
I had done. And I had already grown. I had pushed myself beyond
my self-imposed limits almost every day. I had learned to stand
straighter, now a half inch taller than I used to be just by virtue of my
improved posture. I had changed how I walked, no longer striking
my heels into the wood of the engawa and stomping loudly around
the Dojo. And over time, I was learning to cut straight through my
problems and to sit without moving in the face of my body's pain,
twitches, and spasms.

And now, finally, I was crying. Sobbing, actually. I was still trying
to sit tall, count my breaths, and see the whole room, but every exhale now felt like it was being rung out of me. Riding each of those
breaths was the stale air of grief, anger, and helplessness. As the tears
came up and my body contracted and seized, I felt flashes of the
past. Not clear memories but just their overall feeling distilled down
into an instant, their essence. It was a relief to be finally letting all
this come up and to cry. But it was also embarrassing for it to happen in front of the sensei and other students. None of us had any
choice, after all, but to continue sitting here, without speaking, eyes
to the floor for the next ninety minutes.

From where I sat next to the jiki, I could see all the sensei and
senpai in profile, spines erect and hands locked in cradled fists in
their laps. Two local students who had started training a week after me had also decided to join the all-night training. Seeing them
sitting there, I felt a camaraderie with them and a sense of shared
purpose. We were all committed to training straight through to the

usual Saturday morning sitting at 8:00 a.m. After the tears had finally cleared and I could breathe again, I felt completely drained, emptied out. I had nothing save energy for my most basic functions left. I could only breathe, count my breaths, and wait without expectation or forethought for whatever came next.

Finally, the bell and taku sounded to mark the end of zazen. I rose quickly, bowed, and put away my cushions. My face was slack and expressionless. I went through the Kendo warm-ups without any extraneous thoughts but still fighting upswells of tears at times. Afterward, we skipped the Hojo and went straight into Kendo. When I put on my men and bogu, it was then that the tears really began to flow again.

Immediately, the senpai and sensei swept me up in keiko. There was no more room for tears. They were sharp and bright, and most importantly, they were precise. With deft hands, they snapped me out of my shakiness and the waves of emotions that threatened to subsume me, forcing me to cut straight. Indeed, keiko was the ideal place from which to shed old habits and create new ones, and I had been training for exactly this for the past three weeks. Rather than being hamstrung by overwhelming emotions, I strove to move swiftly and without encumbrances, letting my past go with each sword cut and leap forward. Still dazed, my limbs felt slightly unfamiliar, and I ran as if on new legs, though thankfully this time, they did not falter. Everything felt vaguely new. I found that I did not need to force things as much. I couldn't, actually; I didn't have the energy. All that was left was to give it everything I had, and in doing so, I found a deeper reserve of physical and psychological strength, as if it had just been waiting to be tapped. When my arms and legs felt like I couldn't run and hit any more, I pulled from my heart and found the energy to keep going.

It was soon time for *shiai*, refereed matches that were fought for points. The two students doing all-night training and I cycled in and out of the center of the shiai, each of us fighting seven consecutive matches so that, by the end, we had all fought each other and all the senpai and sensei save Teshima Sensei, who kept score. When he signaled that one side had scored a point, holding one arm straight up in the air, we came back to the center to start again or, after one of us had scored two points, to bow to one another and end the match. Then, the next opponent would enter. With no rest between the matches, we quickly became exhausted. Our movements became slower and more labored, and each attack took more out of us. At some point, the exhaustion seemed to abate, and then each of our unique habits could be seen clearly in how we fought. For me, it was a tendency to give up, get small, and resignedly let myself be hit. For one of the other all-nighters, it was to go wild, slowly losing his discipline and only focusing on survival without any regard for form or decorum. The third of us became tight in her movements, barely moving and taking only defensive actions.

We each became, in a way, a caricature of ourselves under pressure. It was as if the shiai concentrated the whole of who we were into just a few core expressions. What I saw resonated with what I knew of each of our personalities and characters from weeks of training side by side. Here in the face of deep challenge, our habits were laid bare. The promise of the training was that, if we continued, all of this extra stuff would fall away, all the extraneous effort and extra thoughts evaporating so that our fighting would become more direct and clean—because we had become, ourselves, direct and clean. Body, heart, and mind would intuitively economize and, despite whatever exhaustion and chaos we encountered, become brilliant and clear.

Much of what I exhibited at the peak of the shiai that night was admittedly lost on me. I didn't have the self-awareness to recognize the habits that came out, even when they were described to me later; I was so focused on just getting through it. For perhaps the first time in my life, it did not cross my mind to quit, bowing out and resting on the sidelines or trying to find a reason to take it easy. That felt significant. I faced opponent after opponent, mostly getting hit and scored on, not landing any points myself. But I found it in myself to keep going, even when I was no longer driven by excitement or enjoyment. In fact, by the time my turn in the center of the shiai had ended, I found that I could have kept going.

"Yame!" Teshima Sensei announced, and Sayama Roshi made for the front of the room. We all lined up with our shinai by our sides and removed our kote, men, and tenegui.

"Mokuso!" We sat in a few moments of zazen.

"*Yame!*" We bowed to each other, to the butsudan, and once again to each other. And then class was over. We lined up to bow to Teshima Sensei, and then peeled off for cleanup duties. I ran to the kitchen. Rather than cleaning and closing it down, since we would be up all night, I had planned to bake a pan of butter mochi, a local treat full of eggs, butter, and coconut milk. But, as my hands shook and I rattled the mixing bowl and measuring spoons, one of the senpai came in and told me to put the cake aside. He took one look at me, wild-eyed and still on the verge of tears, and knew that I was pouring all my frantic energy and internal chaos into the food that other people would be eating. That was not the Dojo's way.

"Just breathe," he said, and I immediately doubled over in tears. "Get it all out," he said, "but collect yourself before the others get here. It's not going to help them to see you a mess."

I kept heaving sobs, struggling to breathe.

"OK," he said, finally and decisively. "Go up on the hill and do Hojo Walk. Take your slippers off, and do it on the gravel." I nodded, catching my breath. The other students rounded the corner on the engawa and approached the kitchen.

"Go *now*," he said, and I took off running.

At any other time in my life that I had felt similarly overwhelmed by intense emotion, all I had wanted to do was give in and let my feelings carry me away. Let the grief or sadness take over; I didn't care. I just wanted to disappear. But now, my training dictated the opposite. Once I had climbed to the top of the hill, standing next to Omori Rotaishi's calligraphy, I removed my slippers and began walking with my bare feet on the gravel, slowly and with each breath hitched to a step forward or back. I swallowed the night air loudly. Ah'ing and um'ing, I pulled my face into a mask of ferocity and strength. I pushed the top of my head up toward the sky and let my shoulders drop. I set my hara. I did as I had been told, allowing the emotions to be there, the overwhelm and the swirl of feelings I couldn't pinpoint or name. But really, my energy was devoted to my breath, posture, and the Hojo Walk. I stayed in my body, not disappearing and not running away.

The sharp gravel dug painfully into my bare feet. It heightened my senses, pricking them into sharp relief and alertness. My breath steadied. My center of gravity slowly sank lower down into my abdomen, my awareness settling down into my feet as my legs moved in rhythm. My chest stopped heaving and then, over time, stopped quivering, as well. When I felt stilled and my mind was clearer, I finally stopped to look down at the Budo Dojo and the temple grounds. From where I was, higher up, I could see that the light was on in the kitchen. One of the other all-nighters was finishing the butter mochi cake and putting it into the oven. The other was walking down the gravel path.

After I had been doing the Hojo Walk for a half hour and felt recovered, I descended from the hill to continue training. At midnight, we would have a sitting in the Budo Dojo. Then at 3:00 a.m., another. I went to the tea house and practiced making tea, ferrying the various utensils to the front of the warm brazier of almost boiling water. I fudged most of the form, since I had learned little in my three weeks, but at least managed to whisk a cup of matcha. After placing it on the tatami, I rose from the host's position and walked over to where I would have sat as a guest. I sat down and then pulled myself forward, retrieving the cup of tea and bringing it back to my seat. In the cool, still air of the night, the first sip of tea hit me with its brightness. It cleared my head from my palette to my forehead and down to the nape of my neck. I finished drinking, returned to the host position, and did it all again.

At the midnight sitting, my head began to bob, heavy with fatigue. On one bob backward, the jiki suddenly slammed his hand down on the tatami, jolting me awake. I opened my eyes just in time to see the other students also start, eyes wide open. After forty-five minutes of zazen, I practiced more Hojo Walk and sword cuts. And then I sat some more. Although I had imagined that the all-night training would be one continuous fire drill of intensity, I had blown myself out in only the first hour and a half. For the rest of the night, I felt emptied out and calm. There was an ordinariness now to getting through the night. All that was left, I knew, was to keep going, putting one foot in front of the other and rotating from zazen to tea to sword until it was still dark but, according to the clock, morning.

At 6:30 a.m., we sat down for zazen again. This time, our eyelids dropped shut like trap doors, and our heads dipped mercilessly back and forth. The jiki put his hands together, bowed, and stood up. Picking up the keisaku from the butsudan, he walked the room and came to stand in front of each of us. I woke up just enough to realize that he was standing in front of me, his hands in gassho. I returned the gesture, and then, together, we bowed. I knew what came next, though until now I had not yet experienced it for myself. Bending toward the floor, I wrapped one arm under my chest until my hand was behind the opposite armpit. I placed the other hand on the tatami in front of me. I felt his hand push my head to one side, moving it out of the way so that one side of my spine was clear.

"*Whack! Whack-whack!!*" came three hits, the last two in rapid succession. The hits were so hard that my upper body bounced each time the keisaku came down. With the stinging pain and the force of the keisaku, which had knocked a bit of the wind out of me, came a new clarity. I switched arms and received three hits on the other side. Afterward, I slowly sat back up and held my hands up in gassho. The jiki and I bowed to one another, and then he continued down the line. I watched in my peripheral vision as the other students bounced and then woke up and straightened with the keisaku, every set of hits coming down in exactly the same rhythm and with the same sharp sound each time. Afterward, as the jiki returned to his seat, the air remained piercingly still.

By the time the 8:00 a.m. sitting came around, the sun had come up, and I had downed a cup of coffee, hoping to avoid nodding off in front of a full dojo. Sayama Roshi scanned our faces and carried on with his morning, apparently satisfied. The Budo Dojo filled with its usual variety of local students: the seniors in the flower arrangement class, the teenagers in the Aikido class, several calligraphy students, and a few ceramicists.

"*Wake up!*" the jiki yelled a few times during the sitting, prompting one or two of the older members to inquire afterward if the three of us had been up all night training.

"Good times," one of them chuffed as he walked down the steps from the Budo Dojo, laughing to himself and surveying the scene as he remembered his own days of intensive training. And with that, at the close of those forty-five minutes of zazen, my first all-night training came to an end.

"The challenge now is to stay awake until it's dark," one senpai said. "But it was only one night. It should be easy." He smiled and I smiled back.

"Your face is bright," he said.

I *felt* bright. I was also ruddy with accomplishment: *My first all-night training!*

It had not been so hard after all, even after a great deal of apprehension and self-doubt. I had only had to approach it in the right way. And it was also important to be around the right people, I thought to myself. And also, I supposed, to be in the right place.

In many ways, having completed my first all-night training now felt quite ordinary, but I realized that it was also simply extraordinary

that these conditions—right people, right place, right approach—
had aligned so that we could pull it off. I thought then of something
I had heard many times over the previous three weeks, and which
made me appreciate my years of wandering up to this point: that
the hardest thing was walking through the temple gates. If I had
not been ready to do this kind of training; if I had not heard from
Michael at just the right moment; and if I had not had the means to
fly to Hawai'i, I might never have made it to the Dojo. Once I had
arrived, diving into the training was a foregone conclusion. I was
drawn so irresistibly forward that all I had to do was put one foot in
front of the other. As challenging as the training was, just making it
here had been the hardest part.

16

SAYAMA DAIAN ROSHI, MY TEACHER

Sayama Daian Roshi was born in Honolulu to a local Japanese American family that he describes as simple and poor. For much of his childhood, he grew up in a one-bedroom apartment shared by seven family members—his parents and five children—in a Japanese tenement in the Nu'uanu neighborhood. On the ground floor of the tenement were small businesses like the sundries store the Sayamas ran, called the Rainbow Sweetshop. Up above lived a close-knit community of Japanese families.

During the day, Sayama Roshi's mother, Yaeko, would run the store while his father, Etsuo, worked for the US Army Corps of Engineers. A grandmother or auntie would watch the store in the evenings so that the Sayamas could eat dinner together as a family. After dinner, Etsuo would go back to work, this time at the store, where he marked his children's homework in red pen for them to correct before going to school the next morning.

Despite their financial struggles, the children's education was of the utmost importance to Yaeko and Etsuo. They worked multiple jobs and never owned their own house or car, making it a priority instead to put all five of their children through private schools in Honolulu. Later, Sayama Roshi and his sisters, Sandy and Laura, graduated from the Punahou School, the prestigious private school that the future president Barack Obama would later attend. As a senior there, Sayama Roshi became a Presidential Scholar, an honor conferred to no more than 161 high school seniors in the country each year. He then graduated from Yale University summa cum laude in three years, taking a one-year leave of absence to train intensively in Tokyo with the renowned Aikido sensei Tohei Koichi.

Sayama Roshi's father was regarded by many who knew him as having the discipline of a samurai. For a short while when he was small, Etsuo had lived in Japan, and he attributed the integrity and focus for which he would later be known to the traditional Japanese moral education he received there. These were values he passed on to his children, and, together, he and Yaeko instilled in them the traditions and old ways of Japan.

When Etsuo passed away, Sayama Roshi reflected on the immense childhood struggles that shaped his father's character. At only six years old, Etsuo had lost his own father and was, in many ways, left to fend for himself. At fourteen years old, when his mother remarried, Etsuo was sent away to live separately.

When Sayama Roshi eulogized Etsuo at his funeral, he said, "I don't think I could have realized my father's greatness if I didn't have my sons Richard and Jackson. When I try to imagine them without me at the age of 6, or fending for themselves at the age of 8, and then being removed from their mother at the age of 14, the thought is actually unimaginable. Somehow my father endured the unbearable and overcame all manner of hardships to have a full life and when it was done, to feel grateful for everything."[8]

Coming of age at the end of the counterculture movement of the 1960s and 1970s, Sayama began asking big questions about the meaning of life and how to achieve the highest possible consciousness. Even as a teenager, he knew that he wanted to be a serious person who committed himself to the pursuit of a Way.

The word "Way" is a translation of 道 (*Do*, or *Tao* in Chinese). Do describes a path to awakening or enlightenment. In one sense, the word refers to a spiritual discipline or religious doctrine. But within the specific context of Taoism, Do is the undefinable energy that runs through and interconnects all existence and nonexistence. In Japanese culture, Do is also what differentiates the study of technique in arts like Kenjutsu (swordsmanship) or *ikebana* (flower arrangement) from Kendo, the Way of the Sword, or *Kado*, the Way of the Flower. The character and the ideogram from which it evolved depict a path with footsteps on it—a path one has to walk on her own to approach her True Self.

It's a bit of a Zen-ism to refer to enlightenment as "realizing one's True Self." It means to transcend the small, impermanent self that we are so attached to and so easily identify as all that we are. The True Self is bigger, everlasting. It's not a soul but that which existed before we were born and that, after this body is dead, will continue to exist. It is also the entire universe, meaning all existence and nonexistence. These are religious and philosophical concepts, but they're also deeply embedded in traditional Japanese life and culture, as reflected in the role of Do in the arts. As a concept, Do is also often approached in a way that can be surprisingly practical and literal. It is not so uncommon for a Japanese person, for example, to express a desire to train in a particular art because of the way they think it will shape their character or because they want to emulate someone they admire, not necessarily because they want to become skilled in it.

At twenty years old, Sayama went to live in and train intensively in Aikido with Tohei Sensei in Japan. While he had imagined training in a romantic setting—somewhere, in retrospect, like Chozen-ji—he found himself living with four other young men in a small apartment in Tokyo, where he says he was "the lowest man on the totem pole." He was the first to get up each morning, cleaning the toilets and laundering everyone's clothes in an archaic machine out on the patio, even in the winter. This was not far from doing the laundry by hand, as the water and soap had to be put in for the first cycle, drained, then new water put in for the rinse, and drained again. There was no dryer—all the clothes hung on a laundry line on the patio, sometimes taking up to a week to fully dry. Sayama also trained six hours a day and carried the sensei's bags from dojo to dojo, a privilege for which he even paid tuition each month.

Throughout his time in Tokyo, he often asked himself what he was doing. But in the end, the training paid off. By the time Sayama returned to Hawai'i, his skill in Aikido had grown considerably. He had become especially good at taking falls and being thrown. Even the *Aikido-ka* who had previously been his seniors now called him "Sensei."

It was upon his return to Hawai'i that Sayama had a chance meeting with Tanouye Rotaishi, to whom he was introduced by another Aikido sensei. He was so deeply impressed upon meeting him that he asked to train with him immediately. In his biography of Tanouye Rotaishi, Sayama Roshi writes about the gravity of this encounter, which ended up becoming a critical turning point in his life:

> I debated with myself about coming to train with Tanouye Roshi. After my year of Aikido in Japan, I told myself I'd never put myself in that kind of situation again which was taxing physically and psychologically with most of the gratification coming at the end for not having quit. But then I had to recognize that Tanouye Roshi was superior to me physically, intellectually, and aesthetically. So if I was sincere about pursuing the Way and not just an ego trip, I had to train under him. I asked him if I could. He replied, "You better think twice." My saving grace was to be able to immediately reply, "I already have."[9]

After only a short introduction to zazen, Sayama spent several weeks working as a bus tour guide on the mainland before returning to Hawai'i for sesshin. His meager training for sesshin, a week of the most intense training done at Chozen-ji, was doing zazen for ten to fifteen minutes in front of the television in various motels along the tour route.

Once sesshin began, Sayama found his body to be so tight that it tilted stiffly backward whenever he sat in zazen. The jiki would correct his posture, pulling him forward so that he was straight again. But, like a rubber band, his body would spring back. The pain was even worse than the austere, three-day Shinto *misogi* spiritual training he had done while in Japan and that he'd sworn to himself he'd never do again. But sitting in zazen across from a group of young women in the Budo Dojo, he realized quitting or running away was not even remotely an option. He'd have to get up and walk right past these tranquil-looking girls. As a local Hawai'i boy of his day, Sayama knew that he would not be able to live down such a shame, so he stayed.

After beginning his training at Chozen-ji, Sayama attended graduate school at the University of Michigan, where he completed a PhD in psychology. Later, he turned his dissertation into a book that was published by SUNY Press under the title *Samadhi: Self Development in Zen, Swordsmanship, and Psychotherapy*. After school, he moved back to Honolulu and worked in clinical psychology and health care. At thirty-eight, he married Yumiko, and they had twin boys, Richard and Jackson. The first place that the boys went as babies was to Chozen-ji to meet Tanouye Rotaishi, who carried them around the grounds as they squalled.

By the time I met Sayama Roshi on that Tuesday afternoon in early 2018, he was already in his mid-sixties, just a few years from retirement. His boys were graduating from college in New York City and Shanghai. Yumiko was deep into Chado, teaching students in the tea room at their house.

When he wasn't in Hilo on the neighboring island of Hawai'i running a health care nonprofit or at the Dojo, Sayama Roshi spent his free time tending to the bonsai and rock garden behind his house or throwing a ball with the Sayamas' beloved family dog, Mia. As he had for the previous forty-plus years, he came up to the Dojo like clockwork to run his Kendo class twice a week. He was on-site for zazen on Saturday mornings and at other times to tend to plants and odd projects around the grounds.

Pruning trees or giving a talk, the Sayama Roshi I met when I arrived at Chozen-ji was a master in his element who radiated with kiai. Depending on his aim, he could put people at ease or catapult them into action. In many ways, Chozen-ji was his home. As he was now the abbot, to step onto the grounds was to enter his domain. Becoming his student, then, felt less like a conscious step onto a new branch of my spiritual path and more like being sucked into his orbit. Whether I realized it or not, from the first moment I stood opposite him in Kendo class and sat across from him at the kitchen, I was already his student. At long last, I had found my teacher.

17

BECOMING
MY TEACHER'S
STUDENT

Before coming to Chozen-ji, I had mostly met Buddhist teachers at meditation centers or on silent meditation retreats. In these places, I was only one of dozens—sometimes more than a hundred—students sitting in row after row of cushions and chairs facing the dais from which these teachers lectured. I supposed that this was in line with the norm and in keeping with tradition. I had seen pictures of saffron-clad monks sitting in large crowds at the feet of renowned teachers in Southeast Asian and Tibetan temples. However, I had also learned of very different kinds of interactions between teachers and students—ones that were more intimate and interwoven with daily life in a way I did not experience on retreat, and that felt mysterious and inaccessible to me in twenty-first-century America.

In the books they wrote and the talks they gave, the American Buddhist teachers I came to know described their own teachers and the incredible insights they had received from them, their stories often peppered with heartwarming details of spiritual mentorship and care. There were stories of playful chiding and stern rebukes, of how gleeful and childlike these sage masters could be—for example, when interacting with the neighbors as they made their morning alms rounds or when mopping the sweat off their brows as they ate a deliciously spicy meal of home-cooked Southeast Asian food. There were funny stories of lessons lost in translation between Asian teachers and their American students and poignant moments shared when teachers became old and eventually passed away, their students at their bedsides.

This was the kind of teacher-student relationship I wanted: something that serious spiritual students for eons before me had pursued and that today's teachers themselves had benefited from and prized highly. But I could not see an obvious way to find one.

Going to retreats for several consecutive years and trying to establish rapport with specific teachers over email and calls in between did not yield the kind of close relationship I yearned for. Perhaps recognizing that this was a widespread need, some teachers had begun to offer formal programs for serious students to go deeper. These came in the form of "experienced practitioner" groups and mentorship programs, which often spanned one year and included reading and writing assignments, regular group calls, and one-on-one conversations. I spent thousands of dollars on such programs over several years! But whether there just wasn't chemistry, my approach was off, or the conditions weren't right, even twelve years after my first meditation retreat, I still wasn't sure that I had found my teacher.

I did not know right away that Sayama Roshi would be my Zen teacher, as there were in fact several teachers at Chozen-ji, including one I had met a few times prior to my arrival. When I had signed up for one of her day-long intensives in the California Bay Area, I hadn't actually known that she had any connection to the Dojo. It was only after the fact and a month or so before my arrival that I put all the pieces together and asked Michael if he knew her and if she taught at Chozen-ji.

"Ha!" Michael replied over email. "I just taught a class with her last night. No joke."

But as soon as I met Sayama Roshi, I felt a deep affinity with him. He was my father's age and reminded me of him in many ways—a completely modern American man but with a strong streak of the traditional East Asian patriarch running through him. For better or worse, this made being in his presence and what was expected of me feel familiar.

Even though he had gone to Yale and held a PhD, Sayama Roshi was very blunt in sharing his disdain for artifice and intellectual self-indulgence. He joked a lot and pivoted between self-deprecation and a surprisingly direct honesty regarding his own achievements: Presidential Scholar, Yale summa cum laude in three years, student to Tohei Sensei, corporate executive, and so on. And it wasn't simply a matter of past accomplishments—I could see his brilliance directly in the way he could, for instance, artfully explain the principles of Buddhist metapsychology or quantum physics. And in the same breath, he joked about the ways Tanouye Rotaishi cut him down to size when he was a young student: "You'd have better luck getting enlightened being a ditch digger," he was told more than once.

I immediately felt a dynamism, intellectual vitality, and intensity in my interactions with Sayama Roshi. Simply put, he was fun to be around. I was drawn to how not self-serious he seemed and how solid, steady, and reliable this made him, especially in the face of my own emotional ups and downs. Once, wanting to understand what his kiai felt like and what it might literally be like to walk in his shoes, I borrowed Sayama Roshi's slippers from where he'd cast them off outside the kitchen. All our habits, I had been told, are in our feet. Literal imprints of these habits are captured in the soles of our slippers, a physical record of how we walk and move through the world. Wearing Sayama Roshi's slippers out onto the gravel and into the storage shed where I was going to fetch something, I felt a bright beam of energy traveling all the way up through the top of my head. For a moment, the world felt brighter, and I felt more upright, with a buzzing light in my forehead. I simultaneously felt anchored and unshakably grounded—a new and foreign sensation.

Sayama Roshi was also, as local people would say, "samurai." There was an uprightness and a simplicity to the rules he believed should govern human behavior, and he inspired his students to see things the same way. In my first weeks at Chozen-ji, Michael shared how, years earlier when he was young, broke, and had nothing but his physical labor to give back to the Dojo, he had asked Sayama Roshi if he could join his Kendo class. He had already been coming up to do a full day's construction and maintenance work once a week and for sitting several days a week. Kendo, he had heard, was a way to approach training more seriously.

"Yes," Sayama Roshi had responded to his request to join Kendo. "But don't miss a class."

Michael took those words so seriously that, for three years, Sayama Roshi and Michael did Kendo together twice a week without fail. Sometimes, Michael would arrive and find that he was the only student who'd made it to class. Still, Sayama Roshi would devote three hours of his evening to sitting zazen and training with him in Hojo and Kendo. This was even though Sayama Roshi had a young family at home and, in Michael's eyes, better things he could be doing with his time. The sense of obligation and responsibility Michael felt to meet Sayama Roshi's commitment was so strong that, even on the days when he felt exhausted from working multiple jobs and going to school or like he was coming down sick, he would still get on his bike and ride nine miles, much of it uphill, to the Dojo to train. One day, he even got into an accident on the way. He got back on his bike and rode up anyway, leaving a scant trail of blood all the way up Kalihi Street. It was only on very rare occasions—when it was pouring rain and there happened to be a live-in at the Dojo who could drive him home—that Michael wouldn't finish up several hours of intense training only to get on his bicycle and ride the nine miles back home.

Michael's very presence at the Dojo, now living on the grounds and carrying responsibility for the training day to day, was a clear signal of the gratitude he felt for all his teachers and the responsibility he bore for ensuring the future of the training. His devotion to Sayama Roshi was the result of how Roshi had been there for him—dedicated, generous, and constant throughout the years—as well as simply out of respect for Roshi's own lifetime of serious training. If Sayama Roshi was on the grounds, Michael's already sharp attention grew even sharper. He knew where Roshi was and was always a step ahead or at least ready if he needed anything. Michael arranged his work schedule—as, in addition to running the Dojo, he worked close to full-time—so that he'd be available if Roshi was coming by, in case he wanted to discuss temple business or just talk story. They both had a love for training and talked with a warm and easy rapport, often in lockstep with one another.

When Sayama Roshi told me on the morning after all-night training to get dressed for lunch with him outside the Dojo, I hoped for the chance to develop the same kind of bond that he and Michael shared. I trusted him and respected the veracity of his transmission—not only had he been one of Tanouye Rotaishi's core students, but he had trained closely with the Hawaiian spiritual leader Nana Veary and done koan training with Omori Rotaishi, as well. As abbot of Chozen-ji, he was now the eighty-fifth teacher in a line of direct teacher-to-student transmission that could be traced all the way back to the historical Buddha. This authorization to teach was an important factor in selecting a teacher, I had read in Omori Rotaishi's biography. And not only did Sayama Roshi have the right bona fides, he also seemed to like me. Most importantly, he wanted me to train hard, which was what I wanted, as well.

After all-night training, Sayama Roshi drove me to a quaint Chinese restaurant on the other side of Honolulu. Regarding me from across the table, he asked me how the all-night training had gone.

"Did you have a breakthrough?" he asked.

"Well, I'm a little embarrassed that I had such a break*down*," I admitted.

"What breakdown? Oh, when you were crying?" he asked. "What was that about, anyway?"

I nodded, sheepish. I didn't have a good answer for what it was about. I was only able to describe it as "stuff"—emotional baggage coming to the surface. I couldn't place it, and it hadn't been about anything in particular, but I conceded that maybe my crying was a way to release some of the pent-up emotions I had had about my spiritual seeking. I had placed a lot of importance on the all-night training. Perhaps my emotions had gotten ahead of me.

"Well, I don't think that was a breakdown, Cristina," he replied, much to my surprise. What he said next surprised me even more.

"That was a break*through*," he said.

"A breakthrough?"

"Listen," he explained. "It's by design that the training is hard, so hard that it's going to make you want to quit. It's by design! That's how you transcend your self-imposed limitations. You have to remember that. Look at it this way: you faced whatever it was, and you didn't give up. You didn't quit.

"Now," he continued, "if you had quit, it would have just been a breakdown. But you kept going, so you broke through."

"That's all that a breakthrough is?" I asked.

"OK, you're right. It's not the same thing as having a realization. But yes, you should consider it a breakthrough."

I sat quietly and without eating, unsure. I did not feel like I had had a breakthrough. I could recognize that I felt lighter and brighter today and, indeed, had just accomplished something I had not thought possible before. But I felt I was the same person today that

I was yesterday. I felt just as close to crying in the Budo Dojo now as any other day in the past three weeks. I did not feel the beatific glow of a realization or like I had unlocked any earth-shattering insight.

"Cristina!" Sayama Roshi said, interrupting my thoughts. "OK, how about this? I'm the abbot of Chozen-ji, and I'm telling you that you had a breakthrough. Is that good enough?" He laughed loudly, his eyes twinkling.

"Yes," I said knowingly. I understood what game we were playing now. I would just have to trust him.

"It better be!" Sayama Roshi laughed some more. After a few moments, he settled down and, still in a kidding mood, took on a faux air of seriousness. He placed both hands on the table in front of him, which puffed up his chest and pushed back his shoulders. He was no longer just talking. Now he was presiding.

"OK, but one thing, Cristina, and this is very important for you. You have to take yourself less seriously. Don't get me wrong, you have to train hard. But like Tanouye Roshi said, 'Why train if it doesn't make you free and happy?'

"That's your training," he concluded, "to become free and happy." A faint smile returned. "OK?"

"I think that may be a tall order, Sayama Roshi," I offered, smiling back and raising my eyebrows, my attempt to join in on the fun. Sayama Roshi's lips spread into a wide grin.

By the time lunch was over, it was a foregone conclusion that I would live and train at Chozen-ji long-term, beginning with a commitment to stay for one year. A month later, Sayama Roshi fully formalized my training as his Zen student by beginning to do sanzen, or koan training, with me, as he had done himself as a student of Tanouye Rotaishi and Omori Rotaishi decades before.

For him, the matter of deciding to take me on as his student was straightforward. We matched in our idea of what kind of training I should do—physical and vigorous—and I was already training in Kendo with him. I had not been so sure, however, as I was unclear on the proper protocol for becoming a formal Zen student and wondered if some sort of request had to be made. Before the matter had been resolved, I belabored the question in my mind and in our collective process by anxiously voicing my concerns to whomever would listen.

Rather than Roshi approaching me directly, it was one of my senpai who finally suggested that, as I was living in, it was time to start doing sanzen. I did not realize that this, along with teaching me basics like sword cuts and how to wash the dishes, and keeping my mind on track through scoldings and warm encouragement, was part of the responsibility he bore as senpai. As we cleaned up after lunch one day, he explained that sanzen was an appropriate next step in serious Zen training and an opportunity to develop the kind of one-on-one relationship with a teacher I had been seeking. Triangulating, he also brought it up with Sayama Roshi, who agreed that it was a good next step. To allay my concerns about propriety, my senpai also suggested that if I wanted, I could formally ask Sayama Roshi if he was or would be my teacher, maybe on one of the afternoons he was on the grounds before Kendo. The request earned me one of Roshi's hearty laughs, a twinkle in his eye that was more incredulous than mischievous this time—another wordless commentary, maybe, on my numb kotonkishness. But he said yes, of course, and that we would go ahead and start that very evening.

18

SANZEN

Before the end of the second evening sitting, Senpai escorted me from the Budo Dojo to a smaller temple and Zendo on the opposite side of the grounds. With shoji screens on either side, wooden ceilings, a traditional stone entryway, and a more ornate butsudan, it is a beautiful and classically Japanese space that feels warm, healing, and imbued with decades of deep spiritual training.

As we walked in, I was formally presented to Sayama Roshi for sanzen. Roshi sat on a white zabuton and zafu on the floor in front of the butsudan. I had never seen him in his robes before—long, black priest robes, the sleeves and lapels lined with bands of gold. A small brass bell rested by his side, and a single stick of incense burned directly behind him in a pot of ash sitting in the butsudan. The sliding glass windows on either side of the room were cracked slightly, and I could hear the faint crowing of roosters and the brief, clipped chirps of the evening birds outside. A gentle breeze pushed and pulled the plume of incense smoke into delicate circles in front of the wooden Buddha statue that faced us, the palm of one of its hands turned toward me.

I did two full-body bows near the entrance, circling my arms up overhead and then prostrating on my knees, my forehead to the ground. I stood up, took three steps forward, and then completed the sampai with a third bow. Afterward, I remained sitting in seiza. This first meeting, I had been told, would be less formal than subsequent ones, and Sayama Roshi proceeded to use the time to explain how I was to approach sanzen. He assigned me my first koan, Joshu's "Mu"—a common starting point for students in the Rinzai sect of Zen. And then he assigned me to read the first chapter of a book of commentary on the *Mumonkan*, a collection of koan compiled in China in the thirteenth century and from which various schools of Rinzai Zen have drawn their koan curricula in one way or another over the centuries.

The *Mumonkan* describes an encounter with a Chinese Zen monk named Joshu, who's asked if a dog has Buddha nature. "Mu!" (Void/Emptiness), Joshu replies. The koan posed to almost every beginner is, What is this Mu?

Later reading the commentary, I gleaned some conceptual insight into why Joshu might have said Mu, but I remained stumped as to how to answer my koan. Sayama Roshi had also suggested that I review Omori Rotaishi's description of koan training in *An Introduction to Zen Training* and the description of Omori Rotaishi's own koan training detailed in his biography, *Omori Sogen: The Art of a Zen Master*. Having read the latter before my arrival at Chozen-ji, I now recognized a description of how to sit with a koan that Omori Rotaishi had pulled from the *Mumonkan*:

> Don't you want to pass the barrier? Then throw yourself into this "Mu," with your 360 bones and 84,000 pores, making your whole body one great inquiry. Day and night work intently at it. Do not attempt nihilistic or dualistic interpretations. The search for an answer is like having swallowed a red hot iron ball. You try to vomit it but cannot.[10]

Omori Rotaishi had framed his own advice to beginning Zen students approaching koan training thusly:

When you are working on your first koan, just as it is written in the *Mumonkan*, you should *kufu* this koan twenty-four hours a day whether you are awake or asleep. . . .
It is said that the method of solving a koan is to become
a mass of doubt. . . . The person who is doubting and the
object of the doubt unite and become one mass of doubt.
Becoming the mass of doubt is the method of solving the
koan, and breaking through this mass of doubt is enlightenment.[11]

This sense of existential urgency to provide an answer, to know
and embody emptiness, fascinated me. But I also suspected that my
enthusiasm to achieve such a complete state of confusion was another expression of my habitual love for drama. While I should have
been contemplating my koan, I instead spent sittings imagining myself getting dizzyingly caught up in my koan until I seemed mentally
deranged, unable to distinguish up from down. Then—*pop!*—I
would have a realization.

Whatever it actually meant to solve a koan felt out of reach and
incomprehensible. Nevertheless, I did kufu, or struggle, with it, just
not in the way I felt Omori Rotaishi must have meant. At best, as I
tried to understand Joshu's Mu, I felt like I was casting about in the
dark, unable to catch even a glimpse of insight to point me in the
right direction. And yet, nothing about me seemed to change; I did
not feel myself becoming a mass of doubt.

Instead of counting my breaths that night and in the sittings that
followed, I said to myself, "Mu," on every exhale, drawing it out for
twenty to thirty seconds or simply as long as I could. Trying to push
the sound or the thought of Mu down from inside my head so that
it felt as if it originated from my hara. Trying to make Mu suffuse
my whole being.

Every time I could remember outside of zazen, which was not
often enough, I would again kufu my koan, exhaling and trying to

become "Mu." One sanzen, I arrived with enthusiasm and a beautiful, philosophical concoction about Mu meaning both emptiness and everything, a riff on the Heart Sutra's "emptiness is form; form is emptiness." Sayama Roshi said that my response was awfully conceptual. Instead of *explaining* Mu to him, he wanted me to demonstrate to him that I *was* Mu.

Over the course of many subsequent sanzen, I tried to pay attention to everything—180 degrees in every direction, just like in zazen. I would notice many impulses to speak and many thoughts popping into my head. But I was unable to form a statement that felt genuine, direct, or like an embodiment of Mu. I knew it would all come out sounding contrived. I kept trying, but I was not yet Mu.

Sometimes Sayama Roshi's only response to my attempts would be to simply reach for the small brass bell that lay beside him and ring it. The high-pitched *brrriiiinngg!* signaled the end of our encounter. Sometimes with relief, sometimes with disappointment, I would bow, rise, and take three steps backward. One last time, I would prostrate to Sayama Roshi and, after rising one last time, run back to the Budo Dojo to try again.

19

JOKKEI

Weeks at Chozen-ji turned into months, and I began to become a fixture of day-to-day training, present at every sitting, morning and night, and in almost every class. On Monday nights, two or three of us would train the Hojo while the seniors in the Budo Dojo did Tai Chi. On Tuesday and Friday nights, we did Kendo. On Wednesday nights, I did my best to wrangle unwieldy lumps of clay on the potter's wheel in the ceramics studio. On Thursday nights, more Hojo. Saturday mornings were for more ceramics, and Sunday, Chado.

Each weekday morning, we followed up the 5:30 a.m. zazen with some sort of training, either Hojo, boxing, or okyo. A quick NASCAR pit-stop breakfast of granola and yogurt followed. Then, I would spend the day free training and doing work projects around the grounds. As time went on, I also took on duties in the kitchen, trying my hand at some local dishes like stir-fry with cabbage and watercress, beef stew, and Japanese curry, all over rice. I also began to help with Dojo administration, working on the biannual newsletter and piloting programs to attract new students. And I waged an un-winnable war against the weeds growing through the gravel, filling half a bucket each day with the small green shoots.

I was urged to tackle all these activities head-on like training. I learned to chop vegetables precisely, consistently, and without unnecessary roughness. I also learned to plan our daily menus to suit the weather and people's training, and though I plied us all liberally with calories, because of how hard we trained, we were always still able to eat more. Even working on the newsletters felt like Kendo. When Michael and Sayama Roshi gave me the opening, I proposed new approaches to layout, delivery, and how the newsletters could be displayed on the website. Then, they made me follow through vigorously, running the projects to the finish line under their discriminating supervision. I even pulled weeds with intensity, pulling with both hands and squatting close to the ground to build strength and flexibility in my hips; I never surrendered and sat on the ground. I could make it a few hours at most before my low back, neck, and shoulders burned so badly I had to stop.

I also took on more of a role in the training. During zazen, a second cushion was often set next to the jiki's, facing away from the butsudan and toward the other people sitting zazen. This spot was reserved for the *jokkei*, for all intents and purposes the jiki's second in command. As my zazen got stronger and as I became more competent in the forms of the Dojo, jokkei, too, became one of my responsibilities.

Approaching six thirty each weeknight, the jiki would raise his hands in gassho, signaling the beginning of a sequence of actions I was to carry out, starting with ringing the Peace Bell. Returning to the Budo Dojo with two sticks of incense, I trailed a thin line of smoke behind me as I rounded the corners of the engawa and crossed the tatami of the dojo. One stick went to the jiki, the other stick into the big pot of ash inside the butsudan.

Before exiting again, I'd turn on the rest of the lights for evening training. The light over the stairs was straightforward; I only had to flip a switch. But the old, rickety dial that controlled the globe lights had to be navigated with caution. As I turned it, the lights would go on but then dim again before jumping up to an always too-high setting. The first few times, I was alarmed by how bright the room became and then spent what felt like an eternity fiddling with the dial—dimming, brightening, and then dimming and brightening the lights over again until they were just right. It took a week or more to develop a muscle memory for exactly how far the dial needed to go, and I was eventually able to brighten the lights in one, swift turn. I did this with great satisfaction, the same way that I completed other basic forms and routine actions like opening the combination lock on the temple gate in the dark just by feel.

The last of my responsibilities as jokkei was hitting the *han*, a thick block of solid wood that hung from one of the posts of the engawa. Well-worn in the center where students had been hitting it for several decades, the han could withstand far more force than I could dole out. So I was encouraged again and again to hit it harder—always harder—and faster to give the people sitting inside the dojo the feeling that time was speeding away, all the more reason to train hard *right now*. To hear the han when it is hit properly is to feel like your last train home is pulling out of the station, its powerful engine and wheels accelerating in an unstoppable rhythm. And, though you sit perfectly still, you want to muster everything you have to jump aboard.

Perfectly in sync with the last hit of the han—*soft, soft, loud!*—the bell would ring out. Then, the taku sounded and the jiki would say, "*Kinhin*," to announce the beginning of a short and swift walking meditation. After hitting the han, I'd return to the Budo Dojo and stand near the entrance, so I could enter the kinhin line right behind the jiki.

Slow at first, the kinhin line would speed up into a military march as we walked the perimeter of the room. As I did kinhin more and more, I learned how not to lose step with the person in front of me as we took the turns, all of us stepping with the same foot forward at the same time, left-right, left-right.

"Kinhin is basically a clever way to do ninety minutes of zazen," I was told, "but you get to stretch your legs in the middle."

At Chozen-ji, kinhin was vibrant, vigorous, and tightly disciplined. When done well, it flowed like a beautifully choreographed dance that opened and honed the senses, a true moving meditation.

During zazen, I now sat in the jokkei position almost knee to knee with the jiki. This proximity aroused an extra degree of vigilance and conscientiousness in my zazen, except, of course, when it didn't. The long days of training and the physical exhaustion of Kendo, outside work, and my attempts at near-constant awareness—to my posture, breathing, koan, hara, environment, and to the possibility of a scolding coming from any direction at any time—made me drowsy whenever there was a pause in activity. Sitting zazen, especially in the first thirty minutes of the evening sittings when the pain in my knees wasn't yet there to keep me awake, I would come dangerously close to dozing and sometimes did.

The Dojo has little patience for people visibly falling asleep during zazen, even though getting us dog-tired is an indispensable aspect of the training. If I could stay sitting erect, I learned, sleep might be acceptable, as it meant I had cultivated the ability to keep my hara set. But still, sleeping through zazen is mostly seen as a waste of training time. In particular, it is a disservice for less-experienced students, as it gives them the wrong idea about how to train. I had heard a story about one jiki growing so fed up with a student jerking back and forth in the sitting that the girl sitting next to him was assigned to whack him across the chest whenever she saw his head bob. In another story, it was the jiki himself who doled out the whack to wake up a sleepy, teenaged jokkei. The boy had dozed through the subtle gesture of the jiki raising his hands in gassho at 6:30 p.m., something I was also occasionally prone to doing.

The first time, I received only a stern, "Jokkei," which was enough to rouse me and get me going. The second time, I was woken up by the sound of the jiki getting up himself to go and perform all my duties, leaving me to burn with shame and self-recrimination at my cushion. And finally, there came the day when, having dozed off for what felt like just a moment in my seat, I was shocked awake by the *thwack!* of the jiki's arm striking me across the chest. It wasn't that hard, but it was enough to immediately fill me with embarrassment and rage—*How dare he?!*—which conveniently diverted my attention from how I had failed in my responsibilities not only as jokkei but now as one of the more experienced students in the room.

After several months at the Dojo, I was now senpai to a number of local students and even one or two short-term live-ins who had started training after me. As their senior, I was supposed to demonstrate what it meant to train hard, treating our time together as precious and serious, like pursuing a realization was a matter of life and death. My best attempt at this was to foster an intimidating focus during the formal training periods, watchful of where people were and what they were doing inside the Budo Dojo so that I began to learn what it meant to take full charge of a sitting. My demeanor became gruff and serious around training time. I did not smile, I rarely made eye contact except to convey a silent scolding, and I did not make small talk. I responded to questions with clipped, direct answers, and sometimes, if the question was frivolous, I didn't respond at all. Here was a place, I was told, to try out different approaches and demeanors. Nobody would be too offended if I was too sharp or too serious. If I made a mess and got things wrong, it was my training to figure out how to get it right next time. But it was also others' training to figure out how to remain unbothered, to take what was useful from missteps, like an overly harsh scolding, and just discard the rest.

This was about as far as my experience thus far could take me. I was too wrapped up with myself and my own training to be able to truly fulfill the role of senpai for others, even if that was an aim of the training—to learn to take care of others before myself. Every day at Chozen-ji, I had received such care, in the form of sittings, classes, home-cooked meals and cooking lessons, one-on-one instruction in the Hojo, other training sessions, and work projects. Even the continuing existence of the Dojo was evidence of people extending their care to future Zen students like me in the same way that their teachers and senpai had taken care of them. My first real taste of what it meant to care for others before myself—overcoming solipsism, discomfort, and even pain—would come soon enough. As the six-month mark of my training approached, so did my first sesshin.

20

SESSHIN

My first Summer Sesshin began at 6:00 p.m. on Monday, July 2, 2018, and was scheduled to go until late morning the following Sunday. It happened to include the Fourth of July holiday, so, as the week of intensive training approached, a few fireworks could be heard booming from the wooded side streets of the Kalihi neighborhood. They wouldn't ever really pick up in earnest, I was reassured, maybe just a few sounding off at most. Since Hawai'i had been illegally annexed in 1898 and then had only just become a state in 1959, American Independence Day wasn't nearly as big a day for celebration as New Year's, which reflected the strong Asian influence on the islands. Everyone would be saving up their stockpile (especially the large, illegal aerials) for then.

The whole temple buzzed with activity in the days leading up to sesshin. Pulling the training off was truly a community effort, and different groups took on preparing the kitchen and the grounds, moving equipment around, washing all the cushion covers, and making seating and sleeping arrangements. Even six months into my time at the temple, I rarely felt confident in what to expect next. It felt like I just ran from one assigned task to another. So, it was only on that Monday that I finally looked up long enough to realize that my first sesshin was upon me. Even just ten minutes before the 6:00

p.m. sitting, I was still changing out of my blue jumpsuit and into my gi and hakama at a leisurely pace. I arrived at the entrance to the Budo Dojo only to realize that everyone had already been in their seats for some time. I sheepishly took my seat next to the jiki and then remembered that the sitting formally began at six, whereas, during our regular training schedule, there was no opening bell for the first sitting.

Thirty minutes after the jiki hit the taku and the bell, he held his hands in gassho, and I exited as usual to ring the bell, bring in the incense, turn on the lights, and hit the han. This time, I was accompanied out the door by two other students who were to be our meal servers, or *handaikan*, who headed to the kitchen. I finished up the sequence on the han, and, instead of the jiki hitting the bell with the last hit of the han, a different senior student hit together the two giant, wooden taku that usually hung on the wall outside the Budo Dojo. These taku were four or five times the size of the ones that lived on the jiki stand. They made a massive sound as they were hit in a set sequence I had come to recognize. It was the same sequence that we hit on a flat metal gong outside the kitchen called the *un-pan* once in a while so that, wherever you were on the grounds, you would know that lunch was served.

The simple tea ceremony that marked the beginning of training that followed was my first taste of what the rest of sesshin would be like. With an even sharper feel than our day-to-day training, the jiki announced for everyone to sit in seiza. Very few of the participants had done sesshin before, and most had even less experience training than I did, so they moved slowly and uncertainly.

"Hurry up! Sit seiza!" the jiki yelled, and everyone picked up the pace. I walked quickly to get back to my seat, while the jiki rose to place Roshi's cushion at the front of the room, something I had been instructed to do earlier but had already forgotten. The air that permeated the beginning of sesshin was bright and clear, but it had the ability to catapult the mind clear into confusion.

"Pick up your teacups," the jiki instructed as he returned to his seat. We all reached behind us and to the right to pick up the small white and blue teacups sitting behind our cushions and on a small square of paper. I grabbed mine, as well as a second set for the jiki.

Loud-soft-soft. Loud! cracked the taku now, and on the second loud hit, the jiki hit the fast sequence on the bell that I recognized from okyo class as the signal to stand up. In a somewhat Pavlovian response, I got up, and anyone else who was lagging, wondering what came next, followed my lead. Then, still in sync with the big taku, the jiki hit the bell one more time, signaling us to bow and then start walking. Getting in line in order just as we did during kinhin, we walked to the center of the room. As our line snaked forward, the other side of the room followed, and when we came to a stop, we found ourselves standing opposite one another in two straight lines flanking the center of the dojo. More confusion followed as we bowed one more time and the jiki started to sit down in seiza. Some people knew to put their cups behind them, while others put theirs in front of them. It seemed like such a simple thing—sit down and put your cup behind you—but in the tense atmosphere of sesshin, even in just these earliest moments, most of us looked lost, eyes wide like deer in the headlights. We'd become blind to what would otherwise seem so simple and obvious, right in front of us, and to the cardinal rule at the Dojo: pay attention.

"Put your cups behind you!" the jiki finally barked. Everyone did so and then sat mutely again, wondering what would happen next.

Finally, Sayama Roshi walked in—slowly, seriously, and with a slack, intimidating expression on his face. He walked past us, without acknowledgment, straight to the butsudan, where he lit one stick of incense and placed it into the bowl of ashes before bowing and then turning around to sit at his cushion. As soon as he sat down, he said, "*Hai!*" and the jiki and more experienced students immediately bowed. The rest of us followed. When some unknowingly sat back up, Roshi boomed, "Stay down!" And then his voice softened, and he proceeded to tell us in a surprisingly grandfatherly manner what to expect of this sesshin.

"Sesshin means to focus the mind," he said. He encouraged each and every one of us to give this precious time of intense training everything we had. "Think of it as a vacation from thinking," he said. Though he conceded that sesshin would be very difficult, designed to push us past our self-imposed limitations, he encouraged us to recognize how luxurious it also was to take a week off work to develop ourselves and catch a glimpse of our True Nature.

"Everything is taken care of: the schedule, the food. You don't have to make any decisions. You only have to train hard," he concluded.

After one last word of encouragement, he again said, "Hai!" and all of us raised our heads and sat in seiza. Most of us were starting to get the picture: if in doubt, just follow the jiki. As he reached behind him to pick up his cup and piece of paper, we did the same. More corrections were soon to follow though, as not everyone noticed that the jiki's cup was placed so that the side bearing a design faced away from oneself, and the piece of paper was to the left of the cup.

As cups and papers were hurriedly rearranged, one of the students working in the kitchen stepped forward bearing a small tray with a special, lidded porcelain cup and a *senbei* (rice cracker) in a cellophane wrapper. He held the tray up over his head and, coming to a stop in front of the roshi, bowed to him with the tray still aloft. Sitting down seiza, he brought the tray down in front of him and then served the senbei and the teacup. Rising and lifting the tray overhead again, he bowed one more time before taking his leave. Then the handaikan raced to the front of the room carrying trays of more senbei. We new students hesitantly reached for the senbei, only some understanding that we were to put them on the paper in front of us, while those who did not catch on earned yet more scoldings. Then, the handaikan returned for a second pass, each carrying a brass-colored tea pot. As they sat down seiza in front of us, our job was to swiftly pick up our teacups and then, holding them in our left palms, proffer the cups to the handaikan to receive some tea. Our right hands were to be held palm side up just to the right of the tea-cup. If we had paid attention and accurately mimicked the jiki, we flicked our wrists when just a little tea was in the cup to signal that the handaikan should stop pouring. This being the first night and many of us being new to sesshin, we were cut some slack so that, if we failed to give the signal, the handaikan stopped pouring at a rea-sonable time. We were told that, on subsequent nights, they would just keep pouring if we forgot to signal, even if that meant tea over-flowed from our cups and onto the tatami.

Finally, when everyone, including the handaikan and the *tenzo*, or cook, were seated at the back of the dojo and had a senbei and tea in front of them, Roshi leaned down to pick up his cracker. Every-one followed but then halted in a moment of utter confusion when the roshi stuck his senbei into the billowing sleeve of his robes. We were wearing gi and hakama and had no such wide, spacious sleeves; there was nowhere like that to put our senbei. The cellophane wrappers crinkled as some tried to shove them into their narrower sleeves. Finally, though, enough of us saw the jiki sticking his into the front left panel of his gi, which, like all of ours, wrapped around the front of our torsos and then was secured in place by a small tie. This left an opening at the front, above and below the tie, where we could reach in and stow all manner of things, including our senbei. I caught on and then watched to see if everyone else did. I noticed an older man in the other line managing to barely stuff his senbei into his shirt sleeve. I didn't dare signal to him to do otherwise, but he didn't look in my direction anyway.

Next, it was time to drink the tea. We followed Roshi as he picked up his teacup with both hands and drank from it in three sips. As we all went to put our cups back down, the senbei fell with a crinkling pat sound out of the older man's sleeve, but he was so preoccupied with what came next, putting the teacups away again behind us, that he didn't notice.

"Mike, pick up your senbei," the jiki ordered. Several other people pointed at it sitting on the floor before he finally saw it. The rest of the way back to his cushion, as we all rose and marched back to our seats together, he held the senbei in his outstretched hand in a way that reminded me of a little boy.

The jiki said, "Hai!" again, and we all knew to put our heads down and, this time, to stay down. What followed was a short speech on the rules and regulations of the sesshin, and I paid particular attention to the part where we were encouraged to seek out the roshi day or night if we had a question about our training.

Zazen followed, then *sosan*, which was the name for the opening night of sanzen. Now, with so many newer students attending sesshin, I was their senpai, ringing the sanzen bell and bringing new students to Sayama Roshi for their first meetings. After this, Roshi returned to the Budo Dojo to give *teisho*, which he explained was not a lecture but a time at which the roshi demonstrated his realization to the Buddha and to Tanouye Rotaishi, who was represented by his memorial tablet inside the butsudan. Sometime during his teisho, a single firework boomed across the sky, the frighteningly loud noise suddenly pealing across the entire valley.

"What was that?" Sayama Roshi asked, laughing, though he remained composed and unperturbed.

Following teisho, there was more zazen, and even after the closing sequence to signal the end of formal training for the day, more zazen still was expected; we were to continue free training until midnight. Just like my all-night training five months before, I followed a schedule, this time alternating between periods of zazen and ceramics. Shortly after midnight, having brushed my teeth and washed my face but still dressed in my gi and hakama, I laid two zabuton on the tatami in the Budo Dojo, taking care to place them so I wasn't directly underneath the rafters. High above us, the geckos ran along them through the night, sending their refuse down to the floor below. It was wise to be out of their range.

All around the Budo Dojo, more zabuton and sleeping bags were arranged as we all prepared for sleep. It had been a long night of training, and we still had six more days and five more nights to go. The next morning, we would be up at 4:30 a.m. and then back in the room at 4:45 a.m. for a serving of sour pickled plum tea to begin a long day of training. Someone's snoring woke me at some point in the night, along with the sounds of people stirring in their sleeping bags or ducking out the door to go to the bathroom. We were all, it seemed, a little too excited to sleep soundly. After a few more days of intensive training, though, with only a maximum of four and a half hours allotted for sleep each night, we would find that as soon as midnight came, we slept like the dead.

21

2 − 1 = 3

"You have this hang-up where you think because you're tired, your brain doesn't work," the jiki lectured me. We were walking on the gravel path in between two of the longer sitting periods of sesshin. I had heard stories about how monumentally hard sesshin could be for a beginner, and I was indeed finding it challenging. In particular, it was astoundingly difficult to stay alert and to anticipate which among the many forms of sesshin came next.

So, *Why yes*, I thought in response, *that's exactly it*.

The days during sesshin were exhausting. On top of the little sleep and long hours of meditation, we ran through a gauntlet of formal activities that all required keeping track of an impossible number of details and tasks. During certain sittings, the candles and incense inside the butsudan had to be lit. But during others, they did not. The okyo equipment and taiko drum had to be uncovered and set up at specific times, and porcelain teacups and small squares of paper had to be placed behind our cushions for each of the two tea ceremonies performed each day. Papers, brushes, and inkwells all had to be set up for calligraphy in the mornings, just before breakfast. Cushions had to be moved for teisho. A seemingly endless list of forms governed our every activity.

After the first day or two, the forms were no longer announced, and few instructions were given. Instead, we were all pushed to remember or intuit what came next, which often resulted in chaotic scenes of people rushing around the dojo, either in a daze or like chickens with their heads cut off, but always under the discriminating gaze of the jiki. He might bark orders at us if we got things wrong, but at other times, he might just repeatedly observe, "That's not it," goading us to figure out what was wrong but without revealing the solution. The harshest scoldings came when we were caught standing still while others worked. All the scoldings and corrections, which came not only from the jiki but also from Roshi and senior students, were harsher even than what I had become accustomed to day to day. Full-throated yells were delivered across the dojo, and their language was even sharper and more direct.

The meals, eaten while sitting on the floor, were also very formal. They required that we assiduously observe Sayama Roshi and the handaikan, the latter of whom blew by our tables bearing pots of rice and miso soup and baskets of vegetarian sides. Each time they approached, I learned to quickly finish eating and put my *hashi*, or chopsticks, down on the table—but silently, lest I be scolded for making noise. There were right and wrong ways to hand over one of my small lacquer bowls so that only I touched the rim of the bowl, from which I drank soup or the hot, astringent tea used to clean our bowls at the end of each meal. And there were specific ways to signal with my hands that I would like to be served and how much food I wanted to take, without exchanging any words at all. Finally, at the end of each meal, the handaikan would march up, a folded rag held high overhead, to wipe the tables down end to end. Some people dawdled or zoned out, staring into their laps, and failed to put their bowls and hashi away in time. In those rare cases, utensils would go flying onto the tatami mats, the student to whom they belonged at a loss as to what to do next. That was, until they were scolded to pick up their things and put them away, as they were holding up the end of the meal and our return to our cushions.

Some of these forms I thought I had managed to pick up well. I had already been serving in the role of jokkei for months. But now there were extra times to go hit the han, my only cue for these being such subtleties as hearing Sayama Roshi's footsteps approaching on the gravel before morning chanting or at the end of the evening tea.

I took myself to be on the brink of collapse in every sitting, unsure if I would make it through because of the pain in my legs. I found myself wondering many times a day if I could go on and at other times was in a sleepy stupor, the gears of my brain grinding to a halt. As far as I understood it, there was a clear mathematical equation that tied together lack of sleep, physical exhaustion, and mental fog. I was sure that I simply could not pay more attention than I already was nor remember more of the forms than I already did. It did not occur to me to glean some wisdom, or at least tricks, from the senpai who had done sesshin more times than I had and seemed to know their ways around. My condition of dull empty-mindedness, always on my heels, felt like nothing less than incontrovertible and irreversible, the only way that things could possibly be in that moment.

The jiki's criticism—that I believed that, just because I was tired, my brain shouldn't work—was delivered in a withering tone. I could do nothing but stare back at him blankly.

"You have to let go of that," he said.

I wasn't sure what he meant. *Let go of being tired? Let go of my brain not working? How was that even possible?*

"Do whatever you have to do," he continued, as if reading my mind. "Look up, look at the sky. I can't describe to you how bad it is when you're sitting at lunch or walking around with your head down, just looking at the ground. You don't think other people in there are having a hard time? Trust me, they're having a worse time than you."

His last words cut deep, and I felt a familiar sense of guilt. He was right. Most of the people sitting this sesshin had done less training than I had. Others were older, with less energy and more physical limitations. I understood immediately that staring down at my lap in a posture of self-defeat would only make those around me feel worse. Because many new students had come through the gates after me these past six months, suffering through zazen and okyo in the way the jiki now described me, I knew what a terrible drag it was to have someone around, broadcasting their self-pity and sucking all the resolve out of the room.

"Stop feeling bad for yourself, and stop wasting all that energy," he concluded and walked away.

His advice to just let go of my exhaustion sounded impossible. I thought it was simply a biological fact that, as I became more tired, I would become more forgetful, absent-minded, and morose. And yet, whether it was all the zazen we were doing or the amplified kiai of all of us training hard together, something inside me said that I should still try to figure out what he meant.

Just do it, I thought to myself, not stopping to consider whether I believed that I *could* do it.

Why not? I thought. *Just let it go.*

Sesshin had already been one long string of impossible moments. I had survived sittings I'd told myself were unsurvivable. I had begun to intuit some of the sesshin forms even though their logic utterly eluded me. And despite the discouraging narrative in my head that I was too tired and that I could not go on, I still managed to see the end of each day. Wasn't the very purpose of our training to venture the impossible, aiming to become enlightened and realize our True Selves? So much that had seemed impossible over the past few days, I had actually achieved. Why not then try to do one more impossible thing?

I fixed my resolve and became set on simply stopping in its tracks the voice that whined, "I'm so tired," whenever I heard it. I wouldn't give it an inch. Every time it came up, I would look up, see 180 degrees, feel my feet on the ground, and set my hara. I would not tolerate feeling bad for myself. I would fight the urge to collapse my posture and just think, *I'm so tired. I'm so tired. I can't do this.* No matter what, I would be chipper, indefatigable. Having decided on my course of action, as wishful as it seemed, I returned to the Budo Dojo to give it my all.

And, miraculously, it worked.

I could scarcely believe that I had simply wished my fatigue and brain fog away and effectively seen it disappear. That was kind of all there was to it. I had simply decided that I would no longer be bogged down with those negative thoughts and committed myself to challenging them whenever they arose. For the remaining days of sesshin, I found myself to be brighter and more energetic, even while I should have been getting more and more run down. The voice inside me eventually didn't need fighting anymore; it more or less disappeared. No longer was my head filled up with a repeating chorus of discouragement and self-doubt. When I stopped to reflect, I realized that I felt good, and my face was bright. This wasn't torture or even all that unpleasant. I realized, in fact, that having overcome this seemingly insurmountable obstacle through the combined power of meditation, community, and everything else we were doing, I was coming to unequivocally love sesshin.

"I don't know how you're doing it," another student later said to me. This was his second or third sesshin, and he looked rough. "I'm completely wrecked, but you're untouched."

I faltered at trying to explain what I had figured out. But then, I remembered something that Michael had said to me on a previous day when I had been flagging quite badly. It was something about how, if I were to let go of my tiredness and stop holding back, it would become possible to expend energy but still be all right. If it were a math equation, he said, it would be something like $2 - 1 = 2$. With a twinkle in his eye, he'd gone even further and said that it was also possible that $2 - 1 = 3$. I had understood that he was alluding to the potential of tapping into something greater than myself—the

Kozen no Ki, or energy of the universe. By dropping my deeper habits and self-imposed limitations, I could give energy without depleting myself or perhaps even feel more energized by giving energy to others.

I tried to put it into more practical terms: Leading the Kendo warm-ups in the afternoons, I made my voice loud and crisp, and it was evident that everyone else perked up in response, which only made me feel better still. Instead of walking from one place to another, I ran. Whenever I realized that there was a chance for more kiai, I brought more kiai. I couldn't explain why it worked beyond this, only that it did.

By the end of sesshin, I could tell that this same student had been picked up in the current of sesshin, coming out bright and shiny just like everyone else. But I could see that he had not been able to break the code of kiai and $2 - 1 = 3$ for himself. Now that I had figured it out, though, it seemed straightforward. I knew that I had been lucky to get the advice at just the right moment, when I was in the right condition to be able to give it a sincere try, turning the dial up to eleven without hesitation. I also gave credit to Michael and my senpai, noting the gulf between how their advice and mine had been received. I may have figured some things out for myself, but I was not yet in any position, it seemed, to teach or share it with others.

Zen students often romanticize the esoteric idea of "dying the Great Death"—that is, letting go of our egos and our attachments to experience the death of our small selves. This is something that is often repeated in Zen books and lectures, and we are prone to thinking of it in grandiose terms. But learning to silence the self-pitying voice saying, "I'm so tired," during my first sesshin was a real, practical version of this Great Death, albeit writ very small.

"You're gonna die like a rat," was a running joke about what to expect of one's first sesshin at Chozen-ji. I didn't know if the old-timers embellished their stories of the early sesshin in the 1970s and 1980s or if they were really that intense. Quite a few of them talked about the pain and the intensity of the whole thing being so extreme that they could only think about walking out of the sesshin or dying in their seats. Although he hailed from a later generation, Michael also said that he remembered wondering to himself early on if he would really be able to endure this and, in fact, if any human being could.

The following Sunday, July 8, sesshin came to an end. Finishing felt like a triumph. I had survived sesshin. But also, I felt that in this first sesshin, I had only scratched the surface of something, and now, I wanted to keep digging.

After cleaning up, including stripping all the covers off the zabuton and zafu in the Budo Dojo and running them through the laundry, those of us who were staying on at the Dojo endeavored to stay awake, at least until dark. One girl didn't make it and lay snoring, and we decided to leave her out of compassion. The rest of us busied ourselves as best we could, pulling weeds, stuffing the zabuton back into their covers, and talking freely with one another, all feeling a little goofy, emptied out, and vibrant. We laughed easily and found ourselves in a smooth rapport, able to read each other's cues, verbal and physical, after one week of training together so closely and after heightening our senses.

As the day wound down, some of the people who had come in from out of town gathered their things and were shuttled to the airport, though not without long, appreciative goodbyes in the parking lot. Those who had done many sesshin left with a more perfunctory goodbye. Sesshin was a part of their lives, just like visiting family or going in for their annual checkup. They had made the journey many times, and we could be sure that we would see them again.

22

THE WAY
OF TEA

Resuming our normal training schedule the morning after sesshin ended, I felt happy about returning to just another forty-five-
minute sitting, without several more hours of zazen ahead of me.
Sitting down now felt like something I approached matter-of-factly.
I held less apprehension as I set up my cushion. Also diminished
were my soaring, romantic hopes of a mind-blowing realization.
This was one of the most marked impacts of my first sesshin:
that regardless of discomfort or euphoria, I did not give a second
thought to keeping on going. Whether I realized it or not, I was
sinking deeper and deeper into the rhythm and the vibration of Zen
training at the manawa of Kalihi Valley. This would have been impossible if I had only stayed three weeks or three months or flown in
from elsewhere. Having completed my first sesshin, with more daily
training and more sesshin in my future, I was now entering a long
settling in, the training working on me from all sides.

After the sitting, everyone who'd flown in for sesshin departed,
and the regular cadence of training truly returned. Things went
more or less back to how they had been during my first six months:
the same schedule, the same responsibilities, the same people

appearing each day for zazen and class. This return to routine and my emerging matter-of-factness brought a new awareness of some of the merits and failings of my approach to training, and I found myself wanting to get more serious. It wasn't that I had slacked over the past six months, but I felt a renewed commitment to find more sincerity in all my training, whether it was Kendo, zazen, or anything else.

From the beginning, Sayama Roshi had pushed me to train in Chado, the Way of Tea, and while I had done it, I had also resisted. Little did I know that my resistance was evidence of the fact that Chado was some of the most important training I could do. After sesshin, I realized that I had been stubbornly sticking to a limited idea of what warrior Zen was, going to Chado class only out of obligation each Sunday. Being a Zen warrior, I had thought, did not include demurely serving tea, bound up in a kimono that made it hard to walk and breathe. Why, I'd wondered, couldn't I just keep swinging swords and moving rocks?

"Learn strength from Kendo," I remembered being told one day early on in my time at Chozen-ji. "And learn grace from Yumiko."

Some of my resistance to Chado came from the fact that I resented how deeply it challenged me. Learning gracefulness through its forms was, in and of itself, extremely difficult. More difficult, however, was navigating the complex social and political conditions under which Chado existed and the landmines of gendered and racist stereotypes I connected to it. At first, adjustments and corrections in class brought up a sense of failing in me—failing at learning the forms, failing to be graceful, and failing to be feminine. All this combined to create the sense that, in a strangely fundamental way, I was also failing at being a woman. My ego responded with a knee-jerk defensiveness, and Chado class often became a time for me to struggle with much more than just sitting seiza and learning how to serve or drink tea.

The ideal of being easygoing, beautiful, and charming while

serving tea brought to mind for me the racist and sexist stereotype of the obsequious geisha, who is often mischaracterized as a servant or a sex worker rather than a highly trained artist. As an Asian American woman, I had grown up with the hypersexualization of Asian women and the emasculating trope of Asians as a subservient race. Both of these were potent tools of America's pacification of postwar Japan, as well as the American military occupation of South Korea, and they traced back to the nineteenth-century view of East Asian women as sexual temptresses and carriers of venereal disease that justified their being barred from entering the United States. As an Asian American woman, my relationship to these entrenched sexist, racist, and imperialist ideas was complicated, to say the least.

Having grown up a Hawai'i boy in a different time, Sayama Roshi was not aware of, or at least not preoccupied by, any of this. But he had an intuitive sense of my carrying a lot of baggage—and that this baggage posed an obstacle to realizing my True Self. I needed to pursue both strength and sensitivity, courage and refinement, he said. This was why he assigned me to train in Chado. He wanted me to feel comfortable in my own skin and to truly be the master of any situation.

After sesshin ended, I accepted fully that Chado was going to be a significant part of my training. Only then did the grace that had been promised open up to me so that I could see it, both in and beyond the tea room. There was grace, I realized, in how Teshima Sensei dealt a blow with a sword and in how Sayama Roshi shaped his bonsai and the trees on the temple grounds. I saw it in the clean lines of Omori Sogen's calligraphy and in the ceramic pots displayed around the Dojo and which I sought to emulate in my own rudimentary works. Grace, I eventually came to understand, is not just gracefulness. It is another dimension of sensitivity and its related trait, sincerity. To be graceful is to exert influence in a way that can evade notice. This is 無為—Mu I, or the action of nonaction, which Sayama Roshi described to me as the product of successful

Zen training. My education in grace thus continued every Sunday morning in the tea house, and in the days after my first sesshin, I became a more committed and attentive Chado student.

For another six months or more, I focused in Chado class only on learning the forms—which step in the serving procedure comes after the last in what feels like an infinite string of prescribed actions. Even as a guest, there is a correct way to pick up the tea bowl, bow to it, turn it in one's hand, and drink. I also learned different forms for how to sit, walk, touch the utensils, and talk about the utensils. I started getting the hang of the basic forms, though Yumiko still adjusted my body and corrected my procedures ad nauseam. Then, once I had some command of the technicalities of Chado, the emphasis began to shift to the feeling rather than the form of the training. My new focus became refining my movement and learning to generate a warmth and a feeling of welcome that the guests could perceive.

It was around this time that I began to think that referring to our teacher as simply "Yumiko" was uncomfortably informal. As I took my Chado training more seriously, I wanted to address her in a way that reflected that seriousness and conferred more respect, so I began to call her Sayama Sensei in the same way that our Kendo teacher, Dick Teshima, was addressed as Teshima Sensei. One day, however, she told us that she preferred not to be called "Sensei." If we wanted to, we could call her Yumiko-*san*. That was akin, she said, to "Aunty Yumiko" and had a more collegial and friendly feeling. After all, she was only sixty years old! In her eyes, she was too young to be "Sensei."

"When you touch the tea utensils, treat them like a lover," Yumiko-san said one day in class, using what I would soon come to recognize as one of her standard teaching phrases.

"Oh, I love this tea scoop!" she demonstrated, holding one of the thin, curved bamboo scoops between her thumb and forefinger. She looked at it with apparent adoration. "When you put down the tea bowl, don't just use your arm. You have to use your heart," she said, slapping her chest for emphasis.

"Not just," her voice flattening to a mechanical tin, "I am serving the tea.

"We are not the robot," she continued. "I want to see some *drama*."

Our aim was to captivate our guests and envelope them with our kiai. To illustrate her point, Yumiko-san extended a tea bowl grotesquely, as if she were slinging slop in a cafeteria. Then, she did it again, and as the tea bowl touched down, her whole upper body bent toward it tenderly—as if the tea bowl had come to life, a little tea bowl baby tugging on a string tied to Yumiko-san's very heart. The long sleeve of her kimono came to rest on the tatami for just a moment before she pulled away, slowly.

We were often treated to Yumiko-san's creative turns of phrase and this kind of emphatic instruction.

"Like hugging the big tree," was how she described the right way to hold our arms as we brought the tea utensils in and out of the tea room.

While Yumiko-san was a serious teacher, like her husband, Sayama Roshi, she never came across as self-serious. Even in her more serious moments, when she admonished her students to train harder or went about correcting our forms, pushing and pulling our bodies into the right positions, she was indelibly kind. If she ever became angry or frustrated with us, it never showed. Though she commanded attention, it was never borne of aggression or any kind of demand for it. Our respect for her arose naturally, an organic response to her poise, her kiai, and her generosity.

Through observing Yumiko-san's own comportment and through the discipline of Chado, I learned as much about Zen each Sunday as I did about the many components of the Way of Tea: courtesy and manners, aesthetics, philosophy, calligraphy, flower arrangement, cooking, and the tea itself. Because of all these cultural elements could be learned through Chado, it was sometimes called a multidisciplinary aesthetic journey. Chado originated in the sixteenth century as the discipline of a Zen monk, and it continues to this day to be a means of developing oneself spiritually. It is admittedly not always practiced this way, though. Yumiko-san herself spent ten years training more in the way that it is often approached, as a hobby and as something light and fun for Japanese housewives to do. But after spending a year doing intensive training in Kyoto, every day from six in the morning until ten at night, she surpassed what was called *Chanoyu*, or tea ceremony, and discovered Chado, the Way of Tea.

In Kyoto, Yumiko-san met men and women who devoted their whole lives to Chado. They lived tea. And now, teaching at Chozen-ji, she endeavored to show us how to do the same, staking our lives on our Zen and Chado training not only with vigor and strength but also with passion. Once we understood how to capture the essence of the Way of Tea, moving and serving as hosts with kiai, it would be all right for us to let go of the forms. She pointed to her friends from Kyoto who didn't need a formal tea room to serve tea and thus did Chado in all sorts of places and with all sorts of utensils—by a mountain stream or even on a subway platform. Of vital importance was not whether we did things perfectly but whether we had developed ourselves, transcending all those niggling, small self-limitations to be happy and free. That would then come through in our tea.

At the front of Chozen-ji, with the soft green slope of the hill rising behind him, stands the statue of Hotei, the Chinese monk who strode into the marketplace in the sixth century bare-chested, his belly hanging out from his robes, purportedly with fish in his sack and sake in his gourd. Sayama Roshi described him as someone who, despite breaking all the rules, had refined himself through hard Zen training and still upheld the Way. As he would enter the market, consorting with beggars and thieves, everyone around Hotei became enlightened. He is often described as having bliss-bestowing hands.

As my Chado training progressed, I began to imagine Hotei in a kimono serving tea at the foot of the manawa, the Hawaiian sacred energy mountain that is Chozen-ji. His arms held aloft like he was hugging the big tree. Touching each of his tea utensils like a lover. Bringing relaxation and the feeling of care to whomever he encountered. Carrying fish and sake, sure, but maybe also a few small sweets and some matcha in his sack and an old, cracked tea bowl that had passed through many grateful hands. Taking away any passerby's suffering and delivering enlightenment through a bowl of tea.

23

A WARM, PINK LIGHT

The tea house, the most Japanese building on Chozen-ji's grounds, embodies the warm feeling one learns in Chado. It was built as a place to welcome and house Tanouye Rotaishi's teacher, Omori Rotaishi, whenever he was in Hawai'i. What was once the Omoris' living room is now the tea room, with a ten-tatami-mat floor and an alcove on the south wall that is perfect for a scroll and a vase of fresh flowers cut from the grounds. Seasonal flowers bloom throughout the year on Chozen'ji's grounds—purple and white irises, white balloon flowers, hibiscus, orchids, and others. Constant are the bright pink and red azaleas that grow outside the Kyudo Dojo and the pale yellow narcissus irises that were Omori Rotaishi's favorites. A selection of calligraphy scrolls is cycled into the alcove throughout the year, displaying seasonal or tea-related sayings. The one most consistently on display during my first three years at Chozen-ji read, 茶禅一味 (*Cha Zen Ichi Mi*, "Tea and Zen Are One Taste"), and was written by Omori Rotaishi's Zen teacher and the abbot of Daihonzan Tenryu-ji in Kyoto, Seki Seisetsu Genjo.

When I first arrived at Chozen-ji, everyone sat zazen in the tea room on Sunday mornings and remained there for class. But as

Sayama Roshi, Michael, and my efforts to cultivate a new generation of students training at the Dojo picked up steam, new classes
were added to the schedule. Okyo and Karate established a regular
sitting in the Budo Dojo on Sunday mornings. Then, when there
was no longer enough space in the tea room to have the whole
Chado class sit zazen there, we began sitting in the Budo Dojo, as
well. It was quite a sight, the Budo Dojo full of people ranging from
sixteen to seventy years old. Though we hailed from various races
and ethnicities, we were all dressed in samue, Karate-gi, Kendo-gi,
or kimono. Everyone sat at full attention, unmoving for forty-five
minutes, and then, after the final bell and taku, we departed to train
in our various arts. For our part, the Chado class would return to the
tea house, first to clean and then to train.

The thumping of the Karate class on the tatami and the steady
rhythm of the okyo diversified the range of sounds now heard
during our cleaning and keiko. With the rice paper screens, curtains,
and sliding glass doors of the tea room open to the outside, these
new sounds blended with the gurgling of Kalihi Stream and the occasional bullfrog or rooster in the distance. Small birds would flit by
the windows, adding the soft flapping of their wings and chirps to
the atmosphere, their bright colors catching the light in quick flybys
beyond the open doors. The scents of wild ginger, Suriname cher-
ries, and citrus blossoms wafted inside depending on the wind and
the season. In autumn, I came to expect the descent of the bright
yellow leaves of the Albizia trees from the ridges of the Koʻolaus.
When the breeze blew, they gently floated down into the valley and
sprinkled the back of the temple grounds like a light snow.

Especially in the winter, when the morning air had not yet
warmed, the breeze coming through the open doors of the tea
room was cool and refreshing. In the summers, bands of sunlight
migrated slowly across the tatami. By 8:30 a.m. in July, August, and
September, the room would already be warm, and by the time class
ended, my face would be flushed and my clothes damp with sweat.

Sometimes, I would sweat so profusely when practicing being host that a bead of sweat rolled off my nose, only narrowly missing the tea bowl in front of me. In the winter, it was not sweat but *hanabata* dripping from the inside of my nose that I had to worry about.

One day after he had returned home after college, Yumiko-san's son Jackson came to Chado class and joined us in taking turns serving tea as the host and then drinking tea as the guest. Although he had not done much training in Chado, it was clear that he had inherited some of his mother's skill. But more than that, his upbringing by a Zen master and a Chado master produced a different level of poise and sincerity than what is usually found in people his age. Watching his *temae*, or tea procedure, made a deep impression.

It is customary throughout Chado for a host to make conversation to put guests at ease, explaining the calligraphy, flowers, ceramics, and sweets chosen for the day. But there are two times when the room is silent: when the host is making the tea and during the very last pour of cold water into the kettle. By the end of the procedure, the kettle is hot and rumbles quietly atop the glowing hot brazier. The rumbling is silenced only momentarily when the last ladleful of cold water goes into the kettle.

Although the room was already quiet that day, with a sharp training vibe as we watched Jackson intently, a further hush fell over the room as he poured the last ladleful of cold water into the kettle in a thin and steady stream. Everything was still. After seven or eight seconds the kettle began to rumble again and it was only then that the room came back to life. In that short interval, all of us had been holding our breaths, and it was as if time had been standing still.

When my turn came up next, it seemed that some of the kiai from Jackson's temae still lingered in the air. His spine had been so straight as he brought in the tea sweets; his face, so relaxed. His pace was measured—not fast yet giving a brisk and refreshing feeling. In this pleasant rhythm, everyone seemed to grow more still and attentive as the procedure went on. There was a pleasant tension, the kind Yumiko-san described as our aim, translating literally from the Japanese as "a good tense."

As host now, I found my mind clearer and less restricted than usual. I felt oddly at ease, and each of my movements flowed into the next with a calming, steady rhythm. I moved of my own accord but also felt as if I were riding in Jackson's wake. I found each movement carried out with some of his same concentration and feeling. I realized that I felt like some version of myself that was clearer, calmer, and less concerned with getting things right or wrong. That was Jackson's innate skill, Yumiko-san said, that he didn't care, though in a good way. When I was finished, Yumiko-san signaled her approval: "*Kekko deshita*," or "it was fine."

Over time, Chado gelled much more for me. The discipline was helping me make sense of Zen and of the changes that I felt unfolding in my own countenance. I found two things to be exceptionally helpful in this regard, supercharging my training and my personal transformation: wearing kimono and striving to embody *yasashi*, a word Yumiko-san described as the desired feeling in Chado.

A month or so after Yumiko-san first informed me that it was time I started training in kimono, she arrived at the Dojo carrying a long paper package. I knew that, by Japanese and local Hawai'i custom, I should refuse to accept it, but when I saw the two kimono, matching obi, tabi, *setta zori*, and other accessories, I could only restrain myself enough to refuse once, and timidly at that. I accepted them greedily, even though I knew that, for a well-trained Japanese person, this was like snatching the gift out of someone's hands before they were even done saying, "This is for you."

It was gratifying for Yumiko-san to acknowledge my progress and encourage me to go deeper. But what caught my attention most was simply that the kimono were beautiful. One was a light blue-and-white single-layered kimono with a pattern that resembled small branches or pieces of coral. The second was a lined winter kimono, brown on the outside and with a dark red, almost maroon, lining on the inside. The third kimono that Yumiko-san gave me, once the weather started to warm, was a pale white-and-purple summer kimono, thin and gauzy for the hot weather. For several days, Yumiko-san came to the Dojo just to show me how to put everything on. It was far more complicated than I'd expected. I was surprised, most of all, by how many layers of fabric and accessories it comprised. Three thin fabric straps were also needed, one to cinch the kimono tightly around my natural waist. The other two were later removed after the obi, which held everything together, was secured in place with a woven silk rope worn as a high belt. In addition to that and the undergarments beneath the kimono and obi, I also wore two Velcro belts and an elastic band with clips on either end to hold the tops of the undergarments and kimono in place.

Yumiko-san insisted that there was only one correct way to tie the obi: with my hands behind my back rather than tying it in the front and then rotating it to the back. And when I wound the obi around my body, I was to turn in place, allowing the long belt to rest in one place rather than drag along the floor. For five or six weeks, I put on the tabi, undergarments, kimono, and obi every few days just to practice. It took more than a year to be able to put it on correctly and consistently, without forgetting the silk *obiage*, without my obi falling down, or without tripping on the hem of the robe, which I sometimes left too long.

Training in kimono gave me new perspective on the function and importance of the objects of Chado, as well as the proper equipment required for all the Japanese arts. This included the importance of appropriate training clothes, which I had already understood to some degree by wearing the gi and hakama for zazen and Kendo. A hard panel at the back of the hakama supported my low back, so my posture was less likely to collapse while sitting zazen. At the same time, the straps wrapping around my hips and holding the hakama in place put pressure on my hara, providing low-tech biofeedback that I was sending the breath below the belly button and keeping my hara set.

The kimono went further. Everything about it, from the robe to the tabi, changed the way my body sat, stood, and moved. Because I couldn't sit cross-legged in kimono, wearing it on Sunday mornings meant sitting the full forty-five minutes of zazen in seiza. It was a feat to get through the whole sitting, and I often needed a minute afterward for feeling to come back to my feet enough that I could stand.

Wearing kimono, my posture couldn't help but be erect because of the way the obi wrapped around my midbody. Then, the straightness of my spine called attention to other body parts, like my arms, which now demanded to be held with the same loft. Wearing kimono also encouraged small, patient steps. Forward movement had to be propelled by my hara rather than by my head or my legs, and I found that it took conscious effort to move fast. Even if I was moving quickly, my center of gravity was naturally lowered, so I couldn't really rush.

Before wearing kimono, there were only rare moments in which I finally achieved the appropriate pace serving tea. At these times, I'd find Yumiko-san and my senpai laughing or trading knowing smiles, as they knew I was only moving as fast as my feet, which often fell asleep while sitting seiza in the host's position, allowed. As I rose and put the utensils away, the pins and needles in my legs and feet slowed me down to the right speed. The kimono similarly forced the right pacing, but with more consistency, especially as I got used to sitting seiza and my feet fell asleep less and less. This played a significant role in my being able to bring the right feeling of calm into the tea room.

Finally, the soft hug of the kimono was a constant guide as to where to put my mind—not in my head, which led to tense, raised shoulders and too much thinking, but in my hara. Unlike in the hakama, the kimono was tied around the upper diaphragm. The hara remained completely unrestricted, free to rise and fall with each breath in an easy, unbounded way. This made it much easier to access the second thing that greatly improved my Chado, which was yasashi.

Yasashi means easy, simple, kind, gentle, and tender. It feels, Yumiko-san said, like a warm, pink light. Yasashi often eluded me because I approached it conceptually, as an idea to be consciously expressed through the techniques of language and action. But what Yumiko-san described is best understood as just a feeling. Putting on kimono, the constant awareness in my core and in my hara, combined with a beloved regard for the tea utensils, brought up yasashi in me. I could feel it in my heart and in my body. It was a sincere appreciation and warmth toward the objects of the tea room, the people within it, and our shared efforts.

I began to listen anew when Yumiko-san spoke about how our Chado training needed to extend beyond the tea room—we were not just people who did Chado but "Chado people" now. And I reminded myself of her words, lauding the preciousness of being able to train in Chado at a place as beautiful as Chozen-ji and, moreover, for free—as Zen training at Chozen-ji has always been offered without monetary fees.

Yumiko-san's comments also served as a master class in how to push and even scold students with gentleness. I became more aware of my tendency to want to police the students for whom I was now senpai. Enforcing the rules was my nature and my habit. Like an overactive sheepdog, I barked, growled, and snapped at the students who came to train after me and were my *kohai*, or junior students. But yasashi was the key that eventually began to undo this tendency. Once I experienced what it was like to feel and to be yasashi with the kimono on, it became possible to learn to also be more yasashi outside of it, when I was in a work jumpsuit or even in my Kendo armor.

It may not have been meant this way when I was first encouraged to learn grace from Yumiko-san, but another dimension of grace that I came to see was the Christian sense of it, meaning undeserved favor and kindness from God. I felt especially touched with grace whenever I would visit Tenku-an, the tea room that the Sayamas had built in their home. It wasn't just the privilege of being able to train in this space that Yumiko-san had painstakingly built, drawing not just on her own resources but also centuries of knowledge and praxis. Nor was it that this was the space in which she had forged herself through hard training year after year, every ceiling beam and blade of grass in the tatami glowing with that kiai. It was also that the space and everything that took place within it was designed specifically to wrap me up in Chado's core principles of 和 (*Wa*, or Harmony), 敬 (*Kei*, or Respect), 清 (*Sei*, or Purity), and 寂 (*Jaku*, or Tranquility). Every aspect—the flower and the calligraphy in the alcove, Yumiko-san's choice of kimono and utensils, the day and time of a tea ceremony, the tea procedure, the handmade sweets, the ceremony's freshly whisked tea, and more—was chosen for the guest and for that specific moment. I felt lucky to have found Chozen-ji and Yumiko-san and had to acknowledge with gratitude all the circumstances and conditions of my life that had allowed and led up to my being here. All of it, I realized, felt mysterious and wonderful—like grace.

By the time all this was becoming clear to me, I had let go of all my initial resentment to training in Chado and now embraced it fully. I tried, though sometimes without success, to be yasashi all the time, in zazen and in class and in all the moments in between. I even tried to do the Hojo and fight in Kendo like I was doing Chado. For a while, that drive pervaded my whole life. And in this way, Chado lived up to its promise to be much more than Japanese tea ceremony, as Yumiko-san often insisted. Ceremony, she said pointedly, meant something like a performance. Chado was, rather, the *Way* of Tea, a path to knowing oneself and to perfecting a human being. I could not help but getting swept up in her passion as she emphatically explained this, again and again.

One winter, a few days before Christmas, Yumiko-san approached me with a gift. It was another long package, this one in silver wrapping paper with white snowflakes all over it.

"I don't think she got us anything," Sayama Roshi teased. He was right; I had no Christmas gifts for them. But Yumiko-san only laughed.

"Oh, it's OK," she said sweetly, putting me at ease. "Merry Christmas!" She smiled widely, from ear to ear.

Back at the Dojo, I unwrapped the package and stared at the cream-colored kimono inside. It was beautiful, luxurious, and pure silk. I could hardly imagine any occasion I'd have that would be fancy enough for me to wear it, especially since the majority of my days were spent sweating in a blue jumpsuit. The other kimonos that Yumiko-san had already given me were machine washable, so I could use them for Chado keiko, even on hot days when they would get soaked through with sweat. When I thanked her again later, she counseled me that I could only wear this one to a place with air-conditioning.

Already, each time Yumiko-san had given me a kimono, I had felt the weight of responsibility that came with it. I was becoming a senior student, taking on the obligation to share the training with others in the same way it had been shared with me, especially such that it transcended formal training. It bled into intimate daily moments like this, receiving a gift from and being lovingly teased by my teachers.

When I showed one of my senpai the new kimono, he looked at it and immediately knew my own mind. He smiled, looked at me, and, without missing a beat, said, "You better train hard."

24

"JUST CUT IT."

"Just cut it," Yumiko-san said. "You know what comes next, right? So now, figure it out: What can you get rid of? Then, just cut it."

Motioning with her pointer and middle fingers like scissors, she reiterated emphatically, "Just cut it!"

While I understood the words coming out of her mouth, I could not understand for the life of me what Yumiko-san meant. After two years now painstakingly learning the forms of Chado, both at Chozen-ji and at Tenku-an, I was again doubling down on my training. I began taking notes after each class and taking private lessons with Yumiko-san. I had, by this point, memorized almost a dozen temae, including the variations on the basic *hakobi usucha*, or thin tea, temae for the various seasons. I also learned how to use more tea utensils, like a shelved table called a *tana* and a long, formal board called *naga ita*. Now, in an effort to communicate more of the feeling of Chado and not just its procedures or forms, Yumiko-san was saying that something had to be thrown away. But what, exactly?

I had heard Sayama Roshi address this many times before—that part of Zen training was mastering form so that, ultimately, it could be transcended.

"But you have to master a form before you can throw it away," he reminded me.

Common throughout Zen and Buddhism is the idea that spiritual development can be experienced through everyday activities, which include the arts. But Chozen-ji is unique in the all-encompassing martial spirit with which training is approached and in the variety of martial and fine arts people are engaged in. Through this, I had come to realize that I really could learn to maintain my zazen mind with a sword at my throat—or a tea whisk in my hand. Almost anything could become a Way, from sweeping a floor to running a company, when executed by someone who understood what it truly meant to train. The idea of approaching everything, all of life, in this manner was illustrated by something Sayama Roshi often said—an artist transcends the form of their art, while the Zen master's art is life itself.

Understanding all this conceptually, though, was far easier than figuring out how to do it. I looked at the red silk cloth in my hands and the utensils in front of me in the tea room. No amount of intellectual knowledge of the history of Rinzai Zen or even what monastic training in Japan was like could help me understand what, in that moment, should be cut. I was being challenged, in that very moment, to transcend the form of Chado. I was also being challenged to transcend my attachment to various forms and to abiding by and enforcing the rules.

So I tried. I thought, perhaps, that I could intuit what to cut from the procedure in the moment. Without a plan, without thinking ahead, I tried bleeding one movement into the next, my hand releasing the water ladle or the flick of my fingers as I folded the host's red tea cloth. But this didn't work. Nothing came across as transcending the form. It appeared only like I was tripping from one step of the procedure into the next. Transcendence wasn't carelessness.

I struggled. Even at times when I would think I was making progress, feeling into things more than thinking, I would still experience setbacks, realizing that I had just completed the procedure like an automaton, each step carefully spelled out in a plodding, monotonous rhythm. Or if I thought I had just succeeded at cutting extraneous movement, releasing my Chado procedure from a mechanical attention to the details, I would be told after I had finished that it had just come off as rushing. "Just cut it" became my koan, second only to the "What is Mu?" that I was still trying in vain to answer in sanzen with Sayama Roshi.

Just cut it. Just cut it, I wondered to myself as I went through my days. I tried to approach it from every which way but only came up blank.

It finally fell into place on an unremarkable Sunday while I was washing dishes. Out of the blue, I imagined Yumiko-san saying, "Just cut it!" And at that moment, I remembered watching her make ceremonial thick tea for me a few days before at Tenku-an. Seeing it for the first time, I had been totally enamored with the thick tea procedure. I was drawn in by its additional ritual, the host breathing in sync as she just slightly creased and released her red host's cloth on each of its four sides to symbolically purify the four corners of the tea room. The thick tea was bright, emerald green and had the consistency of melted chocolate. Meant to be shared, each guest taking one small mouthful and then passing it along, the *koicha* slid languorously down the side of the tea bowl and left a slight coating of dark green on one's upper lip. The sweets that accompanied the thick tea were the pressed sugar kind, each one like a precious jewel and decorated to evoke a seasonal theme, though much simpler than the elaborate *wagashi* made of sweetened bean paste that Yumiko-san would make for her private students.

I remembered noticing something slightly different that day, even before the tea was served. Just a slight change that shifted my experience subtly but completely. It had been several months since I had last seen Yumiko-san in the role of tea host. With a steady stream of new students at Chozen-ji, our Chado classes had been taken up with each of the students practicing being host in a revolving scene. Yumiko-san's temae struck me as a stark contrast to what

I had been watching for some months. However, it wasn't until I was soaping and rinsing dishes that Sunday that I saw it all clearly, in a flash.

When Yumiko-san had turned around after bringing out the tea sweets, she had not paced her exit as I had learned: *Slide the left knee. Slide the right knee. Scoot once to the left. Rise on the left leg. Cross the threshold with the left foot. Exit.*

Instead, she had slid backward, turned, and rose all in one fluid motion. Later, instead of pulling the lid of the kettle toward her as she removed it, pausing slightly before moving it diagonally toward its resting place, her hand had moved in one long, unbroken, and elegant arc.

Another memory came to mind. Actually, both memories played as if I were watching them side by side. That very morning in Chado class, I had watched a new student as she went through the motions of the host procedure. It had only been a few weeks since she had started, and still new to the forms, she performed each movement with deliberation and a halting rhythm. She was completely absorbed in her own experience, a self-absorption that was understandable given the circumstances. But, watching her, I found myself falling to her level. I succumbed to the same frame of mind, absorbed with my own experience, mine taken up by impatience and aching feet.

Remembering them now, the kiai of these two moments dominated while the details of what had happened faded into the background. The labored, articulated movements of the beginner contrasted with the essentialness of Yumiko-san's. Sitting with Yumiko-san, I had been anchored there, completely at attention and present in the room with her. Even the boundaries and separation between us as host and guest fell down a little because of the "Just cut it" quality of her movements. With the beginner, I had become as focused on myself as she was on herself, and though we were together in the tea room, we could not have been further apart.

In an instant, "Just cut it" became clear to me, not as a rule for what aspects of the procedure could be omitted but as a feeling. I could not put it into words, and it did not lead to a clear plan of what I would do in the next class, when I had to demonstrate "Just cut it." But I perceived it clearly enough that it made me draw breath. I felt it like I thought maybe migratory birds feel the earth's magnetism—a faint guide, an intuition, a feeling of home. I knew that what I had to do now was just keep going, following it like my North Star.

25

ALIVE

By the time July 2019 came around—and with it my third sesshin, marking a year and a half living at Chozen-ji—I realized that sesshin was my new favorite time of year. Preparations started in earnest several weeks before. The tenzo in the kitchen planned the menu and stocked up on vegetables, several kinds of tofu, and all the invisible yet ubiquitous elements of Japanese cooking: dashi, shoyu, potato starch, sake, mirin, and sugar. Work projects were prepared. Various specialized equipment, like the low tables for eating meals, were taken down from the loft above the men's bathroom and given a thorough cleaning, ridding them of the dust and gecko excrement accumulated over previous months. Everyone pitched in, organizing the printed sheets of mealtime okyo, washing teacups, cutting the small squares of paper for the senbei accompanying evening tea, preparing the calligraphy equipment, and assembling the *jihatsu*, the sets of nesting lacquer bowls we would all be eating out of for a week, to be cleaned only using hot tea and a slice of *takuan*, or pickled daikon radish, after each meal.

Sometimes, everyone participating in a given sesshin would be from on island. At other times, there would be airport pickups to coordinate as former live-ins and priests flew in to reup on community and kiai. Seeing the ease with which people I had never met before folded into the rhythm of the Dojo reminded me that there was a whole network of people out there who had heeded Tanouye Rotaishi and Omori Rotaishi's call to do shugyo so that they could be the leaders the world needed them to be. These were powerful people, comfortable in their own skin whether they worked as government officials and executives or as artists and handymen. What they all had in common was the training, which made it so they seemed at ease, ready to respond to any situation, and genuinely themselves. Each time sesshin approached, I couldn't help but feel like I was witnessing some sort of superhero reunion, all of them reemerging from their ordinary lives where they hid in plain sight.

These people were not immune to life's challenges, of course, or its joys. They had babies, and lost pregnancies and children; they got high-profile new jobs and retired; they got married, and their spouses passed away or were lost to disease; they became grandparents and fought cancer. But through it all, they approached life with their belly buttons facing forward, cutting straight through their problems, as often with stoic determination as with smiles on their faces. Nothing, it seemed, was unmanageable for them. Whatever life threw at them was where they put their attention and energy, and they wasted little time on things that were unnecessary.

It appeared that they had broken through and let go of much of their baggage and habits. Yet they kept on returning for sesshin because there was always more to let go of and more training to do. Sayama Roshi would sometimes illustrate this while we talked story on the engawa. He spread his arms out wide to measure his forty years of Zen training and then indicated how the span of my few years could fit between just the thumb and first digits of one of his hands.

"If my realization is this big," he'd continue, gazing off to where the wooden planks wrapping around the building ended, "then Tanouye Roshi's was somewhere over there at the end of the engawa. And Shakyamuni Buddha's . . . who even knows?"

The point was that, unless we had achieved the realization of the historical Buddha himself, training was a lifelong endeavor that could just keep going and going.

Remarkably, these older students and priests in their forties, fifties, and sixties still had the energy and taste for training. It wasn't as if sesshin at this point was easy for them, of course. Some of them were slow to get up off their cushions, especially after the longer sittings. They were susceptible to the same fatigue that knocked us beginners around, and they would stoically nurse cups of coffee before the day officially began at 4:30 a.m. They felt it all. But in the face of the stresses of sesshin, they were able to keep their bodies and their minds remarkably relaxed. They would say that, of course, they were tired and their legs hurt, too. But they roused a deep well of spiritual strength to transcend it all and to be pleasant and focused through everything, which was a great inspiration to those of us sitting across from them in the Budo Dojo.

At one point during the sesshin, I was enduring one of the long stretches of sittings, a block of two and a half hours broken up into intervals of sitting and brisk walking meditation. I was in a lot of pain. So much so that it felt like I had to marshal everything I had just to breathe deeply, count my breaths, and survive until the bell rang. In my head, a thought—more like an offhand comment—about the pain came to mind.

It hurts so much, was all it said.

And then my own voice immediately shot back, *Well, I'm alive, aren't I?*

In a sudden moment of refreshing clarity, I realized that yes, I was alive. And moreover, that the pain and the suffering I was experiencing were certainly signs, if not the most obvious symptoms, of my being so. It dawned on me that this was one way of understanding the Buddha's first noble truth about suffering—that it is not a sorry consequence but rather a hallmark of the human experience.

Whatever self-pity and aversion I had had a moment before

evaporated suddenly. In that moment, I was able to let go of much of the suffering I had glommed on to my pain. I could now just see the pain for what it was—the pressure, the burning, the piercing feeling in my legs. Noticeably absent were the anxiety, alarm, and mental machinations that usually accompanied these physical sensations and made me wish that the sitting would end posthaste.

When, years before on my very first vipassana meditation retreat, I sat hard to learn how to withstand possible torture inside Burma, I had gotten a similar reprieve from pain as my mental concentration grew. But that experience was less developed and refined. It had been more ecstatic, almost like a high. This, in contrast, felt calm and measured, like a more lasting foundation upon which I could build. I had come away from that first vipassana retreat, more than a decade earlier, ready to proselytize about what a great teacher pain could be. Now I felt more measured. If I had previously been eager to court physical pain for the insight it brought, I now understood that pain was an inevitable part of life and not something to be pursued out of vanity. It was useful, and that was it. Pain was something to be appreciated for its potential to help me grow and transform, and the same, I would later realize, went for any other difficulty in life. If I could approach the challenges I encountered professionally, personally, and spiritually as opportunities to develop myself, I would no longer feel so beleaguered or overwhelmed. Instead, I could face whatever was thrown at me belly button forward, my hara set, and as if I were attacking life. That was, after all, the only thing that there really was to do.

When I asked some senpai about this experience of hearing my own voice in zazen, convinced that it must have been something special, I received only shrugs in response and was told not to dwell on it. It might just be a kind of *makyo*, what people called a hallucination or figment of the imagination. I decided to take what was useful and discard the rest.

What new insight I did hold on to reminded me of one of the

calligraphy scrolls Michael had been working on of late, 直心是道場—*Jikishin Kore Dojo*. It translates literally to "the straightforward mind is the dojo," the word "dojo" meaning a place to train in the Do, or the Way. But taken to its obvious conclusion, if the straightforward mind was a place to train in the Way, so was the whole of human experience. In other words, all of life was training and the whole world was the dojo. Every experience, painful or pleasurable, was fodder for training—or, as Sayama Roshi would call it, grist for the mill. Realizing this cast a different light not only on how to approach pain and suffering but also on how to approach all of life and even how to understand the purpose of being alive.

After running to sanzen with Sayama Roshi, I shared this experience and my new insights with him. But sesshin was always a roller coaster. The feeling of clarity and elation was short-lived, and just as quickly as I'd gained this newfound resolve and understanding, in a subsequent sitting, it disappeared. The next time I went to the sanzen room, I resembled a whipped puppy, again having pushed too hard in a way that Sayama Roshi described as *muri*, meaning "without principle, against the grain, or excessive." Where I had formerly found a distanced appreciation for pain and suffering as a feature of human existence, I was now wallowing in it.

I still had so far to go. The deepest irony, of course, was that Sayama Roshi's response was always to tell me to let go, relax, and be happy. I knew that he didn't mean that I should indulge myself or seek pleasure, but that if I learned to truly relax and be in accord with the Way, these other things would follow effortlessly.

After a year and a half, I felt that I was still progressing in my training and growing as a person. Knowing that I wanted to progress further still, I felt at a loss to find the motivation or clarity I needed from my own internal resources, yet I knew that my training needed . . . something. Some kind of boost. I wanted to find the release and freedom Sayama Roshi described, both for myself and for everyone around me. It was just that I wasn't sure where it could come from. While the training continued to be challenging, the long days at the Dojo were no longer novel. They also often felt lonely. There were seasons to life at the Dojo, I'd learned. There were times when we would get waves of new energy and students and other times when sittings and classes dwindled. While we had experimented with hosting one three-week training period for a group of six live-ins, there were also stretches of time when, outside of the formal training sessions, nobody except for me, Michael, and maybe one other person would be on the grounds.

There were also seasons to my training. The first few months felt like a rapid, upward climb as I learned new forms and became more familiar with this very different sect of Buddhism. Now I struggled to sustain the same energy and vigor through Zen training's doldrums. There had been big peaks, but there were also long plateaus and deep valleys.

One of the most remarkable things about Chozen-ji was that there was an endless variety of creative means by which students could be pushed and challenged. The arts were a big part of that, allowing us to attack our egos and habits from all angles—with brushes in our hands or swords at our throats. While we didn't leave the Dojo often, if someone ever really needed to release some of the pressure of the training, Michael might take them to the mountains or the beach for a vigorous hike or swim. If our training had gotten stale, there were always ways to shake things up, and we were given latitude to be creative and try crazy things like different kinds of projects and, of course, all-night training.

One still had to pull from deep inside oneself to find the motivation and ability to be creative and push forward, but I struggled to marshal that next big push from within. It felt necessary for at least a bit of pressure to come from something outside and bigger than me. It was partly for this reason that, one day when speaking to Sayama Roshi, I found myself blurting out that I wanted to ordain as a Chozen-ji priest.

The thought had kept coming up the past few months. Each time it had, I'd tried to banish it from my mind. Michael had described to me how he'd trained for fifteen years before ordaining, rejecting it earlier on in his training because he'd never felt like he needed the title; it wouldn't change how he approached the training or how he lived his life. The day that Michael was ordained, two other people ordained with him, both of whom had also been training already for decades and had said no to invitations to ordain several times. The way they described their own journeys to priesthood, it seemed as if I should reject the idea, as well. By feeling pulled to it and wanting it, I thought I was only indulging my own ego, grasping after the title like a merit badge or trophy.

"I know I shouldn't want it or think about it," I said to Sayama Roshi, the words spilling out of me. "But I can't help but think about becoming a priest."

"Why shouldn't you think about it?" Sayama Roshi asked with genuine curiosity. The tone of the room suddenly shifted.

"Well, because I shouldn't want it. Aren't I supposed to wait for you to suggest it to me? Otherwise I'm attached to it?"

Sayama Roshi smiled, letting out a small laugh.

"Actually, I've been waiting for you to ask," he said. "Whatever attachment is there will get worked out. I'm not concerned about that."

Oh, I thought with surprise. Especially after my internal drama, my self-doubt, and the ways in which I was convinced I was being egotistical by wanting to be a priest, this was not the response that I had expected.

Sayama Roshi smiled at me and then continued, "Consider it aspirational. It'll be good motivation for your training."

My ordination was scheduled soon after for the end of the following sesshin, December 2019.

26

MYSTERIOUS PEACE ARISING FROM THE GREEN WATER

In the fall of 2019, we held one more three-week live-in period and decided at the end of it that it would be our last. As the program closed, we were exhausted and wondered what there was to show for it. There was so little that one could learn in three weeks, only a tongue-tip taste of Zen. It was maybe only enough time to change just one or two superficial habits, like how someone walked or their posture. And who knew if, once people went home, these changes would last. Perhaps most importantly, only one of the participants in the two three-week programs we had run had been local. After the program ended, all our hard work to teach the basic forms of Zen training flew away with them out of the Honolulu airport. Only some small donations, basically enough to cover the costs of groceries and utilities for that month, were left behind. We had even had to send one participant home as he had proven too immature and disruptive to the group.

It was with far more caution, then, that we accepted one more three-week live-in that November, and we only allowed her to come because it truly seemed that she had a karmic connection to Chozen-ji. Like had been the case for me, she also came recommended, and there were too many odd coincidences and shared connections to ignore, including the timing of her being able to come out and train. A nonprofit director in her late thirties and a young leader in the Asian American and social justice communities, she was professionally accomplished and overall quite serious. Perhaps most importantly, while she approached being able to train at Chozen-ji calmly and with a professional level of composure, she also gave us the feeling that her being able to come and train hard was a life or death matter. Like me before her, she would also be the only new live-in during her time here.

Moreso now than with other junior students, I stepped into the role that my senpai had played for me. We spent long hours pulling weeds together, during which I kept a close eye on her posture and energy, offering corrections as well as the occasional bottle of water and granola bar. I taught her the Hojo—first, the Hojo Walk, with the shinai between us, and then the kata, one season at a time. During many of the sittings now, I served as jiki, and I would correct her and others' postures as I walked with the keisaku, sometimes also doling out hits when they were requested. I cooked for almost every meal, and though I made sure we always had ample rice, protein, and calories, no matter how much I fed her, the pounds kept melting off her petite frame and soon, she was muscly and lean.

I also took on the role of senpai and even sensei for others. Sayama Roshi, Michael, and I had redesigned the pathway into training for new, local students, and it now included a beginning zazen class that I more or less ran. It was through this class that I began to learn how to tailor the training to individuals and their specific needs. Some of the more promising students needed even more than the accelerative effects of the martial and fine arts and benefited from additional, creative measures. I invited them to join me for training outside of the beginner's class and spent extra hours in the afternoons and on weekends teaching them to yell by the stream, do the Hojo Walk, and do outside work.

In general, they were young, with great potential. But they were physically, emotionally, and spiritually frail. I took great satisfaction in helping them discover what their bodies could do and in witnessing their bodies transform as we worked side by side and as I plied their growing appetites with hearty home-cooked food. During our time together, they also found their voices. They learned to yell with resonance from their hara rather than constricting their voices so that they were strained and small. They found new vitality and senses of purpose, going from sluggishly pulling weeds in a circle to plowing through whole swaths of gravel until they were weed-free and sparkling with kiai. And, sometimes talking as we worked, they learned to take stock of their lives and approach their challenges and opportunities with a new, samurai-on-the-bridge, belly-button-forward kind of view.

Two years into my stay at Chozen-ji and approaching ordination at my fourth sesshin, I felt that I was being swiftly carried along by the stream of Zen training. I was still very much caught up in the currents of my emotions and mental machinations most days, and I was tired all the time. Sometimes, I felt like I was barely keeping my head above water. But at least I had a better handle now on how to swim. Up ahead of me, expertly riding the currents, were my senpai and Sayama Roshi. While I couldn't carry my kohai on my shoulders, I felt like they were at least able to stay afloat more easily with my help, and they could look in my direction and then beyond to see where their training might be headed.

During my second and third sesshin, I had served in the role of handaikan, or meal server, and sometimes also jokkei or *inji*, the roshi's attendant. I did so again as my fourth sesshin began. Being handaikan was physically challenging. To serve food during each of the three meals and tea during the opening and closing tea ceremonies every day, we carried trays and heavy pots above our heads and then sat seiza, repeatedly sitting and standing to serve all the way down the line. If twenty people were doing sesshin, that meant lowering to and rising from the floor more than one hundred times a day. This physical activity combined with the long hours of zazen and lack of sleep so that, by only the second or third day of sesshin, our legs burned. The physical strain and the level of attention that being handaikan required increased our intensity, and we brought a sharpness to the whole sesshin just by doing our jobs with more exacting efficiency. This, too, was a 2 – 1 = 3 situation. Out of necessity, we found ways to offload anything unnecessary. Because it was our job to open and close the kitchen, we rose in the morning before everyone else and went to bed after them. We were constant in seeking out ways to deliver the most impact with the least amount of effort. We had little energy to waste, and our attempts at efficiency in this regard included not wasting utensils, trips to and from the meal tables, food, and, most importantly, time.

As this sesshin progressed, I also found I had less energy and interest in conversation. That was how, at the end of the week, nobody participating in the sesshin aside from Sayama Roshi, Michael, and I knew that I was being ordained. Roshi said his closing remarks, and then the jiki closed the sesshin with two final hits of the taku. And afterward, instead of going into our usual informal breakfast, we immediately went into setting up chairs and cushions for the ceremony.

"Wait, I thought sesshin was over?" I overheard someone saying as I made my way out the door and to the tea house to change. But that relentless feeling of attacking the unknown continued.

As I changed into my white kimono, I was preoccupied with the upcoming ceremony and did not have extra space in my mind to contemplate what I was embarking on. I trusted in the guidance I was receiving from Sayama Roshi and my senpai, but personally, I felt like I was tumbling forward with only a modicum of control on the Path— not taking measured, well-considered steps forward. When I had asked what exactly it meant to be a Chozen-ji priest, I received two answers. Essentially, my job as a priest would be to continue to train for the rest of my life and to make the training available to others. In its highest form, this also meant stoking courage and removing fear.

Before I'd arrived at Chozen-ji, I had read Omori Rotaishi's biography, and I took special note of a section entitled "*Se Mu I* (Giving Fearlessness)." Omori Rotaishi recounts a story of someone asking the famous samurai swordsman and later Zen priest Yamaoka Tesshu what the secret of swordsmanship is:

> Tesshu answered, "It is entrusted to the Asakusa Kannon." The student at once went to Asakusa, searched everywhere in the temple and came to realize that the sign with the phrase "*Se Mu I*" (*Se*—give alms, carry out, conduct; *Mu*—void; *I*—fear) must be it. When he repeated this to Tesshu it is said that Tesshu answered "*Kekko*," (very good) and laughed.
>
> *Se Mu I* comes from the sutra of the Bodhisattva of Great Compassion (Jpn. Kannon, Chin. Kwan Yin). In the sutra the Bodhisattva Kannon (Kanzeon Bosatsu Makasatsu) gives fearlessness in the midst of calamity of any kind. Consequently people call this bodhisattva *Se Mu I Sha*—the "Giver of Fearlessness."
>
> The gift of fearlessness is the removal of fear or anxiety from the *kokoro* (mind, hearts) of people. To say it another way, to give fearlessness is to give absolute peace of mind. If the highest stage of swordsmanship is to give fearlessness, then without doubt it is identical to Zen.[12]

Just like Mu and "Just cut it," I knew that, rather than gaining just a conceptual understanding of this "Se Mu I," I needed to approach it as a koan. I could not just interpret it but had to struggle with it and embody it. Although I knew that I was on the right path, I was still lost as to how to actualize this. But I felt with confidence and conviction that if I kept training, it would get figured it out.

As the ceremony came to an end, Sayama Roshi gave me my rakusu and shared my Buddhist name, explaining its meaning to the small crowd. He finished, and the okyo began, which was my cue to walk over to my seat among the other priests. As I walked over, things didn't quite feel real. I was also still so unsure of what came next in the ceremony and, in a larger sense, where my training was headed. Scanning the people assembled, I locked eyes with one Chozen-ji member who had become like a sister, mother, and friend all in one over the past two years and whose father had been one of the Dojo's founding members. Framed by long salt-and-pepper hair, her face routinely startled me with its simple beauty. This morning, I was again struck by its glow and sweet arrangement of features. Exhausted and wide open as I always was at the end of sesshin, and with the emotions of the ordination on top of it all, I burst into tears. Never in my life had I seen anyone look at me with such understanding, pride, and joy, sympathetic to the culmination of years of hard work and self-searching that had gotten me here, including all those years that I had felt so lonely in my spiritual seeking and so lost. It utterly overwhelmed me. Here I was, supposed to be chanting and impressing those assembled with the contribution of my loud, brave voice to the row of other priests and giving peace of mind. But instead, I was sobbing.

"*Shu jo mu hen sei gan do.*" I could barely make the words out, which meant, "however innumerable beings are, I vow to save them." My voice was shaking, and tears streamed down my cheeks.

Thankfully, the ceremony soon ended, and I was able to pull

myself together. I was quickly led outside for some photos so we could truly finish the sesshin with our usual informal breakfast of leftovers, clean up, and send people home. With a fragrant *pikake lei* draped over my neck, I stood by the Hotei statue and posed with the Dojo members who had come for the ordination—leaders of the Dojo and the Honolulu community who were happy to see someone from a new generation taking up the same kind of training they had done decades before.

Looking at the photos later, I could still see the complicated emotions of the moment painted across my face, a frown-smile betraying the fact that I was still on the edge of tears. My size and presence expanded by the billowing black robes, I could not but notice how top-heavy I also seemed. Walking out of the tea house that morning after getting into my white kimono, I had forced my clothed feet into two tightly fitting setta zori. Although I had received quite a trove of items along with my priest robes, one thing that I was missing was the proper footwear, two wide and flat zori with straw-colored soles and white thongs. All I had, instead, were my zori from training in Chado. Compared to the priest's zori, they were daintily tapered. Instead of straw-colored and white, they were a blushing pink. Nobody said anything that day or seemed to notice, but to me they were an obvious wrinkle in my priestly presence.

After the ceremony, Sayama Roshi gave me a certificate verifying my ordination. Now, he said, I was formally in his lineage. On the certificate were the characters of my full Buddhist name, 緑水妙安 (*Ryoku Sui Myo An*), or Mysterious Peace Arising from the Green Water. Referring in part to my training in Chado, Yumiko-san had helped find the right Japanese characters that conveyed the nuances and depth of my full potential.

"It's aspirational," Sayama Roshi said, referring to the "mysterious peace" part of my name. When I expressed concern about not knowing how to do that, how to be the mysterious peace, which seemed just another way of saying giving fearlessness, Sayama Roshi reminded me that it wasn't a matter of doing.

"It's arising, remember?" he asked. Then, his eyes twinkling with mischief, he added, "Mysteriously."

27

WHAT A ZEN PRIEST DOES

I was still getting used to the ebbs and flows of people and activity at the Dojo. So this time, as sesshin ended and we immediately transitioned to a limited holiday schedule with a skeleton crew, I was again taken by surprise as the Dojo abruptly emptied out. Somewhat automatically, I went back to my daily routine of cooking, working outside and in the office, and training. It was only a day or two afterward that I looked up and all of a sudden realized that everything was over and everyone had gone. Perhaps I felt left behind as everyone else returned to their homes, families, and lives and prepared for the holidays. Having expected life after ordination to somehow feel different, I was also disappointed by the fact that everything around me seemed to feel the same.

Four months before, at the end of August, I had paid a short visit to my father in rural Virginia. He had retired there from New Jersey, seeking a quiet, country life. One day, the pastor of the small church across the street from his house came over for lunch, and it was with genuine curiosity that he asked, in his silver-tongued old Southern drawl, "Now, what exactly does a Zen priest do?"

As I had only a month before received the news that I was getting ordained, I didn't know exactly how to respond. I described our daily schedule of training and, in particular, the role that I played as senpai to other Zen students, helping and guiding them in their training. I talked about how each person was really assessed individually: *Was Kendo the kind of training this person needed? Or Chado? How is their zazen? Their posture? What kind of training trajectory did we expect her to be on, fast or slow?*

I also described how sometimes the jobs of the teachers, priests, and senpai was to give support and counsel and to push forward someone's development in life, not just Zen. When someone lost a family member or was launching a new business, we mobilized whatever we could, whether it was a reassuring word or a community of customers, to help out. Especially for serious younger students (whose numbers were slowly but steadily increasing), we sometimes made introductions to influential Chozen-ji members in whatever field of work they were in and in other ways helped to create opportunities that challenged and helped them grow.

The country pastor nodded with understanding, though he also seemed disappointed that my responses didn't suggest a more exotic vocation. We weren't so different, he admitted. He remarked that I could have been describing the pastoral work he himself did as a Protestant minister. The pleasant lunchtime conversation quickly moved on but, for months and, in fact, years afterward, I continued to ask myself, *What does a Zen priest do?*

I asked myself this as I went through my daily routine back in Hawai'i—cooking, cleaning, working, and training. It sprang into my mind while I was pulling weeds. While I was making ceramics. While I waited for a recipe to finish in the oven. While I set up the cushions in the dojo for zazen. While I updated the Chozen-ji website.

Is this *what a Zen priest does?*

In those same months running up to my own ordination, I also followed along on the ordination journey of a young woman I'd met almost ten years before. She had still been in college then. When we met, she was a passionate activist participating in a leadership program to build a youth movement for global nuclear disarmament. I had designed and run the program, and after it ended, we'd stayed connected. I still thought of her as a young college student interested in international affairs, so it was with a lot of surprise that I learned about her upcoming ordination as an Episcopalian Christian minister. She was traveling to England at the time, apparently part of her ordination process. Between pictures of the stunning cathedrals she'd visited was one post on social media, written in gorgeous detail and tastefully punctuated with praise to God and his divine grace, describing the process of picking out a custom-made stole from a specialty shop for priests. I gazed at a photo of the shop populated by mannequins wearing what looked like long, brocade bibs embroidered with biblical themes and symbols. When the young woman described the design she'd specified for her stole, she shared that it would be sewn with gold thread.

A few weeks later, she shared about teaching Sunday school to a group of children at her church in Maryland.

"What do you want to pray for?" she'd asked the kids, and they called out the names of various animals they felt needed prayer. She described one of the children coming up to her and whispering conspiratorially in her ear that he wanted to pray for the elephants. And then she ended her post with a beautifully crafted, almost lyrical, blessing for the children.

Yet another post documenting her exquisite priest-in-training life described her giving a guest sermon and being thanked afterward with cake and other sweets made by the parishioners. Her youthful face glowed in the accompanying photo above a slice of white cake and her black vestments, white collar and all.

In contrast, most days, my responsibilities as a Chozen-ji priest had me wearing navy-blue coveralls I'd bought online for sixty-five dollars. I did not give sermons, and although the local Jodo Shin

Buddhist temples did have Sunday services and Sunday dharma school, Chozen-ji did not. At best, during formal training, I put on my blue gi and hakama or samue. My priest robes, with their own touch of gold—but decidedly secondhand, not custom-made!—had been folded, wrapped in fabric, and stored away in the closet. There they remained for a month until it was time for me to stand for a scant twenty minutes at Tanouye Rotaishi's memorial service at the back of the grounds. And then back into the closet they went.

One time when I thought of this other young woman priest, it was not too long after my ordination and the end of sesshin. I was up to my elbows making potato salad. Later, about forty houseless community leaders from around Oʻahu would be coming to Chozen-ji at our invitation for a kind of summit. All day, I had been occupied with things like cleaning and stocking the bathrooms, moving folding chairs to the Budo Dojo, setting up a tent in the back, and making lunch. Mixing heaping spoonfuls of mayonnaise into the boiled potatoes and chopped celery, I paused and thought of my Episcopalian acquaintance, my sister priest in training. And I looked at the potato salad and thought to myself, *Is this what a Zen priest does?*

The holiday break at Chozen-ji was particularly quiet, with no evening classes and few people coming up to the Dojo except to drop off New Year's donations, cards, and gifts that slowly piled up on the kitchen table. After the summit ended, the Dojo again became empty.

The quiet lent itself to reflecting on the many students who had come through the Dojo in the past year. A few days before Christmas, I found out that one of them, a brilliant young local girl, was in the hospital. When I asked if it might be helpful for me to pay her a visit, I was told that yes, she'd probably love that. The first visitor's hours would be the day after Christmas.

I waited at the Dojo for Christmas to pass, thinking about the time I'd spent with this student pulling weeds, raking gravel, yelling, and swinging swords. The first time I'd met her, she'd barely been able to speak above a whisper. But within a few months, she was coming to the Dojo several days a week by bus, staying almost the whole day working and training. She had been beginning to open up. Her voice grew, and she learned to stand taller, appearing bigger and more vibrant each time I saw her. Each time she ate with us, she piled her plate higher and higher, a sign of her growing appetite not just for food but for life.

The day after Christmas, I drove over and navigated the maze of hospital wings and hallways, finally finding the wing she was in off to the edge of the hospital complex. Behind a heavy door at the top of a short flight of stairs was the reception desk for the wing, staffed by two local nurses.

"Hi," I said, "I'm here to visit a patient."

The nurse brought out a ledger to write down my name and the patient's. And then she asked, "What is your relation?"

I paused for a moment and could see the nurse taking in my appearance. I knew that I looked young, and I was dressed casually, in jeans and a buttoned shirt. Would she understand if I explained how I'd spent months with her patient teaching her how to train in Zen? That we squatted close to the ground pulling weeds out of the gravel, a healthy burn in our legs, the sun on our backs, and dirt collecting under our fingernails? Would she even know what zazen was, and could she imagine her patient swinging a wooden sword?

A long moment passed while I decided how to respond. And then finally, the right words emerged.

"I'm her priest," I said.

The nurse seemed relieved and wrote something down matter-of-factly in the ledger—maybe just the word "priest," I imagined—before pointing the way down a short hallway.

Once by the student's side, I found that there was little in the way of comfort or Zen wisdom I could offer. It felt like there was really nothing I could do beyond simply sharing my kiai, and most of the time, we just sat together, silent. My young student was out of it, heavily medicated, but she expressed appreciation that I was there. Later, she'd hardly even remember that I'd visited, only knowing I'd been there because her family told her about my visit.

Driving back to the Dojo that afternoon, I asked myself again: *Is this what a Zen priest does?*

This time, I answered back. Yes, visiting a Dojo member in the hospital was what a Zen priest did. So was making potato salad, raking gravel, doing Kendo, and shepherding a younger generation through Zen training so that they may better be able to face whatever challenges they encountered.

Navigating the turns of the highway under the towering cliffs of the Koʻolau Range, I realized that I'd been looking at this priest thing all wrong. All this time, I had been asking what being a priest meant for *me*. I had wanted to know how it might change what *I* did, how *I* trained, and who *I* was. I realized now that being a Zen priest wasn't actually for me. What was important about my being a priest was that it meant something to other people, like the registration nurse taking notes in the hospital ledger. It gave them a name for what I was and some understanding of what I did.

I could see, of course, that the responsibilities of being a priest were challenging me and creating new external pressure to train more deeply, which was what I'd hoped. So, in some sense, while it wasn't for me, it also wasn't *not* for me. But from that day forward, I looked at being a priest very differently.

If I had initially wanted to be a Chozen-ji priest because I thought it would make me fearless, I realized that, sitting in the hospital, I'd actually been plenty afraid—in no small part because I was so focused on myself and whether I could live up to the idea of what I thought a priest should be able to contribute. The path to fearlessness, I now began to think, wasn't in thinking that fearlessness was something I would attain or achieve. "Se Mu I" was the sign above the Asakusa Kannon—giver of fearlessness. To give fearlessness rather than obtain it for oneself, I reminded myself, was what a Chozen-ji priest did.

And how to give something that I didn't feel like I had? The answer was somehow in this fearlessness being so big that it could only be shared, not possessed. I would have to grow into it—if I tried to define it too tightly, whatever concept I'd arrive at would surely fall apart. Though its mechanics still eluded me, I knew "Se Mu I" had something to do with the definition of Zen that Omori Rotaishi wrote down in Chozen-ji's canon, which was that Zen is to transcend all dualism—life and death, self and other. I couldn't wrap my hands around how it worked and what it meant yet, but I could feel it in the way you might see something far away, just beginning to glint on the horizon. It was a beautiful and mysterious wonder that was unmistakably out there, and something to strive for, though not for myself.

28

THREE YEARS ON THE GREAT MOUNTAIN

News of the growing pandemic approached from afar. We read about it and felt a little closer to it than most Americans probably did, being in equal proximity to Asia and the continental United States. We were all relieved that, so far, no cases in Hawai'i had been reported. Our health care system simply would not be able to handle mass infections like those that were sweeping New York and California. The neighbor islands were especially vulnerable. As it was, people on Moloka'i, Lanai, Kauai, and even Maui and Hawai'i Island already often flew to Honolulu for medical treatment.

Rumors abounded about the possibility of a nationwide lockdown, so we were not all that surprised when the order finally came down. I knew that such a measure was unprecedented in my lifetime and had never happened at this global scale at any point in human history. So I wondered if my relative calm and adaptability in the face of the historic news was due to my Zen training over the previous two years. Many people seemed to be freaking out, making runs on the grocery stores and causing shortages. But Chozen-ji felt like an oasis of calm.

This isn't to say that we didn't respond appropriately. In fact, the Dojo immediately went into preparation mode. It was our good fortune that, right before the lockdown order, multiple people had accidentally purchased toilet paper. We were well stocked, if not overstocked, and did not worry about the panicked runs on all the paper goods and many frozen foods at the stores. We also already had a healthy supply of nonperishable food items, as we were always prepared to feed a crowd, and I began working through the expired and close-to-expired goods in the pantry just to see what I could make.

Because so much was unknown about the virus at the beginning of the pandemic, we instituted the same drastic measures that some doctors treating COVID-19 instituted in their homes. Every box that arrived in the mail or came from the store was wiped down with disinfectant, and only the people with the strongest immune systems were allowed to go shopping. When they returned, an open path to a hot shower awaited them, all the doors ajar so they wouldn't touch any knobs and a laundry hamper close by so their clothes could go into a hot, disinfecting wash.

We didn't see any of our local students for months. So, in April, seeing that the lockdown might continue indefinitely, we realized that only a hard pivot would make it possible for the training at Chozen-ji to continue for the foreseeable future. We had been in conversation with a young couple in Seattle for several months whose pre-COVID plan had been to come out for a three-week live-in in early April. We had all but assumed that these plans were canceled, but they let us know that flights to Hawai'i were still available and that they had been quarantining at home since before the lockdown even began with the hopes that, if they did so, we might still let them come. There was a seriousness and a sincerity to their approach, and it felt evident that being able to train in Zen was that important to them, that much a matter of life and death already, that they were willing to do whatever they could to get here.

Taking stock of the separate living quarters we had at the Dojo and the ample outside space on the grounds, we realized that we would be able to quarantine them for the required fourteen days to keep ourselves and the local community safe. They would just have to commit to a longer stay. Three months seemed like the minimum that would make sense, and they readily agreed. They arrived within days. And then, after their quarantine was finished, we'd basically doubled our numbers. Operating then as a household, the five of us had almost no contact with anyone outside the Dojo, which meant no chance of contagion or spread. This meant that we were able to return to all our normal activities, from cooking and eating meals together to sitting zazen and doing full-contact martial arts training.

Meanwhile, the governor of Hawai'i stopped all incoming flights to the islands. Hawai'i's tourism industry ground to a halt, and places like Waikiki and Hanauma Bay, usually filled with tourists, suddenly became empty. Food distribution centers helped out where stimulus money fell short, and the existing movement to increase our food security by growing taro, sweet potato, and bananas—food plants originally brought to Hawai'i by early Polynesian navigators—experienced a resurgence. Families who had always been at work or school started venturing out together for walks and exercise at various times of the day. From inside the gates of the Dojo, we began to recognize neighbors who timed their evening walks so they could watch us ring the Peace Bell.

After the lockdown ended, flights restarted with heavy restrictions, but they were restrictions that the Dojo could still accommodate. Seeing that we could safely welcome trustworthy people for live-in training, we allowed a handful more live-ins to come in August and September. These were all people who had either trained with us before or with whom we'd been in conversation for more than a year. Perhaps if their lives had not been so disrupted by COVID, they would not have been able to make a three-month commitment to Zen training. Maybe if it weren't for being confronted by actual life and death in the form of a pandemic, they wouldn't have wanted to.

By the end of 2020, eight of us were living and training at the Dojo, and our local students were beginning to return to regularly scheduled training, as well. We began group sittings again, though with masks, hand sanitizer by the door, and social distancing in the form of extra space between the zabuton. We took advantage of the extra time during the pandemic to take on new improvements we wouldn't otherwise have had time for. We built a new awning for the stairs in front of the Budo Dojo and renovated the kitchen, updating the electrical and appliances. When supply chain disruptions delayed the arrival of our new gas range by eight weeks, I made do with one electric oven and a giant wok heated over propane burners in the carport to prepare three meals and two snacks a day for eight or more people every day.

At the end of three months, the live-in period for that cohort came to an end, but they did not leave. All five of them had decided that they wanted to continue their training and deeply appreciated living in Hawai'i. So, after completing Winter Sesshin, they moved to apartments in Honolulu or simply continued living on the grounds, becoming permanent fixtures at Chozen-ji and stalwart Zen students under Michael, now Kangen Roshi, who had received *inka* from Sayama Roshi the previous summer. The former live-ins made plans to help anchor training once the holidays were over and came up regularly to trim the irises, pull weeds, and otherwise beautify the grounds before New Year's, the most festive time of year at the Dojo and in Hawai'i. For the first time since I had started serving *toshikoshi* soba on New Year's Eve, I had help topping each steaming bowl of noodles and broth with the traditional red and white fish cake, seaweed, and green onions. The former live-ins served the Dojo members, neighbors, and guests on the engawa, where all of us gathered to "talk story" and watch the growing numbers of fireworks light up the night sky. They also helped man the Peace Bell, guiding the way with flashlights, accompanying the kids and the *kupuna*, and keeping count so that the 108th ring coincided with the start of our New Year's ceremony at midnight. And when it was all over, they were there to clean up and to help restore that sense of quiet ever-readiness to the Dojo.

Not long after, following the return of regular Kendo classes in early January, we all sat around the engawa again, drinking in the night air and engaging in some social Kendo. Then, Michael cut into the chatter.

"Things have been so busy," he said, "that we missed Cristina's three-year anniversary of living in."

Indeed, I had completely lost sight of it! So much had happened in the world and at the Dojo that the anniversary had passed me by, completely unnoticed, a few days before.

"Oh, Cristina!" Sayama Roshi exclaimed. "Three years! We should all toast to that!"

About a dozen of us—teachers, local students, and live-ins—raised whatever we were drinking and said, "*Kanpai!*" Everyone's face was sweet. From early twenties to seventy years old. Japanese, Filipina, Chinese, Native Hawaiian, haole, Korean, Mexican, Ecuadorian, and Pakistani. High school dropout and PhD. Schoolteacher, construction worker, social justice activist, and medical school professor. What they said to me without words was that they knew how challenging it was to live for three years at Chozen-ji, which was in and of itself something that few others had done. But more importantly, I saw that they had no doubts about my continuing commitment to the Dojo and to the training. I felt warm and connected to everyone present, our faces flushed and bright from Kendo and from the pleasantly refreshing air of winter in Hawai'i.

"OK, Cristina," Sayama Roshi prompted, pointing at the other students, "share with them what you've learned from three years of Zen training."

If the anniversary had not snuck up on me, if I had felt in the weeks running up that a turning point was coming around the bend or a new chapter was beginning, I would have prepared some words. Really, from the moment Michael called attention to it, I should have known this was coming, since putting people on the spot to give toasts was one of Sayama Roshi's favorite things to do.

"Well," I started, "after three years, the thing that is most clear to me is that I still have a lot of training to do. Not that I haven't made progress, but now I can see what I need to work on that much more clearly."

I still felt so deficient and clung to the forms of training too tightly. I had not resolved my koan, "What is Mu?" I wasn't yet the effective teacher or priest that I wanted to be.

Then, thinking ahead, I added, "I can't imagine what it will be like to look back at ten years, or thirty . . . " and was poised to continue rambling on without a whole lot of direction.

What could I sum up from my three years? I wasn't sure. Not because I had not learned anything, though I knew that, if Sayama Roshi were to stretch out his arms to measure his forty-three years of training, he'd still be able to cover the span of mine in one hand. I had learned little, in that sense, but I'd also learned quite a lot. There was no way to put it into one succinct toast. Words continued to roll out of my mouth, and my eyes fell to look at the gravel and the rock garden in front of us.

Then, at just the right moment, Michael interrupted and saved me from myself.

"That sounds about right," he said. "After three years, now you should know how to train."

Everyone laughed, and I thought to myself, *Yes, that's it.* That was exactly what I had wanted to express. I just didn't have the words yet, though I could at least recognize them when I heard them. I hoped that maybe one day soon, I'd be able to express my Zen understanding so succinctly and effectively.

Satisfied, Sayama Roshi redirected the conversation. And if he was satisfied, I was also content to leave things where they lay. I could have been much more eloquent. I could surely have thought of something better—something more erudite and more Zen—to say, but this was good. And though I had so much more ahead of me, still so new and with so much more to learn, I was confident of the company I was in and the path I was on. I could feel the ground beneath my feet and where to step next. My breath was in my hara, and I knew how to see 180 degrees in every direction, seeing, hearing, and feeling everything. I took in the rich and satisfying life of training stretching out before me. I had the confidence that if I just kept training, putting one foot in front of the other, I might one day find that I had become the source of the mysterious peace Sayama Roshi and Yumiko-san seemed confident I could become.

That winter, Sayama Roshi began to push me to learn how to be a teacher to others. I had played some of that role when I ran the beginning zazen class, spent extra time training with young local students, and taught the Hojo Walk and the many other forms of the Dojo to other live-ins. Yet I knew that I was nobody's teacher. I was satisfied to be a student and to focus on my own training, knowing, of course, that part of my own training was to learn to help others. But teach? I was nowhere near that. Sure, I could guide someone in the Hojo and some forms. But what did I have to teach about Zen? I looked at all my own faults, and they seemed ample evidence that I did not deserve to be seen as a teacher.

"A teacher isn't somebody who's perfect," Sayama Roshi responded when I voiced all of this to him over bento boxes at his home in St. Louis Heights. "People have this idealistic impression that the teacher has to be perfect. And when they're not, they get disillusioned, and they quit.

"Clearly you don't think I'm perfect," he continued, flashing his signature, mischievous smile. "But you're still here!"

Sayama Roshi paused, thinking, and then looked me dead in the eye. The intensity of his gaze would have contradicted the boyish curl of his lip, but after these three years of living and training side by side with him, I was all too familiar with both.

"Cristina, if I disillusion you, you should just feel, 'Well, I'm going to be greater than Sayama Roshi.'" He paused with dramatic emphasis and then continued, "And don't quit. If you quit—for whatever reason—I'll be really disappointed in you!"

Our rowdy laughter filled the kitchen of the Sayamas' home. So much so that their fourteen-year-old beagle, Mia, stirred on the grass outside, looking up at us with her large, brown eyes. Her ears swung in the breeze beyond Sayama Roshi's bonsai trees, and she harrumphed before turning away again and laying her head back down. I reflected on how content I felt, fully engaged and so at home living a life of training and laughing with my teacher. It was true that, for the moment anyway, I was all the happier for his imperfection. It reminded me that, though he was my perfect teacher, he was also still a human being. Perhaps it was even his deep imperfection that made him the perfect teacher for me. Even roshi and abbots, I had to admit, were still works in progress. If life really were training, then as long as he was alive, that would continue to be the case. Which also meant that it was my job and mine alone to take responsibility for my own training each and every day and to never give up.

Sayama Roshi noted my somber look and laughed at me.

"Cristina, don't take yourself so seriously!" he teased. "You're definitely not going to realize your True Self that way."

I laughed, knowing that this perennial admonition to not take myself so seriously—but to still be totally sincere—was one of the most important lessons Sayama Roshi had to teach me. It was at least the one I needed to be reminded of most often.

"Your priest name is Mysterious Peace Arising from the Green Water," he said definitively. He then let fly his oft-repeated, immeasurably precious teaching, said with the same matter-of-factness with which he'd instructed me in Hojo, Kendo, and the fundamentals of breath, posture, and concentration over the past three years.

"It's being, not doing," he said. "Being, not doing."

I smiled and got up to put the plastic bento boxes and disposable chopsticks in the trash. I washed the small shoyu dipping plates and glasses and then dried and put them away, having learned by now where all the dishes went in the Sayamas' kitchen. Mia barked as I walked down the steps to the driveway, as she always did. She hated it when guests left.

And then, it was time to head back to the Dojo. As always, there was a lot of training to do.

EPILOGUE

As I stood in front of a sea of saffron, maroon, and black robes, I listed the names of the six Asian American women killed on March 16, 2021, in a mass shooting in Atlanta, Georgia:

Tan Xiaojie
Feng Daoyou
Hyun Jung Grant
Park Soon Chung
Kim Suncha
Yue Yong Ae

My voice broke as I said their names, and tears threatened to flow—not the image of spiritual strength that I had hoped to offer the thousands of people tuning in to the livestream of May We Gather, a pan-Buddhist forty-ninth-day memorial for those killed in the March 16 Atlanta spa shootings and all other victims of anti-Asian violence.

In the months before May We Gather, I had published a few articles in Buddhist magazines about the value I'd found in the martial and fine arts and in the other aspects of Asian culture that I had come to see as indispensable elements of my Zen training. When the organizers of May We Gather asked me to fly to Los Angeles, it was with the hope that I could bring some of that martial kiai to help the Asian American community repair what had been broken by a rising wave of violent and racist attacks. My assignment that day was to speak on the *paramita*, or Buddhist virtue, of *virya*, which is often translated as "meditative vigor." But I'd decided to describe it as "spiritual strength."

As I prepared what I was going to say and rehearsed walking up to the enormous, golden butsudan of the Higashi Hongwanji in Los Angeles, I wondered how I could bring people some energy, reinvigorate their depleted spirits, and give them some hope. Forty-nine days after the Atlanta shootings, the news of violent attacks targeting people of Asian descent, particularly women and the elderly, was not slowing. If anything, the attacks seemed to be picking up. People around the country were heartbroken, exhausted, and angry—and they were afraid.

Standing at a podium in front of several dozen Buddhist clergy and several massive cameras broadcasting my remarks, I encouraged people to find spiritual strength within our own Buddhist traditions and Asian cultures and in the courage exemplified by individuals within our community. But first, I gave my own appeal for the importance of spiritual strength as the first among the six Buddhist virtues.

"Without it," I said, "the other paramitas of generosity, patience, ethics, wisdom, or concentration fall flat. Without strength, our patience fizzles, our concentration is dull, and our ability to act ethically withers in the face of hardship or severe consequences. . . .

"We clearly need strength, in moments like these, to help us forge a path ahead through racism, patriarchy, and other oppressions and inequities. But we also need it to meet the suffering caused by injustice or just the vicissitudes of life with compassion.

"After an exhausting year," I finished, "many are probably wondering, where can we find such spiritual strength? . . . Well, we can start here, in temples and dojos like this. Here, we can forge our strength through the methods passed down to us, teacher to student, over two thousand years. We can learn how to take the hard experiences in our lives and turn them into opportunities for growth. We can train ourselves to transcend the dualism and separation that leads to suffering."[13]

As a COVID precaution, only a select number of us were in person in the *hondo* that day. Much of the Buddhist clergy—monks, nuns, and priests from many different countries and sects—were very solemn, so it was hard to know immediately how my remarks were received. But after the ceremony ended, several of the clergy approached me, enthusiastic to meet and with many questions about my training and about my temple in Hawaiʻi. The bishop of the Higashi Hongwanji even produced a photocopy of one of my recent articles, waiving it in the air and explaining that he had circulated it to his parishioners when it first came out.

I also received emails from around the country that my message about spiritual strength had been a kind of balm or, in some cases, a shot in the arm. They were inspired by seeing a young Asian American woman priest speaking to their experience and calling on them not to dwell on their grief but to find strength from deep within and from what was already around them. People said they felt ready to feel something more than just brokenhearted—they wanted to feel strong and, in the face of hate and loss, to find their fighting spirit. They were also moved by seeing my own expression of emotion, interpreting it as evidence that one could be both sensitive and strong.

On the flight home, I found myself thinking about my time in Los Angeles and then reflecting on the contents of my carry-on. It included the requisite *omiyage*, or gifts, for the folks back home, but most of it, about 75 percent, was priest robes. This was the first time that I had appeared in public anywhere outside of Chozen-ji in those robes, and the experience had felt daunting, heavy with responsibility. Yet even being a very novice Zen priest, I received all these messages of support, which told me that I did, indeed, have something to offer. They motivated me to go further and deeper and to share what I had to say with others.

If I had not had the title of priest, I would not have been invited to May We Gather. And if not for my training at Chozen-ji, I would not have been able to adequately fill those robes or the role others needed me to play. I felt that many more people could benefit from the kind of training I had done, gaining the courage and calm that is the result of deep spiritual training. I had seen these traits among my teachers and seen them grow with training in my senpai, fellow students, and myself. And not just the Asian American community—and not just Buddhists—but everyone seemed to need it, and profoundly.

Pathways for rigorous and immersive spiritual development—in other words, shugyo, the deepest possible spiritual self-discipline—have existed for almost all of human civilization. In the form of monasteries, apprenticeships, and the military, young people have long had places to forge their characters and their spirits and become the leaders the world needed them to be. As a young person looking for places offering this kind of training, however, I'd thought that they'd all but disappeared.

As Oʻahu finally became visible from the plane, its welcoming green cliffs rising above the vibrant, blue ocean, I felt overwhelmed by a deep sense of homecoming. It wasn't just a return to the back of Kalihi Valley that I found myself looking forward to but a return to our particular way of living. It's a way that is full and vigorous—one in which I feel strong on my own two feet and free, bound only by an invisible but unbreakable tether to the truth I see at the horizon. That truth is so big and irrefutable. It exists beyond self and other, life and death, and everything else that keeps us small and separate. And that, I told myself as the plane started its descent, was where I was heading.

ACKNOWLEDGMENTS

For anyone who helped shape my story and this book but whom I may fail to acknowledge here, please accept my sincerest apologies.

My Zen teacher, Sayama Daian Roshi, spent many afternoons in St. Louis Heights reviewing my early drafts and came up with some very creative means to make our deadlines count. Thank you, Roshi, for showing me what it means to be sincere and for being my perfectly imperfect teacher. Yumiko Sayama, Dick Teshima, and Terry Ueno—thank you for the many graces you've given me, in particular for your generosity in teaching me.

Thank you, Michael Kangen Roshi, for all your guidance and for reading every version of this manuscript, but thank you most of all for leading the way to Chozen-ji and for making a home for me here. None of this would be possible without you.

Thank you to my parents, Kunduck and Min-Hye Moon, for giving me an exceptional head start in this world in so many ways.

Thank you to Anna Knutson Geller of Write View and Matt Zepelin and the rest of the team at Shambhala Publications for shepherding my story out of the back of Kalihi Valley and into the wider world. My two writing groups—Peter Haas and Matthew Hahn; and Geraldine Abergas, Seth Colby, and Chad Kamei—were also crucial to making this book a reality.

Thank you to Bill Kaneko, Colbert Matsumoto, and Cathy Kawano-Ching for your enduring mentorship and support and to everyone at Chozen-ji who continues to make my training and my life what it is. I am grateful to Scott Kiel and Anita Taylor for being rare friends who can relate to the very specific joys and challenges of running a Zen dojo. None of us would be here if it were not for the vision, efforts, and sacrifices of Tanouye Tenshin Rotaishi, Omori Sogen Rotaishi, Mrs. Mieko Tanouye, Mrs. Yoshie Omori, and their families.

Chenxing Han has been an encouraging friend ahead on the path of both writing and combating the erasure of Asian people and cultures from American Buddhism. My grant from the Hemera Foundation's Two Tara Fund has been of great support as I have grown as a Buddhist teacher. And I have been waiting a long time to be able to thank Mr. Mike Brown in print for recognizing a young girl's karmic affinity for the Way.

My heartfelt gratitude to Noland Chambliss and Rich Robinson for being there when I doubted most deeply. And thank you to the friends who never forgot to think of me, even when I disappeared to a Zen temple in the back of a valley in Hawai'i. Nicole Aro, Michael Whitney, Ed Hong, Ivan Lvov, Natalia Lvova, Cindy Phan, Christine Hendrickson, and Andy Kim, I am grateful and lucky to have you in my life. *Mahalo.*

GLOSSARY

TERM	LANGUAGE	DESCRIPTION
-ka	*Japanese*	When appended to some words (usually the name of a martial or fine art), refers to a person who trains in an art—e.g., "Aikido-ka" means someone who trains in Aikido, or an Aikido person
-san	*Japanese*	A polite honorific appended to a person's name—e.g., Cristina-san
aloha	*ʻŌlelo Hawaiʻi*	As in chapter 5 of the Hawaiʻi Revised Statutes: "'Aloha' is more than a word of greeting or farewell or a salutation. 'Aloha' means mutual regard and affection and extends warmth in caring with no obligation in return. 'Aloha' is the essence of relationships in which each person is important to every other person for collective existence. 'Aloha' means to hear what is not said, to see what cannot be seen and to know the unknowable." (https://www.hawaii.edu/uhwo/clear/home/lawaloha.html)

aloha shirt	*English*	Light, often short-sleeved dress shirt originating in Hawai'i and worn as business attire—collared, buttoned, and usually worn untucked with trousers (never shorts)
arahant	*Pali*	An enlightened person
arigato gozaimasu/ gozaimashita	*Japanese*	"Thank you"
Benzaiten	*Japanese*	In mythology, the goddess or guardian deity of culture, music, money, water, wind, and anything else that flows; also referred to as Benten
bogu	*Japanese*	Armor traditionally made of padded, indigo-dyed cotton, lacquered bamboo, metal, and leather worn in Kendo
bokken	*Japanese*	A wooden sword used for practicing Japanese martial arts—at Chozen-ji, primarily the Hojo
bokuto	*Japanese*	A thicker, heavier version of bokken
Bu Do	*Japanese*	Japanese martial arts. Short for the Japanese word *bushido*, which refers to the ethical and cultural aspects of samurai (or warrior) culture
buddha-dharma	*Sanskrit*	The collected teachings of Buddhism

Budo Dojo	*Japanese*	The main training hall at Daihonzan Chozen-ji used for zazen and martial arts
butsudan	*Japanese*	An altar, traditionally displaying religious artifacts
Chado	*Japanese*	The Way of Tea; also, Japanese tea ceremony
daihonzan	*Japanese*	Literally, "big central mountain"; central headquarters temple or monastery in Japanese Zen, which is the seat of its own line of Zen and presides over a network of subtemples
dharma	*Sanskrit*	*See* buddhadharma
Do	*Japanese*	The Tao, the Way
dojo	*Japanese*	Literally, "a place to train in the Way"; a hall or other space used for spiritual and/or martial arts training
the Dojo	*English*	A nickname for Chozen-ji used in casual conversation
engawa	*Japanese*	A feature of Japanese architecture that is similar to an outdoor hallway
enso	*Japanese*	Circle
fukusa	*Japanese*	Square of silk cloth used in Chado
gassho	*Japanese*	A gesture of respect that consists of holding the palms together in front of one's body

genkan	*Japanese*	A traditional entryway in a Japanese building, usually made of stone
gi	*Japanese*	Top garment worn for training in Japanese martial arts
Goenka-ji	*Indian Name*	S. N. Goenka; the appellation "-ji" suggests familiarity and respect in India and other parts of South Asia
Hagakure	*Japanese*	An eighteenth-century samurai manual
hakama	*Japanese*	Traditional trousers dating to the sixth century in Japan, worn commonly for training in the martial arts
hakobi usucha	*Japanese*	A basic procedure in Chado
han	*Japanese*	A wooden board struck at a Zen training temple to mark the passage of time
hanabata	*Japanese*	Nasal mucus, a runny nose
haole	*'Ōlelo Hawai'i*	A person of European descent; White
hara	*Japanese*	The trunk of the body below the belly button
hashi	*Japanese*	Chopsticks
Hawaiian Pidgin	*English*	Creole language developed on Hawai'i's plantations, a combination of Native Hawaiian, Japanese, English, Portuguese, Chinese, Korean, and Filipino words

Hitsuzendo	*Japanese*	Traditional Japanese calligraphy trained in as a Zen discipline (in contrast to calligraphy approached as more of an art)
Hojo	*Japanese*	A classic sword form from the Jikishinkage-ryu school of Japanese swordsmanship
hondo	*Japanese*	Main worship hall
'Ōlelo Hawai'i	*'Ōlelo Hawai'i*	Native Hawaiian language
ihai	*Japanese*	Memorial tablets bearing the name of the deceased, usually displayed in a butsudan
ikebana	*Japanese*	The art of flower arrangement (vs. Kado, the Way of the Flower, which is pursued as a spiritual discipline to train in Zen utilizing the techniques and principles of flower arrangement)
inji	*Japanese*	Attendant to the roshi
inka	*Japanese*	Literally, "mind stamp"; receiving authorization from one's Zen teacher to become a teacher and steward a Zen lineage
ippuku sashiagemasu	*Japanese*	"I will serve tea now"
jihatsu	*Japanese*	A set of five nesting lacquerware (today, plastic) bowls and chopsticks wrapped in a cloth napkin used for eating

jiki	*Japanese*	Short for *jikijitsu*, the student who leads zazen and sesshin (weeklong intensive Zen training)
Jikishin Kore Dojo	*Japanese*	A poetic phrase meaning "The straightforward mind is the place to train in the Way"
Jikishin-kage-ryu	*Japanese*	A famous Japanese fencing school, full name Kashima Shinden Jikishinkage-ryu (鹿島神傳直心影流, かしましんでんじきしんかげりゅう) founded in the mid-sixteenth century
jokkei	*Japanese*	A student leader role during zazen and sesshin (weeklong intensive Zen training)
Judo	*Japanese*	A Japanese martial art; literally, "the Way of Yielding"
juzu	*Japanese*	Buddhist beads
Kado	*Japanese*	The Way of the Flower
kage	*Japanese*	Shadow
kanji	*Japanese*	Japanese logographic script based on Chinese characters
kanpai	*Japanese*	A common toast
Karate	*Japanese*	A martial art developed in Okinawa

kata	*Japanese*	A detailed choreography of movements in Japanese martial arts; e.g., the Hojo kata
kotonk	*Hawaiian Pidgin*	A person of Asian descent raised on the American continent
keiko	*Japanese*	Practice
keisaku	*Japanese*	A flat wooden sword used in zazen; literally, "the stick of wisdom" or "the stick of encouragement"
kekko deshita	*Japanese*	"It is fine" or "good job"
Kendo	*Japanese*	The Way of the Sword, or Japanese fencing
kenjutsu	*Japanese*	Kendo sword technique
kesa	*Japanese*	Rectangular garment worn formally over a Japanese Buddhist monk or priest's robes; also "okesa"
kiai	*Japanese*	The expression of ki, or vital energy; the subtlest form of which ki can be perceived; a yell in martial arts
kimono	*Japanese*	Traditional clothing dating from the fifth century; literally, "clothing"
koan	*Japanese*	A spiritual training tool used to help Zen students transcend the limits of the rational mind

kohai	*Japanese*	A junior student (vs. senpai)
kōlea	*ʻŌlelo Hawaiʻi*	Pacific golden plover; a migratory bird seen in Hawaiʻi in the winter months
kote	*Japanese*	Wrist, gloves
Kozen No Ki	*Japanese*	A poetic phrase referring to the fundamental energy of the universe
kufu	*Japanese*	Struggle, as in "kufu one's koan"
kulolo	*ʻŌlelo Hawaiʻi*	A delicious sweet made of steamed and pounded taro, sugar, and coconut milk
kupuna	*ʻŌlelo Hawaiʻi*	Elder or elders
Kyudo	*Japanese*	The Way of the Bow; traditional Japanese archery
lanai	*ʻŌlelo Hawaiʻi*	Porch or deck
lau lau	*ʻŌlelo Hawaiʻi*	Salted fish and pork wrapped and steamed in taro and banana leaves
live-in	*English*	Translation from the Chinese for a layperson who lives at a Zen Buddhist temple
makiwara	*Japanese*	Practice target used in Kyudo
makyo	*Japanese*	Hallucination, or figment of the imagination

mana	*'Ōlelo Hawai'i*	Energy or spiritual power
manawa	*'Ōlelo Hawai'i*	Sacred energy mountain
mei fun	*Chinese*	Flat Chinese rice noodle
men	*Japanese*	Head or helmet
metta	*Pali*	Practice of loving-kindness
misogi	*Japanese*	Shinto purification practice and spiritual training
mizusashi	*Japanese*	Cold water container
mochi	*Japanese*	Steamed and pounded sweet rice, eaten plain or shaped into a small bun with a variety of fillings
mokugyo	*Japanese*	Wooden drum used to keep time during okyo (Buddhist sutra chanting)
mokuso	*Japanese*	Meditation
monkeypod		Hardwood common in Hawai'i, as well as Central and South America
Mu I	*Japanese*	Fearless or fearlessness; literally, "Void Fear"; depending on Chinese characters, also action of nonaction; "Void Action"
myo an	*Japanese*	"Mysterious peace"
nana dan	*Japanese*	Seventh-degree black belt

nio	*Japanese*	Japanese guardian deity
obi	*Japanese*	Wide cloth belt
obiage	*Japanese*	Silk belt worn with kimono
okyo	*Japanese*	Chanting of the Buddhist sutras
omiyage	*Japanese*	Gifts, usually from one's travels or brought when visiting someone
onegaishi-masu	*Japanese*	A phrase used as a greeting or to request someone to do something for you
paramita	*Sanskrit*	A Buddhist term for the noble qualities of someone who is enlightened
the Path	*English*	The Tao, the Way
pau hana	*Hawaiian Pidgin*	Casual celebration of work being completed, happy hour; literally, "work is finished"
rakusu	*Japanese*	Garment for priests and laypeople worn hung around the neck; a smaller version of the kesa
roshi	*Japanese*	Zen master, one who is authorized to carry on a Buddhist lineage; literally, "old teacher"; an honorific title—e.g., Sayama Roshi
rotaishi	*Japanese*	Honorific title for a Zen master after they have passed away
sampai	*Japanese*	Set of three full-body prostrations

samue	*Japanese*	Matching top and bottom garments traditionally worn as Japanese casual or work wear or as pajamas
sangha	*Pali*	Community of Buddhist clergy or monks and nuns; colloquially used in the West to refer to a spiritual community
sanzen	*Japanese*	Private interview with a Zen master or going to instruction with a Zen master; usually focused on answering one's Zen koan
sara-sara	*Japanese*	Onomatopoeia referring to the sound of leaves rustling and falling through the air in the autumn
seiza	*Japanese*	A way of sitting on the floor with the tops of the feet and shins on the ground, sitting on one's heels
senpai	*Japanese*	Senior student (vs. kohai)
sesshin	*Japanese*	Weeklong intensive Zen training that includes long hours of zazen, formal meals, and little sleep
setta zori	*Japanese*	One variety of traditional Japanese sandals with a toe thong and slight platform
shiai	*Japanese*	Scored match or contest in martial arts
shin	*Japanese*	"mind-heart," spirit, mind

shoji	*Japanese*	Sliding screens that function as removable walls or doors in traditional Japanese architecture, usually made with wood and paper
shoyu	*Japanese*	Soy sauce
tabi	*Japanese*	Split-toe socks used in the training and practice of Japanese arts such as Chado and Kyudo or worn with traditional Japanese kimono (clothing)
taku	*Japanese*	Two wooden blocks struck together to indicate the beginning and end of zazen
takuan	*Japanese*	Yellow, pickled daikon radish named after its inventor, the Zen master Takuan Soho from the sixteenth century
tana	*Japanese*	Small formal table used in Chado
tare	*Japanese*	Placketed cloth armor worn in Kendo over the hips, groin, and thighs
tatami	*Japanese*	Traditional flooring material made of woven rice straw, rush, hemp, or cotton
teisho	*Japanese*	Demonstration of a Zen master's realization, often mistakenly referred to as a Zen "lecture"
temae	*Japanese*	Formal procedure of serving tea in Chado

tenegui	*Japanese*	Long, rectangular cotton cloth usually printed with calligraphy or other inspirational design worn on the head for various activities, including training in Kendo
tokonoma	*Japanese*	Alcove where artistic items are displayed
True Self	*English*	Term in Japanese Zen Buddhism for enlightenment
unpan	*Japanese*	Flat metal gong used to signal mealtime at Chozen-ji
virya	*Sanskrit*	One of the ten paramitas, spiritual or meditative vigor
Wa Kei Sei Jaku	*Japanese*	Harmony, Respect, Purity, and Tranquility—four virtues that are central to the philosophy and practice of Chado
wagashi	*Japanese*	A type of sweet made with sweetened bean paste, often colored and shaped to fit with a seasonal theme
Yakushi Nyorai	*Japanese*	Medicine Buddha, or Buddha of Healing
yame	*Japanese*	"Stop" or "halt," used by a teacher during Kendo keiko
yasashi	*Japanese*	Sweet, thoughtful, warm, caring
yosho	*Japanese*	Expression accompanying physical exertion

zabuton	*Japanese*	Large square cushion used for sitting on the floor
zafu	*Japanese*	Small, flat, rectangular cushion used for sitting on the floor, usually on top of a zabuton
zazen	*Japanese*	Seated meditation; literally, "seated Zen"
Zen	*Japanese*	Transliteration of the word *jhāna* (Pali) and *dhyāna* (Sanskrit), a state of nondual, meditative absorption; in the Chozen-ji canon, Omori Sogen Rotaishi defined Zen as a verb: "To transcend all dualism, life and death"

NOTES

1. John M. Koller, "Oxherding: Stages of Zen Practice," ExEAS Teaching Materials and Resources, Columbia University, accessed May 25, 2023, http://www.columbia.edu/cu/weai/exeas/resources/oxherding.html.

2. "Jim Carrey Shares His Terrifying Experience of Hawaii's 2018 False Missile Alert," The Tonight Show Starring Jimmy Fallon, posted on July 17, 2020, YouTube video, 6:21, https://youtu.be/T8LlB3psUtM?t=256.

3. Hosokawa Dogen, *Omori Sogen: The Art of a Zen Master* (London: Kegan Paul, 1999), 48–50.

4. Daian Sayama, *Ten Shin Myo: The Mysterious Wonder of the Universal Mind, the Way of Zen Master Tanouye Tenshin* (Honolulu: Daihonzan Chozen-ji, 2019), 13.

5. Omori Sogen, "Canon of Daihonzan Chozen-ji / International Zen Dojo," October 1, 1979.

6. "Iverson Practice!," gordievsky, posted on April 15, 2006, YouTube video, 2:22, https://youtu.be/eGDBR2L5kzI.

7. D. T. Suzuki, *Essays in Zen Buddhism, First Series* (York Beach, ME: Samuel Weiser, 1985), 303.

8. Mike Sayama, "Etsuo Sayama: A Life of Perseverance and Principle," April 28, 2007, privately printed.

9. Sayama, *Ten Shin Myo,* 10.

10. Dogen, 125.

11. Dogen, 126.

12. Dogen, 112.

13. Cristina Moon, "May We Gather: A National Buddhist Memorial Ceremony for Asian American Ancestors," May We Gather, posted on May 6, 2021, YouTube video, 1:12:41 and 1:39:40, https://youtu.be/665Gf6yyzVQ?t=4360.